WOMANISM AND AFRICAN CONSCIOUSNESS

Mary E. Modupe Kolawole

Africa World Press, Inc.

P.O. Box 1892

Trenton, NJ 08607

P.O. Box 48

Asmara, ERITREA

Africa World Press, Inc.

P.O. Box 1892
Trenton, NJ 08607

P.O. Box 48
Asmara, ERITREA

Copyright © 1997 Mary E. Modupe Kolawole

First Printing 1997

Book design: Jonathan Gullery
Cover design: Aaron J. Wilson

This book was composed in Cheltenham and Nofret Regular

Library of Congress Cataloging-in-Publication Data

Kolawole, Mary Ebun Modupe.
     Womanism and African Consciousness / Mary E. Modupe Kolawole.
       p.   cm.
     Includes bibliographical references and index.
     ISBN 0-86543-540-5   (cloth : alk. paper). – ISBN 0-86543-541-3 (pbk. :
alk. paper)
       1. African literature–20th century–History and criticism.
2. Women in literature. 3. African literature–Women authors-
-History and criticism. 4. Women and literature–Africa. 5. Women-
-Africa–Intellectual life. I. Title.
PL8010.K58   1997
809'.8896'082–dc21

                                                                    97-3478
                                                                    CIP

To my husband Boye, my son Temi Boyewole,
and my daughter Folake.
Also to my mother,
Adeyoyin Odeyiola-Adewoye, a true symbol of
women's resourcefulness and resilience.
And to Mary Harvey, an emblem of women's sucess,
whose dynamic leadership formed a strong foundation
to my early vision and womanist success.

CONTENTS

ACKNOWLEDGEMENTS

I am indebted to many people for the success of this book, most especially to my husband, Boye, and my children, Folake and Temi, to whom this book is dedicated.

I acknowledge the financial support of the Rockefeller Foundation and the Africana Studies Center at Cornell University, Ithaca, New York. The motivation for this book came when I was a Rockefeller Visiting Fellow in "Gender, Poltics and African Cultural Production" during the 1991/92 academic year. I have been much inspired by my interaction with such renowned scholars as Carole Boyce-Davis, Molefi Kete Asante, and several others during that year. I wish equally to show my appreciation to all my colleagues at Cornell: Locksley Edmundson, Ann Adams, Bob Harry, James Turner, Nwalimu A. Nanji, and others. The special privilege of exchanging ideas with Ali Mazrui, Tsitsi Dangarembga, and Micere Mugo, who were also visiting colleagues\writers at Cornell, provided tremedous impetus for this book. I also thank my former student Iyun Osagie, and her husband, Sylvester, who provided inspiration at Cornell.

I also acknowledge the financial assistance provided by the Association of Commonwealth Universities and the facilities provided by the University of Kent in Canterbury when I was updating and putting finishing touches to this book. I am particularly grateful for the opportunity to be a Visiting Fellow at the Women's Studies Centre. I was greatly encouraged by my colleagues at Kent, Mary Evans, Lynn Innes, and Meredy Harris. I thank Clarissa Dhiwayo and her friend who gave me materials about Zimbabwean women. I also thank my friend Adepeju Jolayemi for her moral support.

I thank my former principal, Mary Harvey, and her good friend, Pat McCabe of Maidstone, Kent. My reunion with Mary and the positive comments from her and from Pat were sources of encouragement.

My views and ideas have been enriched by many other scholars and writers who can not be mentioned individually. They have been duly cited and acknowledged in this book. Special appreciation goes to Nina Mba, Amina Mama, and my sister and colleague, Molara Ogundipe-Leslie. To my sister, and precursor of African womanism, the late Zulu Sofola, I give my tributes. A sister in many ways, she gave me much encouragement and copies of her plays in progress, *The Shower* and *Lost Dreams*. My views have also been nourished by responses to my paper at the Southern University, Baton Rouge, Louisiana, March 1992, and for this I am grateful for interactions with my friend and sister, Gloria Braxton, and also with Obioma Nnaemeka. I can not but acknowledge the exchange of ideas with many colleagues at Nsukka, Nigeria during the first international conference on "Women in Africa and the African Diaspora: Bridges Across Activism and the Academy." My meeting with the dynamic womanist Clenora Hudson-Weems at the Nsukka conference, where we both shared ideas about our ongoing works on womanism, was of tremendous importance.

Finally, I thank all colleagues, especially, Professor Oyin Ogunba, Simi Afonja, S.A. Ekundayo, Tanwa Odebiyi, Femi Akindele, and many other colleagues at Obafemi Awolowo University, Ile-Ife, who have in diverse ways encouraged the research that gave birth to this book, directly or indirectly. I am equally indebted to Mr. J.O. Bamigboye and James Odelade for technical assistance.

PART ONE

GENDER THEORIES AND AFRICAN WOMEN'S MOBILIZATION, PAST AND PRESENT

CHAPTER ONE

THE CONTEXT OF AFRICAN WOMEN'S STRUGGLE

The space occupied by African women in contemporary discourse on women is still a domain that has not been adequately explored despite an increasing interest from the continent and from outside. The invention of the African woman is being interrogated by several women writers but a hiatus still exists and this gives the impression of voicelessness and absences even when history presents alternative realities. Several African women scholars are challenging the way African women's mobilization and the question of self-assertion and empowerment are glossed over or effaced from mainstream women's theorizing. Oppositional discourse has emerged in various ways and it is necessary to probe the unexplored areas of the African woman's audibility and visibility to assess the limits of her voicelessness. Much of the emphasis has been to underscore the liminal voiceless African woman with the result that she is still predominantly portrayed as a victim in various ways.

The call for African women to break the yoke of silence has been made by African women who are genuinely concerned and this call is based on objective realities to a large extent. Since Awa Thiam cried out in 1978 in her classic work, *Speak Out, Black Sister* (trans. 1986), women writers from the continent have responded to the challenge. Women like the Sierra-Leonian activist, Daphne Williams-Ntiri and Molara Ogundipe-Leslie did not need to be prodded since they have always spoken for African women in theory, in creative works, and in political-ideological commitment. Others include Bolanle Awe, Helen Kuzwayo, Rebecca Njau, Micere Mugo, Nina Emma Mba, Chikwenye Okonjo-Ogunyemi and (more recently) Helen Mugambi, Obioma Nnaemeka, Irene Assiba D'Almeida, Abena Busia, and Siga Jajne. These women occupy different ideological spaces but the condition and need of African women is the crux of all their work. How do these women relate to the question of voicelessness, marginality, oppression and self-retrieval of African women?

Several factors mediate the location of African women in gender discourse and some of these are personal, others are communal. One faces a problem in any attempt to generalize about all the women on a continent as diverse and vast as Africa. Colonialism brought different kinds of affiliation to different parts of the continent. National, ethnic, and regional idiosyncrasy, predominant religious influence, tradition, modernism, and post-colonial conditions intercept the writers' perception and consciousness. Nonetheless, these women are not only speaking back, they are fighting back as they deconstruct existing distorted images or misrepresentations of African women. These voices are not monolithic but multiple and the relevance of this outlook to African indigenous beliefs and attitudes also highlights the varying reactions to western feminism as a universal or universalizing theory.

In her recent work, *Francophone African Women Writers: Destroying the Emptiness of Silence,* Irene D'Almeida problematizes the silence and voicelessness of African women and her position is a good starting point in discussing the emergence of African women's femin*ine* (not necessarily femin*ist)* ideology:

> Silence represents the historical muting of women under the formidable institution known as patriarchy, that form of social organization in which males assume power and create for females an inferior status.[1]

This scholar has brilliantly touched on central issues in African women's discourse. She reiterates two reasons for African women's silence as elicited by Carole Boyce-Davis, Mineke Schipper, and others: colonialism and African traditions. Contending that women were vocal in orature but silent in literature, D'Almeida provides an extensive study of the emergence of Francophone African women's writing and their dealing with feminism since "the sudden burgeoning of women's writing in the 1970s." She emphasizes the role of literature for self-expression, self-definition, self-discovery and as a liberating force as exemplified in the works of Francophone African women like Ken Bugul, Calixthe Beyala, Aminata Sow Fall, and Werewere Liking.

Much has been written about African women's voicelessness and D'Almeida's work has clearly enunciated several conditions that explain and validate the efforts to destroy this silence. African women's silence is taken for granted by many scholars while others probe and challenge this claim. This trend is central to African women's dealing with the concept of feminism as well, as D' Almeida's work emphasizes. I will locate my discourse on the terrain that in African world-view, there are many roads to the same goal. The Yorubas strongly believe in the world as a metaphoric and or allegoric marketplace as scholars like Ropo Sekoni have posited (Sekoni 1995). As a follow-up from this world-view, the Yorubas also maintain that there are diverse routes leading to the marketplace: *"Ona kan o wo oja."* A similar Igbo philosophy gives expression to the same thought: "There is no absolute way to anything." Identical concepts exist in many other parts of Africa. I do agree with Obioma Nnaemeka's contention during a recent African Literature Association conference (Columbus, Ohio, 1995), that counterdiscourse is a healthy approach in African women's search for acceptable feminine aesthetics. This versatile writer underscores the centrality of dualities, paradoxes, and simultaneous existence of values in African thoughts—or, in Nnaemeka's words, a "live and let live" philosophy.

The importance of simultaneous discourse and a dialogic position in enhancing African women's voices is central to this discourse. The experience of modern alienated westernized African woman often muffles the voice of the majority of African women including the much denigrated rural women. Speaking out through the written or electronic media is taken as the measure but African women's self-actualization predates the written and electronic media. Their dynamic mobilization in some parts of Africa predates colonialism, feminism, and other 'isms' that are being held up as the norms for evaluating African women's awareness. This will be the focus of another chapter. Nonetheless, in diverse ways, African women have emerged from "silence," transcending the many limiting borders imposed on them by patriarchal-traditional or post-colonial structures, and have taken positions as the mouthpiece for their gender even from various polar ideological stances. They are dealing with African women's questions in different ways but there is room for each in the collective 'compound.'

Micere Mugo maintains that the average African woman is not invisible: "The African woman is not invisible. She is visible on the farm, she is visible in the market place...."[2] A younger scholar, Siga Jajne, agrees with D'Almeida that African women have been silenced and suppressed by colonialism and patriarchy and that they must force their viewpoint on existing discourse by "voice-throwing." Identifying with the Senegalese traditional concept of intrusion or voice-throwing known as *Sani Baat,* she observes:

> I would like to offer an alternate reading and locate myself within the concept of "voice throwing." I believe that by "throwing" in one's voice, a disruption of discourse can take place. The act of "throwing" one's voice can create an epistemic violence to discourse that will create a space for hitherto unheard voices. The problem that will arise from such an action will be the appropriation of this voice within the particular discourse it interrupts, an act that may or may not render it mute.[3]

Senegalese women have been some of the most active in articulating and getting mobilized to reject all the forces that oppress women. The high level of consciousness is revealed in the activities of the women's group, *Yewwu Yewwi.* Their journal, *Fippu,* has equally been a means of strong feminine expression.The deliberate choice of the name, *Yewwu Yewwi*— "Wake up and then wake someone else up" — is a manifestation of the new wave of consciousness, while the title of their journal, *Fippu* (meaning "rebellion"[4] in Wollof), points to the determination and level of awareness that informs this group. Senegalese women are indeed throwing their voices like several other groups in other parts of the continent.

AFRICAN WOMEN AND FEMINIST DISCOURSE

The Senegalese concept of *"sani-baat"*or voice-throwing raises important issues. Jajne's view presupposes that African women are rendered voiceless by certain factors. In a subsequent conversation with Jajne, she affirms that patriarchal, colonial, and post-colonial situations are some of the factors. So, African women need to force their voices into existing male and Western feminist discourse, in her view. This further implies that African women who have transcended the borders of silence are intercepting certain existing notions. A closer look at existing feminist discourse, its validity to African women's reality and the way several of these women are negotiating their own space is an important area that needs to be further investigated.

One can not discuss African women's position *in vacuo.* These women are throwing their voices within an existing context. Throwing one's voice is one of the best things to have happened to African women in recent years. It is identical to the issue of moving from the margin to the center that has become an important issue to African scholars, male and female, globally. Bell Hooks problematizes this in several works and Ngugi wa Thiong'o's most recent treatise is an emphasis on moving the center (Ngugi Wa Thiong'o 1995). Jajne sounds a note of caution, that African women's voices may get appropriated, drowned out, or become a tag to the existing feminist voices. Consequently, some African scholars are uncomfortable with a situation that may cause African women to sing other people's song and dance other people's dance, as Micere Mugo warns in an interview with Adeola James:

> There is nothing wrong with singing about women but I think that we must be careful to define and specify which women we are singing about. I still insist that we must sing and sing and sing again about our mothers and those in the rural areas....and their poverty. (James, p. 98)

A major problem emerges from throwing one's voice unless the African woman is firmly determined not to allow her voice to be submerged by existing feminist discourse. While some are assertive in identifying with feminism, others are cautious, while some will have nothing to do with feminism as it is presented from the West. The Swahili concept of *kikusuku* is rel-

evant here. *Kikusuku* is the concept of parroting or rote imitation of other people's voices. Some African women maintain
that by accepting feminism or Black feminism one faces the
danger of parroting as opposed to speaking out creatively.
Anthony Appiah recently draws attention to the problem of
hybridization as the problem of singing traditional songs in
Babylon and theorizing about African people's condition from
"within the belly of the beast."[5] Some women see concepts
such as African feminism and Black feminism as identical to
singing African songs from the belly of the beast.

Are the fears of African women who reject Western feminism justified and what are the alternatives being proposed?
From personal discussion with several African sisters, they
are not rejecting the process of fighting for women's self-definition and self-assertion, but they have problems with the definitions and conceptualization of feminism as it is transmitted
from the West with the presumption that this perception of
women's issues is universal and relevant to all women globally.
Others feel sufficiently comfortable with feminism as a concept. This is not always understood when such women are
called backward, retrogressive, ignorant or cowards for denying western feminism. These women insist that there are other
ways of eliciting women's positive self-esteem without the tag,
feminism.

Let us look more closely at the issues raised as we attempt
to probe the question, "Are African women parroting or recreating themselves?" Some feel sufficiently satisfied with feminism and will identify with it as a concept. Abena Busia feels
comfortable to be called a feminist. In my recent interview
with this vocal dynamic Ghanaian scholar, she affirms her
commitment to feminism:

> I am comfortable with the term 'feminism.' If we con-
> cede the term feminism, we've lost a power struggle. As
> a strategy, we might be conceding grounds that we
> shouldn't.... Feminism is an ideological praxis that gives
> us a series of multiple strategies (of reading, of analysis)
> and what those strategies have in common is that the
> woman matters.[6]

Abena Busia nonetheless sees the term, "African feminism" as
negative. While stressing the fact that centralizing women is at
the heart of her commitment, she admits that her way of conceptualizing her world as an African is different from that of

North American women. She laments that much of existing approaches are based on a "divide and rule" philosophy.

Molara Ogundipe-Leslie is one of the most prolific and bold theorists that the continent has produced. Her works are as diverse as her activities in the attempt to mobilize African women over the last three decades. She condemns African women's persistent rejection of feminism in strong terms in line with her humanist Marxist orientation. Significantly, she interrogates the question of African women's voicelessness in *Recreating Ourselves,* her *magnum opus.* Like Carole Boyce-Davies, Ogundipe-Leslie believes that African women are not voiceless if one cares to search for and listen to their voices in the right places as she raises salient questions:

> Are African women voiceless or do we fail to look for their voices where we may find them, in the sites and forms in which these voices are uttered?.... We must look for African women's voices in women's spaces and modes such as in ceremonies and work songs....[7]

Ogundipe-Leslie reiterates her conviction that African women have always spoken out and decries simplistic false images of African women, especially the so-called muted rural women portrayed as having no mind of their own. She maintains that the problem is the refusal of scholars to search for African women's voices:

> We neither look for their voices where they utter them nor do we think it worthwhile to listen to their voices. We sometimes substitute our voices for their own and we do not even know when we do this nor are we able to recognise the differences in the mixed or substituted voices. Women of European descent are most prone to these ventriloquisms, frequently calling on African women to play the role of ventriloquists' puppets, speaking to other people's agenda.[8]

Although this critic condemns writers who deny feminism, these are some of the reasons why several women dissociate themselves from feminism. Perhaps some of the anti-feminists are too absolute in their conceptualization of the woman's needs. This great scholar opines, "For example, currently in Nigeria, right-wing women, most men, and apolitical women, like to quip that African women do not need liberation or feminism because they have never been in bondage." There is a meeting point, however. African women, like all women and all

oppressed groups, continue to utilize all avenues for augmenting their position. To argue that African women do not
need liberation is to present a false picture of them, an illusion
that emerges from over-romanticism. All over the continent,
there are areas of women's marginalization that call for a re-
ordering of the social order, and African women have peculiar
needs in this area. But many who struggle for African women's
self-realization are reacting against the condescending attitude of some feminists and the misdirected emphasis of others. We therefore need a deeper probing of the issues being
raised concerning the relevance of feminism to African women
and how these women are creating their own voices and space.

For too long, the African woman's reality has been
inscribed from the West or by men. Yet, African women did not
learn about self-assertion from the West. My maternal grandmother was a very strong personality, firm, strict, and feared
by both men and women. She took no nonsense from anybody,
male or female, and was often invited to help discipline other
people's children. She was the first symbol of firm self-assertion that I grew up to know. During the last decade of colonial
power in Nigeria, many parents feared teachers and in particular, headmasters, who were seen as representatives of the
white man who was to be respected and obeyed. My grandmother was different. She would follow any grandchild to
school if she noticed cane marks, an evidence that the child
had been beaten (a fact that was common in those days). She
would demand from the teacher why her grandchild was
treated so cruelly, ask if there was no other way of dealing
with the situation, and march to the Headmaster's office to
seek redress if she was not satisfied. My grandmother never
heard about feminism or Western actions against child abuse
until her death. She was not a feminist but simply a strong
African woman. At the collective level, instances of collective
actions by African women in pre-colonial and colonial times
confirm the strong concerted actions by women towards liberation and self-actualization.

Let us look at a few examples of writers who have rejected
feminism to keenly assess the bone or bane of their contentions. Important women writers who spend their lifetime in
dealing with women's issues who have denied being feminists
at various times include Ama Ata Aidoo, Bessie Head, Miriama
Ba, and Buchi Emecheta.[9] In the well quoted interview with
Marie Umeh, Buchi Emecheta sounds a cautious note and qual-
ifies her relation to feminism:

I am a feminist with a small 'f', I love men and good men are the salt of the earth. But to tell me that we should abolish marriage like the capital 'F' (Feminist) women who say women should live together and all that, I say No. Personally I'd like to see the ideal, happy marriage. But if it doesn't work, for goodness sake, call it off.[10]

This comment has attracted much criticism from many scholars but a revisionist critique of Emecheta's view is important. She emphasizes some of the issues in Western feminism which she considers anomalous to an African world-view. There must be numerous other Africans who agree with her. Her view is reflective of a slice of African position which many non-educated ordinary Africans will subscribe to. Ama Ata Aidoo's opinion is put forward more strongly, but it touches on the centrality of the family to Africans as well:

Feminism. You know how we feel about that embarrassing western philosophy? The destroyer of homes. Imported mainly from America to ruin nice African homes.[11]

African women's location within existing feminine discourse and reactions such as we see in Aidoo and Emecheta can be best understood within proper cultural contextualization. Secondly, one needs to assess such views against the backdrop of larger issues such as post-coloniality and Third World issues. Despite the varying reactions to feminism, many African women seem to agree that the way African women perceive their reality and the exigency that shape their consciousness and mobilization has to be different from the way western women perceive and react to their situation.

None of the Euro-American schools of feminism is adequate for expressing the yearnings of all women at all times. Rose-Marie Tong rightly contends that:

feminist theory is not one, but many theories or perspectives and that each perspective attempts to describe women's oppression, to explain its causes and consequences and to prescribe strategies for women's liberation.[12]

The implication of the diversity of views and the desire by Western women to prescribe "strategies for women's liberation" for others has far-reaching effects on the reaction of African women to feminisms. Tong's detailed analysis of the diversity of feminisms raises curious questions in the minds of people of non-Eurocentric cultures. One wonders what the concentric "isms" will mean to the average Zulu woman in South Africa, the Ijaw fisherwoman of Nigeria, or the Asante woman of northern Ghana, for example. The same question is equally relevant to the Singaporian, the native American, the rural indigenous woman in Venezuela, the peasant woman in Equador, and the ordinary woman in Papua New Guinea or Nepal. Yet these women have been known to have their own forms of self-expression and collective mobilization.

African Reality and Western Feminist Discourse

Let us look more closely at some central contentions of feminisms to situate them in the African world-view. Liberal feminism emphasizes the impact of legal strictures and custom on women's subordination and advocates gender justice. But Marxist feminists maintain that gender justice is not possible while class stratification is not eliminated. The latter therefore blame capitalism for women's oppression. It is necessary to critique these issues in the light of their relevance to African women.

To the African woman, many forms of oppression exist around her simultaneously. Imperialism as well as the inescapable influence of post-colonial conditions such as the invincible hands of the World Bank because of the side-effects of the International Monetary Fund are often more real to her suffering than gender division. The internationalization of racism and the progressive feminization of poverty are equally important. Many African nations are still under the yoke of frequent political unrest, turmoil and instability. Women receive the butt end of these because in the final analysis they are the ones who are confronted with hungry children who must be fed particularly in polygamous situations. As the African female scholar recognizes these facts, she is convinced that she must look beyond her middle-class privileges and so she becomes the spokesperson for her sisters irrespective of class. Yet many of them prefer not to be circumscribed by a particular feminist 'ism' as they are conscious of the existence of gender inequality in pre-capitalist, capitalist, and socialist societies as well.

Some issues that are central to radical feminism underscore the question of cultural relevance. The role of patriarchy as it undermines women's sexuality is dominant in radical feminist discourse. Many such scholars have proposed very overt demonstrations of sexuality and sexual freedom. They often probe conventional concepts of biological and reproductive roles. Shalsasmith Firestone suggests a neutralization of reproductive role in line with lesbian calls for *in vacuo* reproduction. Others like Marge Pierson envision a utopia in which male and female have the option of "agendered" child-bearing.

Many African and other Third World women have problems with this orientation. African world-view is predominantly family-oriented and this is an aspect of the positive legacy that Blacks in the diaspora have sustained vigorously and self-consciously. Some radical feminists further advocate an overturn of patriarchy and patriarchal symbols. Many African women recognize the way patriarchy has been manipulated to put them down and they are struggling against these forms of subjugation and intimidation wherever they exist, as we see in the agenda of Yewwu Yewwi. But at the same time, many also recognize the need to unite with men in a concerted effort to reject racist and imperialist subjugation. The Nigerian group 'Women in Nigeria' has men participants to confirm this. This recognition of the many tiers of struggle accounts for the caution and scepticism revealed by many Africans in relating to western feminism. In spite of certain strengths and weaknesses in diverse shades of feminism, they address western realities and not African women's peculiar situation.

As post-modernist feminism recognizes, a simultaneous existence of various feminisms is inevitable. Tong also suggests a conciliatory position:

> It is a major challenge to contemporary feminism to reconcile the pressures for diversity and difference with those for integration and communality. We need to have a home in which everyone has a room of her own, but one in which the walls are thin enough to permit a conversation.[13]

This is expressive of the yearning of many African women, but one cannot gloss over difference. It is significant that many women now recognize the need to exalt the positive side of difference. Audre Lorde brings out this need to enhance the "creative function of difference" explicitly:

> But it is not those differences between us that are separating us. It is rather our refusal to recognize those dif-

ferences, and to examine the distortions which result from our misnaming them and their effects upon human behaviour and expectation.[14]

The starting point for Africans is the search for and enunciation of Africaness as a pre-requisite for any coalition with other women globally. Feminism, like any ideology, is socially constructed and the intertwined nature of gender, race, culture, class, and nationalism are central to African women's notion of self-assertion. Uprooting any single agency of oppression will not solve their problems. Many Western scholars are making a conscious effort to recognize and respect this difference by not only including but underscoring the difference in African and other Third World women's needs (Mary Evans, 1994; Maggie Humm, 1994). As Maggie Humm focuses on African and Third World women's issues, she brings out some basic differences. She reiterates the position of African women like Abena Busia by acknowledging the uniqueness in African women's perception of their world. She therefore recognizes the centrality of the family as she acknowledges,

> Black feminism has a different relationship to dominating social policies than does white feminism. For example, a Black woman's family and labour market experience might shape her economic equality but also, and often, the family might be a source of succour and collective support.[15]

Contrary to this recognition of cultural idiosyncrasy we have a host of critics who still consider feminism as the master key to all women's problems and the tool for judging their values, as we see in Gayle Greene's comment:

> We came to recognize that feminism is a new worldview, a comprehensive framework of ideas through which all experience can be measured, judged or evaluated.[16]

Because of the emergence and the increase in the activities of many non-western theorists, women's self-expression is no longer a Eurocentric domain, but many of these women are advocating different versions of feminism. This comes out clearly in the contention of Kamla Bhasin and Nighat Said on the relevance of feminism to South East Asian women:

> ... feminism is based on historically and culturally specific realities and levels of consciousness, perceptions

and actions. This means that feminism meant one thing in the seventeenth century (when the word was first used) and that it means something quite different in the 1980s. It can also be articulated differently in different parts of the world and within a country, differently by different women depending on their class, background, levels of education, consciousness....[17]

It is the failure to recognize this that has caused many African women to doubt the authenticity of Western feminists and propose other terms of self-expression.

DIFFERENCE, CULTURE, AND THIRD WORLD WOMEN'S IDENTITY

One of the most fundamental dilemmas for African and other non-western women is western definitions of feminism. An extreme but common attitude is revealed in certain radical definitions. Jill Johnson's definition involves liberating women for women only. "We don't have to have anything to do with men at all. They've taken care of themselves." She further opines, "Feminism at heart is a massive complaint, Lesbianism is the solution... Until all women are lesbians there will be no true political revolution." Peggy Kornegger considers feminism as "A many-headed monster which can not be destroyed by singular decapitation...."[18] It is therefore hardly surprising that many other non-European women have problematized this attitude. To the majority of ordinary Africans, lesbianism is a non-existent issue because it is a mode of self-expression that is completely strange to their world-view. It is not even an option to millions of African women and can therefore not be the solution as Jill Johnson and many other Western or westernized women propose.

Several other issues are at the heart of the rejection of feminism, not only by African women but by many Third World and non-Eurocentric women. An Asian-American was asked whether she will consider herself a feminist or not. Her reply is representative of the reactions of many and identical to the position of many African women:

> There is feminism where all the problems in society are seen as caused by men. I don't believe in that. I don't believe men are the creators of the problems in society.... I do believe that men and women have to work together to solve the problems in society.[19]

Many African women maintain this position as they refuse to make men the scapegoat for their problems. The danger of non-western women being circumscribed by western ideologies has been succinctly put by Madhu Kishwa, an Indian woman activist who is involved in a women's journal:

> Feminism was an outgrowth of eighteenth-century humanist thought in Europe and the USA, reinforced by thinkers from other schools of thought, such as utilitarianism and Marxism.... While I stand committed to pro-women politics, I resist the label of feminism because of its overclose association with the western women's movement. I have no quarrel with the feminist movement in its own context and feel strengthened by the existence of women's movements in Western as in Eastern countries.... However...feminism, as appropriated and defined by the west, has too often become a tool of cultural imperialism.[20]

Madhu Kishwa speaks the mind of many Third World women and provides the basic reasons for their rejection of feminism as a concept. She has strongly detached herself from feminism because of the horror of imposed 'isms' and the inherent danger of their not being adequate in solving women's problems in a country where millions of women are struggling with more fundamental problems relating to caste, class, poverty, and/or starvation. In spite of her rejection of feminism, she devotes her life to bringing out positive qualities in women as she fights against women's subjugation. Similarly, many African women who are committed to women's issues reject feminism as a label.

The crux of the matter transcends definitions as Kishwa affirms. The condescending gender imperialism that manifests in various ways is another point that many Third World women are highlighting. Trihn Mihn ha is one of the most articulate critics of otherness:

> ... a group of mighty men attributed to itself a central, dominating position vis a vis other groups, overhauled its particularities and achievements, adopted a protective attitude toward those it classified among the outgroups and wrapped itself up in its own thinking, interpreting the out-group through the in-group mode of reasoning while claiming to speak the minds of both the in-group and the out-group.[21]

Leela Dube reiterates this as she condemns the Eurocentric bias that informs many of the positions taken by several scholars. She sums up the trend as the

> ethnocentric bias of western feminist scholars who tend to interpret data from other cultures in the perspective of the experiences acquired in their own cultures and their understanding of female-male relations from them.[22]

An American critic, Philip Burnham, also pins it down rather succinctly; "But writers from non-western traditions have for too long been compared to the Greeks so as to westernize and domesticate their strangeness."[23]

So, many Black women are suggesting a redefinition and Sandra Harding speaks for many in maintaining that feminism as "a political movement for the emancipation of women" must foreground cultural issues. In a similar vein, Bell Hooks and Adrienne Rich maintain that women's writing entails a re-vision and looking back in search of new perspectives. Alice Walker's classical search for our mother's garden has become an aspect of Black women's manifesto. Similarly, Patricia Hills Collins is an important audible voice in enunciating Black women's consciousness. African women writers have always derived inspiration from past prototypes in their creative works. Molara Ogundipe-Leslie has repeatedly called for a critical but progressive probing of the past to understand the present.

Several other points have emerged in this quest for more acceptable and inclusive theories and actions. The de-establishment of binary oppositions is crucial as the world is divided into oppositional imperialistic categories of white-black, north-south, east-west, left-right and similar concepts. These dualities are often deployed and exploited to foster ethnocentric domination and African women always find themselves on the periphery. Lynette Turner has recognized the need to move away from these dualities as many Third World women are advocating the same:

> ... what has become increasingly evident in analyses of colonial discourse is a general move away from a binary model of colonial relations to an acknowledgement in the words of Henry Louis Gates Jr. that the 'structures we have taken to be characteristic of colonial discourse are 'heterogeneous and conflictual'.[24]

The importance of ethnocentric values is being emphasized not to heighten the binaries but to decentre feminism, deconstruct existing bias, and reconstruct a new ideology that bridges the chasm that exists across the imperial divide. Africans require theories that remove gorges without glossing over cultural specificity in order to build meaningful coalitions. Post-coloniality has mediated their experience so substantially that many are seeking new theories that recognize their humanity first and foremost.

African women are at an important intersection in their awareness of the problems of speaking back. Questions are being raised to establish their peculiar canons of womanhood. The longstanding record of African women's mobilization on the continent are still largely ignored as the impression of her passivity and invisibility becomes even more dominant in western academia.

Universalization of womanhood therefore becomes a dilemma and new configurations are emerging. Western feminism is being challenged for posing to be global while in reality it is racially construed and culture specific. The general temper of Black women is well defined by Evelyn Brooks Higingbotham:

> ....women's studies for so long rested upon the unstated premise of racial (i.e. white) homogeneity and with this presumption proceeded to universalize 'women's culture' and oppression, while failing to see whites' own investment and complicity in the oppression of other groups of men or women.[25]

Floya Anthias and Nira Yuval-Davis maintain that not only is western feminism culturally and historically specific but it is also middle class. Bell Hooks has spoken for many in her observation that only the dominant group, the white race, can ignore the centrality of race in women's discourse since they are the privileged.[26] Another vital canon of oppositional discourse is the collective consciousness which is inseparable from the construction of womanhood by Africans and other non-western women (Angela Davis, 1993; Chinkwenye Okonjo, 1985). Black women are unanimous on the inseparability of the individual and communal experience as well as private and public areas.

In all these, difference is being delineated in more positive ways by these women. As they reject hegemony, many are recreating new tools of self-consciousness in their works.

Writing becomes a tool of self-liberation, self-preservation, and self-healing. African women writers are presenting alternate voices globally as an aspect of the increased awareness of Third World women. It is essential to situate African women's struggle and self-expression within African cultural context as well as within the larger struggle of Third World and all Blacks. Chandra Mohanty rejects trite stereotypes that enhance tools of oppression. Like Harding and Mohanty, Gayatri Spivac condemns deliberate effacement of the history of non-western women from their historical documents on feminism (Evans, 1994). This is a serious omission and many women are calling for new tools for representing Third World women's yearning because, in the words of Audre Lorde, "the master's tool will never demolish the master's house." This elicits the two major trends in African women's polemics—they are not only criticizing western hegemonic methods, they are formulating new definitions and world-view. In this process, the emphasis is on enhancing cultural identity even as they reject the image of Black women as victims.

Some white feminist critics are now addressing this issue as it becomes inevitable to revisit their position. To some others, it is almost an act of restitution to demand a rethinking of the woman question. Angela Miles' position in advocating transformative feminisms represents this trend:

> Feminism's difficult but exhilarating political challenge is to build sisterhood/solidarity across differences, using the differences as resources in developing shared critiques and visions.[27]

THE SEARCH FOR A CULTURALLY VALID WOMEN'S THEORY

But many African women's demands go beyond transformation. These women are more interested in a womanist ideology that addresses their specificity and one is convinced that some brands of western feminism are too uncompromising to apprehend the African cultural peculiarity. A new wine in an old wineskin will only heighten existing scepticism. Nonetheless, African women globally have forced mainstream feminists to continue the process of self-interrogation and some have been sensitized by the unrelenting writings of African and other Third World women. In recent years, our sisters in the diaspora have become so prolific in writing back that a new direction has been charted. Inevitably, being on the frontline of racism has accelerated the scope of response. African women on the continent are not completely silent and the emergent voices need to be identified.

Convinced that Francophone African women have broken "the emptiness of silence," D'Almeida elicits certain crucial achievements of these women writers that are true of other African women and their efforts in the direction of self-expression, "as writing becomes a key to self-representation, self-definition, a means of proposing an alternative way of knowing, of doing and of being in the world, women fill some of the pages that formerly were blank. Writing is a means of transgression, of resistance, of exposure."[28] One can see the rejection of the tag 'feminism' by women writers like Aidoo, Emecheta, and Aminata Sow Fall as a process of re-definition and a desire for a new mode of self-retrieval.These women are not denying womanhood or womanity, as their writing clearly illustrates.

There is still a lot that the West needs to know about Africa. I do agree with an English graduate student who lamented, "We don't know enough about African women on the continent and their mobilization and resistance."[29] This is partly because the mode of publicity differs, apart from the basic problem that Africans have in dealing with feminism. Women's concerted effort is not an academic exercise to the majority of Africans. They fight for their rights in different ways and for different reasons. The westernized middle-class woman in academia has to adopt the method that the West can understand—theorizing women's questions as an aspect of intellectual mode of singing about her womanity, and many have responded to this necessity. Yet her efforts remain largely effaced from feminist history.

Many African women resist subscribing to feminism as a rejection of the imperialistic attempt to force them to accept a foreign "ism" that is superfluous to the needs of the majority. Here, even silence is a weapon, as Nana Wilson-Tagoe confirms in discussing Africa's post-colonial conditions. These women saw such a close link between the struggle of all Africans, male or female, against colonialism, neo-colonialism, class, racism, and gender struggles that they do not wish to pigeon-hole their priorities. Nonetheless, women like Ama Ata Aidoo, Daphne Williams-Ntiri, Molara Ogundipe-Leslie, Micere Mugo, Bolanle Awe, Rebecca Njau, Ellen Kuzwayo, Chikwenye

Okonjo Ogunyemi, Nawal El Saadawi, and Amina Mama have been crying out against all forms of oppression as women and on behalf of women as an aspect of the struggle.

Some African women have attempted to paint feminism through terms like "Black feminism" or "African feminism." This has proved problematic, as we see in Alice Walker's definition of both feminism and womanism which draws attention to some salient ambiguities:

> Feminism is the political theory that struggles to free all women: women of colour, working-class women, poor women, disabled women, lesbians, old women—as well as white, economically privileged, heterosexual women. Anything less than this vision of total freedom is not feminism, but merely female self-aggrandizement.[30]

Her classic definition of womanism addresses the question of racial focus and specificity and makes this concept more valid to African women than the omnibus definition of feminism. In her work, *In Search of Our Mother's Garden,* she defines womanism within a Black context and an emergent femaleness or feminine coming-of-age. She defines a womanist as:

> A Black feminist or feminist of color... who loves other women, sexually and/or asexually. Appreciates and prefers women's culture...sometimes loves individual men, sexually and/or nonsexually. Committed to survival and wholeness of entire people, male and female.... Womanist is to feminism as purple is to lavender.[31]

This distinction is not a sharp one and one could easily confuse the two colours. A clear cultural delineation is essential to make continental woman's self-definition relevant.

The corrolary to rejecting feminism as a mode of defining African women's collective self-consciousness is the quest for new terms. They are trying to detach themselves from ideologies that they can not defend, as Ogundipe-Leslie confesses. One of the most outspoken African women, Daphne Williams Ntiri, has succinctly brought out the dilemma:

> For years Africana women have found themselves in a serious ideological predicament. In the absence of viable organized women's groups they have been invited to embrace feminism as an instrument of emancipation and as a new-found source of empowerment and status-building. Unfortunately, the majority of

Africana women on public platforms have rejected feminism for a multiplicity of reasons. First there is the
unquestionable need to reclaim Africana women; second, they are perplexed over the racist origins of the
feminist movement; third, they have found little solace
in the doctrines and mission of the feminist movement,
the realities, struggles and expectations of the two
groups remain on different planes. The privileges and
advantages still belong to the dominant group.[32]

African women's collective bonding and mobilization reveal
unique traits, as we see in the works of Nancy Leis and Nancy
Tanner (Rosaldo & Lamphere,1974). Nina Mba's research has
confirmed the strength of traditional African women which
sufficiently challenged the colonial administrators "to study
the causes of the riots and to uncover the organizational base
that permitted such spontaneity and solidarity among the
women."[33] Since pre-colonial periods, African women have
been mobilized to fight for their rights and even on behalf of
the whole group. Modern African women who are actively
speaking for other women did not necessarily take a cue from
the West. Using literary writers as an example, most of the
early African women writers from the continent confess that
they were motivated by traditional African oral literature and
historic powerful women (Aidoo, Nwapa, Njau, Sofola). Their
literary works make them gender mouthpieces also because
most of them were motivated by the silences in early African
literature which was largely patriarchal. Many agree that the
West can not speak for Africa.

It is this awareness that has prompted many Africans to
search for alternatives. The quest for a different terminology
that more adequately addresses the specificity of African
women's yearning as opposed to an imposed or dogmatic position is a wholesome one. It is a way of 'recreating ourselves,'
to use Ogundipe-Leslie's expression. This scholar who has
strongly reacted to the rejection of the term feminism has also
found it expedient to adopt a conciliatory position by substi-
tuting the term 'Stiwanism,' and this is best explained from
the horse's mouth:

I have since advocated the word "Stiwanism," instead of
feminism, to bypass these concerns and to bypass the
combative discourses that ensue whenever one raises
the issue of feminism in Africa.... The new word

describes what similarly minded women and myself would like to see in Africa. The word "feminism" itself seems to be a kind of red rag to the bull of African men. Some say the word by its very nature is hegemonic, or implicitly so. Others find the focus on women in themselves somehow threatening.... Some who are genuinely concerned with ameliorating women's lives sometimes feel embarrassed to be described as "feminist," unless they are particularly strong in character...."Stiwa" is my acronym for *Social Transformation Including Women in Africa.*[34]

This observation and detailed definition of this new terminology confirms the uneasy attitude of many African women whenever the word feminism is used to denote African women's self-consciousness, self-expression, or conditions of struggle. Even a radical like Ogundipe-Leslie recognizes the possibility of taking feminism as an imitative nomenclature that may be seen as something imposed on African women. This reiterates the problem of parroting or *kikusuku* that I consider central to this discourse. She gives further clarification of the term "Stiwanism" that elucidates her theory as well as her active commitment:

This new term describes my agenda for women in Africa without having to answer charges of imitativeness or having to constantly define our agenda on the African continent in relation to other feminisms, in particular, white Euro-American feminisms which are unfortunately under siege by everyone. This new term allows me to discuss the needs of African women today in the tradition of the spaces and strategies provided in our indigenous cultures for the social being of women.[35]

Perhaps the combative attitude will be eliminated with new terms but better still with a new attitude that accommodates diversities through a dialogic stance. Others who are genuinely preoccupied with augmenting the opportunities and improving the conditions of women may still prefer to do so without a tag or an 'ism,' even those with the strength of character that this writer talks about.

Womanism and Black Women's Search for Self-Definition

Moving from the initial caution, many African women have spoken out in favour of the emergent concept of *Womanism* as a valid African ideology. What then is womanism? To Africans, womanism is the totality of feminine self-expression, self-retrieval, and self-assertion in positive cultural ways. It is generally believed that Alice Walker brought the word into focus as an aspect of African Americans' appreciation of mature womanhood in a girl. Chikwenye Okonjo also used the word around the same time. The consciousness that informed womanism, however, transcends individual awareness and is not new to African women. Nonetheless, Walker's attempt to ground Black feminist or womanist consciousness is a part of the growth of awareness that seeks a unique identity for African women's separate consciousness. Madhu Dubey recognizes this: "The term womanism, coined by Walker, may be interpreted as an attempt to integrate Black nationalism into feminism, to articulate a distinctively Black feminism that shares some of the objectives of Black nationalist ideology." It is significant, as Dubey remarks, that Walker derives this concept from Black women folk culture and highlights a commitment to the survival of all Black folks male and female.

To Okonjo, womanism is a global ideology for African women which embraces racial, gender, class, and cultural consciousness:

> Black womanism is a philosophy that celebrates Black roots, the ideals of black life, while giving a balanced presentation of black womandom. It concerns itself as much with the Black sexual power tussle as with the world power structure that subjugates Blacks.[36]

She emphasizes dynamic wholeness and self-healing as well as the unity of all Blacks across gender lines. This is a reiteration of the position of that giant and pioneer of African literature, Flora Nwapa, who was clearly a womanist.

One of the most thought-provoking and perhaps latest contribution to the definition of womanism from the diaspora emerges from the masterpiece by Clenora Hudson-Weems, *Africana Womanism*. This book has come as a relief to many Africans who are not at ease with feminism in its diverse shades of definition. Her bold ideological thrust coincides with the yearning of a majority of Africans on the continent. She sees the starting point of African women's consciousness as the need for self-naming:

> ... the Africana woman, in realizing and properly assess-
> ing herself and her movement, must properly name her-
> self and her movement—Africana womanist and
> Africana womanism.[37]

She underscores a closer affinity among all African women
globally, while emphasizing the centrality of the family.
Hudson-Weems stresses the conviction that Africana womanism is not a men-hating ideology, as all Africans need a concerted effort against racism and all forms of oppression that
undermine Black people. She defines womanism in a very
explicit way and within a distinct African context:

> Neither an outgrowth nor an addendum to feminism,
> Africana Womanism is not Black feminism, or Walker's
> womanism that some Africana women have come to
> embrace. Africana Womanism is an ideology created
> and designed for all women of African descent. It is
> grounded in African culture, and therefore it necessar-
> ily focuses on the unique experiences, struggles, needs
> and desires of Africana women.[38]

Hudson-Weems stresses the need to avoid tagging African
women's agenda onto white feminist values.

A common nexus, therefore, runs through the consciousness of African people in foregrounding collectivism and an
integrative struggle. To most African women, difference
becomes a stepping stone for self-identity and a strong drive
for cultural self-retrieval. They are not advocating solipsism,
since replacing one separatism with another is not productive. Their quest for a positive but distinct identity is often
mistaken for silence and invisibility.

African women are products of multiple subjugation.
Patriarchy, tradition, colonialism, neo-colonialism, racism, and
gender imperialism all combine to act against the African
woman's self-assertion. But the plight of the alienated, divided,
westernized African woman is usually taken as the norm. While
they try to negotiate a path through the multiple maze of
oppression positively, the life of the majority of African women
reveals resilience and not defeat. Many African women scholars are unfolding the visibility of African women as an important step in speaking out. Self-healing entails correcting the
representation of African women as if they exist in some subterranean world, tongue-tied and demobilized.

There is the need to continue unfolding areas of visibility

and power of African women, especially in the traditional context. Nina Mba's work *Nigerian Women Mobilised* is a masterpiece that unravels the unacknowledged invincibility of Nigerian women in pre-colonial and early colonial periods. Their collective actions made them a threat to kings and an obstacle to colonial administrators. One-sided presentation of gender structures have overlooked these historic actions and African women's dynamics of self-perception, their conflicts and ambivalence. The time is ripe for naive representation and invention of African women to be demolished. These women seek a more holistic approach that is sufficiently inclusive to appreciate the specific African cultural definition of womanhood and empowerment. Awa Thiam, the versatile Senegalese woman, has made this point as she rejects western feminists' patronage. In *Black Sisters Speak Out,* she highlights the irony:

> You should think that Black women did not exist. In fact, they find themselves denied, in this way, by the very women who claim to be fighting for the liberation of all women.[39]

So this alternative, a womanist theory, emerged from the increasing awareness of African women that self-naming is fundamental to these problems. A Yoruba proverb hits the nail on the head,

> *Owo ara eni l'a fi ntun iwa ara eni se*

> You have to establish your dignity yourself and not leave it to others.

Self-naming is very central to African world-view. In many African cultures, naming almost assumes a sacred status. One doesn't just name a child in traditional African society. Diverse considerations such as family traits and achievement, lineal peculiarities or divine guidance determine a child's name. A stranger can not be allowed to name the child since he does not have adequate knowledge of these paraphernalia of naming. The Yorubas believe strongly in this as an aspect of their philosophy:

> *Oruko n ro ni.*
> *Oriki nro eniyan*

> Naming affects the individual;
> Encomium shapes personality.

This is at the heart of the search for new terminologies of self-definition. As Ogundipe-Leslie's term, Stiwanism, underscores social transformation, "womanism" is an explicit denomination of the totality of giving expression to positive female and feminine bonding and collective self-assertion. Although many African languages have no synonym for feminism as it is defined in the West, the concept of group action by women, based on common welfare in social, cultural, economic, religious, or political matters is indigenous and familiar to a majority of these women. Modes of enunciating this may differ but, as Abena Busia maintains, womanhood is central and this is neither controversial nor conflictual to African women. It may not imply burning the bra or alienating men. As we see in the agenda of the women's group, Yewwi Yewwu, African women seek an inclusive basis for action across class and ethnic lines. Where patriarchy is responsible for their oppression, these women will fight against it but at other times, they are ready to accommodate men in a concerted effort, as we se in the outlook of Women in Nigeria. It is an indication of a wholesome pride in feminine look and attributes as opposed to the effacement of feminine qualities.

As far as the ordinary African woman is concerned, the expression of femaleness and the struggle for self-assertion did not come from the West. She is aware of her womanism as the totality of her self-expression and self-realization in diverse positive ways. This involves eliciting women's positive qualities, ability, self-enhancement, self-esteem, and freedom within African cultural context. Being a woman does not entail self-negation to many. So, they are not seeking to be like men, look like men, or necessarily act like men. Womanism therefore manifests and enhances African women's collective grouping, and positive bonding as opposed to ideological bondage. Concerted women's actions are so natural to her that she will consider some of the arguments in contemporary feminism superfluous to her experience. For the purpose of an academic re-inscription, however, one needs to highlight some salient issues in womanist theory and the distinction between womanism and feminism.

Since modern academia describes human societies in relational terms, all women bear certain basic traits and this has been subverted by many feminists. So, womanism bears some resemblance to any theory about women but it has very distinct characteristics emerging from African values. African women in the diaspora are retrieving these values in spite of time and regional mediation. They are very specific in their call for an Afrocentric conceptualization of African women's reality; whether they define womanism overtly or not, their celebration of African womanism inheres in their works. Indeed, most of these sisters transcend womanist theory as womanist activism is a part of their lifestyle.

African Women's Priorities and the Negotiation of Space

One important fact needs reiteration in discussing continental African women and their reaction to feminism. A utopia in which the distinction between men and women is effaced as women neutralize their femininity is seen as an aberration in view of African traditions. I do agree that tradition is one of the many mountains on African women's backs. Positive traditions can, however, enhance African women's position. Many issues exalted in radical feminism will be seen as a perversion to many African women in the traditional set-up, and traditional women do have some positive avenues of self-liberation, as we see in Ondo traditional society. The valences of social interaction and self-perception in Africa often derive from externality in a positive way. The African woman's conceptualization of freedom is not based on the erosion of her feminine attributes and outlook but in asserting her feminine qualities. African femininity is manifested in female fashion designs and other physical adornments that are unique to women. The focus on hairstyles and fashions that distinguish her from men is very important to her.

Rather than passively being exploited for their feminine look and nature, these women exploit such features by taking advantage of them. It is sometimes difficult to draw the line between what is feminine and what is not. In many parts of Africa, such as among the Ijaw people of the Niger delta, women are very active in farming but this is an occupation that is more of a man's job in many parts of Africa. Generally, however, women will be glad to let their husbands or sons or other men do the more strenuous aspects of farming such as tree cutting or building and mending fences. A woman will not see it as an erosion of her feminine self when a man offers to do the hazardous work and may even see this as an aspect of her feminine privileges. The reaction to such issues is different in the West, where it is no longer politically correct to open the door for a woman.

It is documented that women have used feminine solidarity to change laws, political decisions, economic order, and social status (Mba, 1982). Unisexual lifestyle is definitely not a prerequisite for African women's mobilization. In the ongoing search for acceptable women's theories, the location of the African woman is peculiar. She refuses to subsume her cultural needs under the universal umbrella of sisterhood. She is constantly battling with misrepresentation or non-representation in addition to national, ethnic, and serious economic problems. In the much acknowledged feminization of poverty, African women carry the burden of the family's survival much more than is generally appreciated. This problem is more significant in several parts of Africa where the hang-over of imperialism and externalized colonialism continue to haunt the people. The situation in South Africa illustrates this issue very clearly:

> A crucial factor in the position of the women of South Africa has been that of the impact of imperial power on an indigenous culture. Inferiority was imposed on the African peoples by the nature of colonialism in Africa. But the woman has the burden doubled: the black consciousness of 'inferiority' ingrained by the colonists, the destruction of tribal structures that gave status to both sexes and the denigration of any culture other than that of the colonists themselves is the first imposition; the second is the inferior status imposed by the relationship of the women and men.[40]

In Southern Africa, one of the obnoxious apartheid laws that has shaped women's reality in a very destructive way is the migrant labor law, which has undermined the family structure in a way that women receive the butt-end of the suffering. The destruction of family housing in many townships meant sending wives and children back to resettlement camps. So, many of the women face the harrowing experience of watching their hungry children or looking desperately for sustenance as their husbands roam the streets of the cities searching for work. Others become victims of family disintegration in view of a high rate of divorce. As people are forcefully removed and relocated, 'black spots' are cleared for whites and many black women are retained by whites as domestic servants. But as soon as they start a family, they have to move to the homeland. Hilda Bernstein's account gives a vivid picture of the suffering of African women under these and other apartheid laws:

> It is impossible to describe adequately what forced
> removals, both individual and mass, and the systematic
> break-up of family life have done to the women of South
> Africa.... Whether they are moved singly, or as part of a
> group from farms of 'black spots', each removal is an
> individual tragedy beginning with the stonewall of an
> official decree and ending in the destruction of home
> and family.[41]

South African women's experience underscores the serious
issue of imperialistic strangulation that is so real to the people that gender theorizing could not have been the priority of
these women. How can any shade of feminism comprehend the
intensity of such women's trauma or address their pressing
need? To many women on the African continent, the men are
not their enemies. Most Africans, male and female, have more
pressing problems that require the concerted efforts of all. So,
when these women call for their rights, freedom and opportunity to be treated humanely, many targets are closely intertwined and gender is very often not the most serious
problem.Yet, these women's consciousness and struggle
against oppression and self-negation supersede the activism of
many feminists. Such women include Debra Nikiwe Matshoba,
who, having been imprisoned together with her husband,
knows that her struggle is inseparable from that of men and all
oppressed Africans and other oppressed people globally.
Others, like Ellen Kuzwayo, who have become dispossessed of
family lands, alienated, and seen millions of Soweto youths,
male and female, killed by the brutal guns of apartheid government will cry out for a more humane society before building gender coalitions. Yet, their unique courage and struggle
against oppression show the hollowness in any theory that
presents African women as passive, suffering victims.

Wrong emphasis and prioritization by feminists who claim
to be fighting on behalf of African women are responsible for
the indifference to or rejection of feminisms by many African
women and those on the continent in particular. These women
are not seeking to replace one subjugation or separatism with
another. African women yearn for a society in which they can
assert their innate resourcefulness by rejecting the fetters of
tradition and any aspects of socialization that puts them at a
disadvantage. They seek to convince men that they can be

productive in the home and outside the home by their resilience and dynamic drive in economic areas. African women are interested in rehumanizing the world by enhancing their roles positively even as they consider themselves more suitable for certain roles than men.

The position of a majority of African women comes out clearly in the call by the Third World group, 'Development Alternatives with Women for a New Era'[DAWN] :

> We want a world where inequality based on class, gender, and race is absent from every country, and from the relationships between countries. We want a world where basic needs become basic rights and where poverty and all forms of violence are eliminated.... We want a world where all institutions are open to participatory democratic processes, where women share in determining priorities and making decisions.[42]

African women scholars recognize the serious implications of poverty and underdevelopment for women. But their multiple burdens are not docilely accepted or ignored. Many are calling for changes under diverse women's groups and umbrellas, as one sees in the Nairobi women's manifesto:

> Women, as the group most adversely affected by the existing development strategies, will have to be in the forefront of the definition of a new self-reliant people-centred development. This strategy will have to recognize and build on their creative potential and render women equal and active participants.[43]

There are many African women's collectives that are working for positive enhancements of African women. These include groups that operate all over the continent like AAWORD as well as regional and national government women's commissions. Major university women's studies groups are actively involved in co-ordinating research on African women, reaching out to communities to conscientize women and influence governments on women's behalf. An important area of contention is the different attitude to the private-public sphere dichotomy. Western feminists' emphasis on the women's space and sphere of influence mainly in terms of public participation is problematic to many African women. This accentuates the distortion of the criteria of judgement of women's freedom and empowerment. The African woman cherishes her role as a home maker as well as her status as a mother or a potential mother. She does not necessarily see these roles as liabilities. Fatma Alloo of Tanzania makes this point :

> Some of you may ask is it possible to talk of all women as one? Is a rural woman's situation the same as say a typist or a permanent secretary's? Of course not....But if you look at the nature of our oppression, our sex does determine our situation in a very fundamental way. As women we all carry a multiple burden. As women we all have to be concerned with reproductive rights. As women we face situations which men do not have to, e.g. sexual harassment at work. As women our role as homemakers gets trivialized and unacknowledged, and our reproductive role is portrayed as our biggest liability. These are some of the issues we face as women.[44]

A mental detour to Africa by those speaking for African women that will elicit a sincere attempt to understand these women's cultural idiosyncrasies is therefore a major yearning by African womanists. Black women have been placed on the lowest rung of the feminist ladder, particularly those on the continent. This inferiorization of black women is not new. On the plight of Black women in 19th-century America, Dorothy Stirling posits this multiple level of inferiorization: "To be a Black woman in 19th century America was to live in the double jeopardy of belonging to the 'inferior' sex of an 'inferior' race."[45]

The centrality of the family is important to Africans, male and female. Women in particular see the family as the nucleus of social development, growth, moral sustenance as well as cultural continuity. They do not see the family as an anathema. They can not adopt the western feminists' attitude such as the position of Zilla Einstein who contends that the family is a tool for entrenching capitalist oppression and individualism. African family set-up is derived from the communal ethos. These women resist opinions that contradict their African values as we see in Ann Oakley's estimation that the family creates gender and generation hierarchies.

Rather than enhance individualism, African family patterns cultivate the spirit of collective consciousness, mutual reciprocity, and role-sharing. It therefore prevents family dislocation and the plague of self-centredness that characterize modern civilization. Many African womanists are happily married without any overt hindrance to their career or occupation. Some are incapacitated by their domestic situation. Others have adapted themselves to the role of mothers or the status of single women and are actively preoccupied with the cause of women. These scholars believe that they have a different agenda to pursue on behalf of Africans.

One cannot put a veneer on African women's needs and cultural awareness or national exigency that are sometimes more pressing than gender problems. In tracing the development of women's consciousness, African women on the continent are usually treated as appendages to others. In relating to their problems and confronting them, they may not necessarily adopt western styles or yardsticks. Yet they address issues such as the marginalization of girls in education, inequalities in job opportunities, discriminatory legal structures, and discrepancies in the rights and privileges of women workers. Other issues include discriminatory allowances for married women. Some of these have now been changed and these women have gained some ground. Laws about children's custody which put women at a disadvantage have also been changed in many places because of women's mobilization and intervention.

The fear of replacing existing imperialism with new models is a major concern. Colonialism did widen existing gender gaps in many parts of Africa. In establishing schools, colonialists did not consider girls' education an important need. Consequently, girls schools were not established until some 50 years after the first boys' schools. The earliest schools for girls in Nigeria were primary schools and domestic science centers for training women to be good wives for the early African teachers and administrators. On the other hand, boys' schools included grammar schools that produced the pioneers of Nigeria as a nation.

John D. Clarke's very recent work on colonial Nigeria has made revelations to confirm this. In *Teacher and Friend: Memoirs of an Education Officer in Colonial Africa,* he gives a vivid and objective personal account that exposes the foundation of women's educational invisibility as well as the link between gender and racial discrimination by colonialists:

> When I arrived and went into my office in the headquarters of the Educational department in Lagos, I found that all the African members of the staff were male. This was so in all the commercial stores. Even in the hospitals the nurses were all men. There was a distinct but largely unspoken policy to keep the races apart.[46]

Clarke's memoir reveals his departure from the norm because he became sensitive to the gender injustice. On one occasion, Clarke had to change existing colonial gendered policy and decorum to force the admission of girls into existing schools:

> I had noticed that, as was often the case in those days, there were very few girls among the pupils in his school. So, I went along and told him to tell all the parents that the new class would be for girls only.... looking back, I am surprised at the success of my high-handed action.[47]

Since the colonial era, African women have continued to experience such a close link between racism and sexism and this informs their rejection of any claim by feminists to fight their cause. African women are struggling against multiple disadvantages; some of these are caused by tradition, and patriarchal set-up. In some specific ways colonialism did not remove the gender inequality but widened it as education created new forms of inequality to crown the existing ones. So African women are contending with all these on their own terms of reference and no single ideology can be thrust on them as the solution to these hydra-headed problems, some of which are gendered while others are inclusive. Several approaches have been adopted by African women in confronting their reality. Some are more radical than others, but no dogmatic imposition of an external 'ism' can be sufficiently inclusive or endogenous to address the problems. Each approach has some logical argument, validity and relevance. But external eye-view cannot fully address the African woman's problem. Introspection and individuality characterize feminism but African thought is largely collective and this entails respecting several approaches to the problem.

A DIALOGIC APPROACH TO AFRICAN WOMEN'S REALITY

Womanism does not require compartmentalization and one does not need to identify radical, liberal, psycho-analytic and other categories of womanism. Any African woman who has the consciousness to situate the struggle within African cultural realities by working for a total and robust self-retrieval of the African woman is an African or Africana womanist. Like identity, the boundaries of human consciousness are fluid and its expression can reveal multiple levels of perception. For any conceptual framework to be valid to African women, African woman's cultural identity, self-perception, and yearning within an integrative collective consciousness needs to be fore-grounded. Believing that the African woman is searching for a space within the collective room is in contradistinction to the quest for a room of her own. Building a wall around herself cannot be the aim of an authentic African woman's theory. There is the need to shift boundaries and construct bridges across ethnicity, gender, and class.

A dialogic perspective is more wholesome and valid to the African woman and Mikhail Bakhtin's theoretical framework is useful here. Many African scholars have advocated a dialogic approach overtly or implicitly. In calling for *nego-feminism,* Obioma Nnaemeka recognizes this need. Ropo Sekoni's emphasis on the world as a marketplace where human values are negotiated is very significant. He emphasizes the popular Yoruba trope of the market as an open place for negotiation:

> The dynamics of interaction in Yoruba markets can be characterized as dialogic, defined by exchange and interaction of signs as means of constructing reality.... Bargaining and haggling over the price of a commodity between vendor and buyer depicts metasemiotically that the value of meaning of any social phenomenon is open to negotiation by the human subjects that value and revalue such phenomena.[48]

Much within African belief systems is predicated on this philosophy of life as a negotiation of values, as a continuum, an intersection between the past, the present and the future. The world is conceived as a negotiation of diverse convictions and so heteroglossia is more valid to any African thoughts as opposed to monovocality. No wonder the market in most traditional African settings is an open place, a space characterized by active dialogues and negotiation. It is also a space characterized by fluid boundaries as each person's space is not rigidly divided but the borders of one woman's space marks the beginning of another with hardly any fixed dividing walls. The numerous points of entry and exit make room for everyone to confirm the Yoruba belief that there are diversities of routes into the market place, "*Ona kan o wo oja.*" Sekoni opines that:

> The transformation of the market into a communicative/diplomatic space in which both sides exchange notes on their interests and constraints as prelude to the determination of the prices of goods and services,

mimes, in a metasemiotic sense, the notion that social life depends on exchange and negotiation. More importantly, negotiating the prices of the means of biological and social continuity in the market depicts the importance of the complexity and plurality of perspectives in the construction of culture.[49]

This underscores the plurality of perspectives as a logical sequence from the African nego-theory. The valences of conceptualization of human values are therefore multiple and this sometimes assumes a metaphysical importance. African womanist ideology derives from this dialogic outlook. This approach accommodates all perspectives to the problem as bearing some relevance to the solution. It is not based on tension or arguments but on a recognition that diverse approaches can exist side by side. African women's search for self-realization is identical to the quest of all oppressed, marginalized or undermined groups. It is therefore open to a diversity of approaches as opposed to a monovalent imposition of a perspective.

The African woman seeks self-fulfilment within this plural cultural context. The average African woman is not a hater of men; nor does she seek to build a wall around her gender across which she throws ideological missiles. She desires self-respect, an active role, dynamic participation in all areas of social development, and dignity alongside the men. This necessitates a dialogic stance, a mutual understanding and not a dogmatic or diachronic ideological posture. There is the need to break existing barriers caused by Africans who have identified with some brands of feminism and have constructed walls separating them from other African sisters. This is an aspect of the alienated consciousness of modern middle-class Africans that is a departure from strong female bonding by traditional women. Many African women maintain that the time is ripe for shifting boundaries for positive interactions. The African everywoman suspects the valorization and reification of philosophies considered unnatural in the African context. Even among the middle class, this is at the heart of the rejection of the term 'feminism.'

The African wo/man's quest is to eliminate externalized colonialism in all its forms, subtle or overt. Modern literary scholarship is polarized as critics pitch tents between relativism and perspectivism, structure and context, autonomy and commitment. African woman's need is, therefore, first and foremost, a search for dignity and a rejection of neo-colonial strings that retard Africa as a whole, and the woman in particular.

In the on-going yearning, an inward search is also essential, to eliminate all the forces that cause the interiorization of negative values. Untangling the intricate web of culture is also pertinent, but it calls for a clear vision and not a one-eyed perception. A great deal of distortion of the ideals, yearnings, and goals of the African woman exist in modern academic research. African women's reality has suffered much from jaundiced critique. There has been an outcry against this and a call for relocating African womanity (Nnaemeka, 1992).

One needs historical hindsight for proper self-retrieval. This is what women like Angela Davis, Maya Angelou, Alice Walker, Zulu Sofola, Molara Ogundipe-Leslie, Chikwenye Okonjo-Ogunyemi, Amina Mama, and Clenora Hudson-Weems have achieved in diverse ways in their redefinition and reinscription of African womanhood. They identify womanism as deriving from African values. African women are visible in particular areas. They are much more visible, vibrant, and dynamic than the passive image of them that is recurrent in modern academia. Their roles are not passive but dynamic and protean, in line with the changing demands and reality of their situation. Mainstream and malestream concepts need to be reviewed for the emergence of an authentic African feminine theory. The African woman is still largely marginalized; but she has not accepted her predicament without struggle as some critics contend.

Several African women writers and critics are pre-occupied with the African woman's problems, whether they admit this or not. Adeola James has achieved a distinction in bringing out salient viewpoints from outstanding women writers across the continent which draw out the diversity of position. Putting these varieties of attitude side by side emphasizes the dialogic nature of womanist concepts whether the writer overtly defines it or reveals it in theory or praxis. It is important to present African women's consciousness through a discursive framework, a dialogue. This is different from the argumentative or dialectic method of logical disputation. It is also a departure from a dogmatic imposition of a single viewpoint, perception, or definition. It involves mutual respect of each other's views and attitude.

African culture is complex and it is as variegated as the leopard's skin. It reveals common denominators within the heterogeneous components in that the Fulani woman's experience is similar to the Ijaw, Ewe, Buganda, Sotho, or Nuba woman's in several ways, but the uniqueness of each cultural or regional sub-group cannot be erased. Similarly, the experience and needs of the rural in contrast to the urban, the educated as opposed to the uneducated, the lower as different from the middle class African woman, cannot be subverted or subsumed under a single frame of reference.

According to Zulu Sofola, womanism needs to seek genuine liberation of the African woman which involves probing African culture, values, and tradition and understanding the real location of the woman. Sofola maintains that the woman in the traditional set-up who made history did so through traditional institutional roles. This is confirmed by women giants—queens, and political activators and leaders from all parts of Africa (Sweetman, 1984; Awe, 1992). To Micere Mugo, a meaningful perception of African womanism entails the liberation of the ordinary rural woman, in line with her Marxist orientation. She expects African women writers to raise the consciousness and identify with the suffering, oppression, and poverty of the ordinary woman. She decries the failure to relate to these women or analyze "the condition of the majority of oppressed women among the workers and peasants." Mugo sees the on-going research on womanism as valid but she insists on relevance.

One can therefore see that these writers are emphasizing different aspects of the essence of African womanhood, whether they make overt theoretical claims or not. Rebecca Njau highlights strong women's roles in Kenyan history to prove that there have always been proofs of women's self-assertion that are not acquired from outside Africa. This is the motivation for her work, *Kenyan Women and Their Mystical Powers*. She is very firm in her convictions:

> I have always been disturbed by people who say that the women who are highly educated have copied western ideas, knowing that my own strength comes from inside myself and from my own background, from my mother whom I respect very much and from my grandfather.... I wanted to go back into history to find out if there were any strong women who were respected by men and who were not just seen as women. I wanted to prove that there must have been. (James, 1990: 104).

Her opinion is confirmed by the resilience and dynamic power of Kenyan women confirmed by their actions, ranging from their roles during the "Mau Mau" struggle to the determination of the Kenyan women on hunger strike in 1992.

In the opinion of Zaynab Alkali, presenting women's reality is not an option but an imperative. Yet, she sees the women's movement as an interference that has not had much influence on African women. She says that one needs not look at literary works by African women as 'feminist literature' exclusively because to her, "Preserving a certain image of the African woman comes naturally." She was motivated to write by the treatment of women as the weaker sex, "I am irked by the fact that most women have been trained to see themselves as 'weak' and 'incapable' of attaining the highest peak of intellectual development" (James, 1990:29). Her womanist inclination is therefore confirmed by her creation of strong women confronting destructive traditions but coming to terms with the limits of individuality.

African women's consciousness is not static but protean and dynamic. This also varies in different parts and from one class to the other. African women's perception of the need to speak out on behalf of their gender is therefore equally varied. Often, the myth of African women's experience is confused with the reality. It is important to identify and foreground hidden areas of African women's strength and audibility as a departure from current over-emphasis on their voicelessness and helplessness as victims.

NOTES

1.   Irene D'Almeida, *Francophone African Women: Destroying the Emptiness of Silence* (Gainsville: Florida University Press, 1994), p. 1.
2.   Micere Mugo during a seminar on "Gender, Politics and African Cultural Production" at the Africana Studies and Research Center, Cornell University, March 1992.
3.   Siga Jajne, "African Women and the category 'WOMAN' in Feminist Theory," a paper presented at the annual conference of the African Literature Association in Columbus, Ohio, March 1995. This theory is a part of a larger work in progress emerging from this writer's doctoral research.
4.   D'Almeida, *op. cit.,* p.15.
5.   Kwame Anthony Appiah," Africa's Post-Colonial Past," a plenary session at the African Literature Association Conference, Columbus, Ohio, March 18, 1995.
6.   Abena Busia in my interview with her in her office at Rutgers University, New Brunswick, March 22nd, 1995.

7.   Molara Ogundipe-Leslie, *Re-creating Ourselves: African Women & Critical Transformation* (Trenton, N.J.: Africa World Press, 1994), p.11.
8.   Ogundipe-Leslie, *op. cit.,* p. 10.
9.   See Hans Zell, Carol Bundy, and Virginia Coulon, eds, *A New Reader's Guide to African Literature* (London: Heinemann, 1983).
10.   Marie Umeh, "Women and Social Realism in Buchi Emecheta," Ph.D thesis submitted to the University of Wisconsin, Madison.
11.   Ama Ata Aidoo, "Unwelcomed Pals and Decorative Slaves—Or Glimpses of Women as Writers and Characters in Contemporary African Literature," Ernest Emeyonu, ed., *Literature and Society: Selected Essays on African Literature* (Oguta, Nigeria: Zim Pan African Publishers, 1989).
12.   Rosemarie Tong, *Feminist Thought* (San Francisco: Westwood, 1989), p. 1.
13.   Tong, *op. cit.,* p.7.
14.   Audre Lorde, *Sister Outsider* (Freedom, Calif.: The Crossing Press, 1984), p. 111.
15.   Maggie Humm, *Feminism, A Reader* (London: Harvester-Wheatsheaf, 1992), p. 122.
16.   Gayle Greene, *Signs,*Vol.9, No.1 (Autumn,1983): 4.
17.   Bhasin, Kamla et al., "Some Questions on Feminism and its Relevance in South East Asia" (New Delhi: Kamla Bhasin, 1986), p. 2.
18.   Jill Johnson in *Feminist Dictionary,* ed. Cheris Kramarae & Paula Treichler (London: Unwin, 1985), p. 158.
19.   Cited in Susie Ling's dissertation and reproduced in *Feminist Dictionary,* p. 158.
20.   Madhu Kishwa, in Mary Evans, *The Woman Question* (London: SAGE, 1994), p. 23.
21.   Susie King in her reaction to feminism in *Feminist Dictionary, loc. cit.*
22.   Leela Dube, et. al., *Visibility and Power* (Delhi: OUP, 1986), p. 8.
23.   Philip Burnham in an unpublished paper in progress delivered at a seminar organized by the USIA at Obafemi Awolowo University, Ile-Ife, 1990.
24.   Lynette Turner, *Women,* Vol. 2, No.3 (Winter 1991): 239.
25.   Evelyn Brooks Higingbotham, *Signs,* Vol.17, No.2 (1992): 255.
26.   Bell Hooks, *Ain't I a Woman* (Boston: Southend, 1981).
27.   Angela Miles, "North American Feminisms/Global Feminisms: Contradictory or Complimentary?"—paper presented at the *Women in Africa and the Diaspora* conference, Nsukka, 1992, 11.
28.   D'Almeida, *op. cit.,* p. 176.
29.   This profound admission came out of a discussion during my seminar presentation on "African Myths of Gender," at the Women's Studies Post-Graduate Seminar Series, Darwin College, University of Kent in Canterbury, February 1995.

30. Alice Walker, loc. cit.

31. Alice Walker, *In Search of Our Mother's Gardens* (San Diego: Harcourt, 1983), p.xii.

32. Daphne William Ntiri, "Introduction" to Clenora Hudson-Weems, *Africana Womanism* (Troy, Mich.: Bedford Publishers, 1993), 1.

33. Nancy B. Leis, "Women in Groups: Ijaw Women's Association," in Michelle Rosaldo and Loiuse Lamphere,eds., *Women, Culture and Society* (Stanford, Calif.: Stanford University Press, 1974), p.223.

34. Molara Ogundipe-Leslie, *Recreating Ourselves,* pp.209-230.

35. *Ibid.*

36. Chikwenye Okonjo Ogunyemi, "Womanism: The Dynamics of the Contemporary Black Female Novel in English," *Signs,* Vol. 11, No. 1.

37. Quoted in *Africana Womanism,* p. 2.

38. Weems, loc. cit., p. 22.

39. Awa Thiam, *Black Sisters Speak Out* (London: Pluto Press, 1986) (translated).

40. Hilda Bernstein, "For Their Triumphs & for their Tears: Women in Apartheid South Africa" (London: International Defence Funds, 1975), 28.

41. Beinstein, op. cit., p.15.

42. Gita Sen and Caren Grown, *Development, Crises and Alternative Visions* (New York: Monthly Review Press, 1987), pp. 80/81.

43. Association of African Women on Research and Development in "Nairobi Manifesto," during the Nairobi Conference, 1985, p.5.

44. Fatma Alloo, Chairperson of the Tanzanian Media Women's Association,"The Need for a Women's Magazine," *Sauti Ya Siti,* No. 1 (March 1988): 2.

45. Dorothy Stirling, ed., *We Are Your Sisters: Black Women in the 19th Century* (New York: Norton & Co., 1984), p. ix.

46. John D. Clarke, *Teacher and Friend: Memoirs of an Education Officer in Colonial Africa* (Pittsburgh, Pa.: Allies Behavioural Center, 1993), p.32.

47. Clarke, op. cit., p. 34.

48. Ropo Sekoni, "Yoruba Market Dynamics and the Aesthetics of Negotiation in Female Precolonial Narrative Tradition," *Research in African Literature* Vol. 25, No. 3 (Fall 94): 35.

49. *Ibid.*

Chapter Two

African Women's Mobilization— The History and the Myth

African women's mobilization and struggle is older than many scholars acknowledge. History, sociology, anthropology, oral testimony, and oral literature confirm the long-standing nature of these people's rejection of subjugation and dynamic self-assertion and empowerment that have remained largely unnoticed in modern academia. Looking back has become an imperative for African women seeking true self-retrieval and self-healing. There is a catalogue of African women rulers and leaders who have charted their people's history in a remarkable way while the marks left by collective group actions remain indelible (David Sweetman,1984; Bolanle Awe, 1993).

There has been a more conscious effort to unveil the actions of these women giants, to correct the impression that African women have accepted oppression with dignity and so have made negligible impact on social change. Writers in the West who have made significant contributions in this regard include Michele Rosaldo, Louise Lamphere, Jane Parpart, and

Kathleen Staudt. Women historians, sociologists, literary writers/critics, and folklorists of the African continent, have had a major input in deconstructing the role of African women in the struggle for total emancipation of their race and gender. These include Bolanle Awe, Laureta Ngcobo, Simi Afonja, Omolara Ogundipe-Leslie, Ellen Kuzwayo, and Nina Mba.

In her recent work, *Nigerian Women in Historical Perspective,* Bolanle Awe touches on the increasing focus on African women's contribution to history past and present:

> The study of women's history and their contribution to the development of their society has gained recognition as a genuine and significant area of study and therefore worthy of its own literature. Previously, the role of women in African history had been virtually neglected. Most writings on the African past tended to concentrate on the spectacular achievements of men and gloss over the contributions of women.[1]

So, there has been a definite increase in research activities and efforts by scholars and women's studies centers to correct the situation.

Western feminists trace the history of first-wave women's mobilization in the West to the 1880s. It is not often acknowledged that at the same time, and in some cases earlier, women in Asia, Africa, and other parts of the world were mobilized to fight against oppression, and their struggle sometimes influenced the whole society. The 19th century was a volatile period in African history when women were resisting colonial incursion and women's groups became a formidable threat to colonialists. Indeed, women's resistance could be traced to pre-colonial times as women also struggled against slave traders in certain parts of Africa (Kolawole, 1994).

WOMEN AND SOCIAL TRANSFORMATION IN
PRE-COLONIAL AND COLONIAL AFRICA

Women's challenging leadership since the first century in some parts of Africa has been well documented by Sweetman. This includes women prototypes of self-assertion such as Kahina of the Maghreb in North Africa, a powerful ruler between 575 and 702. The reign of Queen Candace of Meroe-Ethiopia in the second and third centuries further reveals a woman's strength as well. The north of Nigeria has some revealing records of women rulers as early as the 9th century, but this fact has not been documented in a systematic way. It is largely believed that before the 9th century, there was a female dynasty in Daura on the northern border of Nigeria. The queens were called *Magajiya* and this tradition only stopped after the invasion by Arabs or Berbers through North Africa. In Borno, queen mothers known as *Magira* had strong influences on the rulers. According to Sa'ad Abubakr:

> Women have been quite active socially and politically, in the affairs of their community in Nigeria. The northern part of the country is full of many examples. In Borno, women officials such as the Magira (Queen Mother), the Gumsu and the Magaram, the official elder sister of the Mai (ruler), wielded tremendous power and influence right from the time of the establishment of the Sefuwa dynasty.[2]

Significantly, one of the most famous rulers of Borno, Mai Idris Aloma, is believed to owe his success to the political education that his mother gave him.

In Zazzau (modern Zaria), also in the north of Nigeria, two—possibly three—very powerful women ruled over this Hausa kingdom and it may have acquired its present name, Zaria, from Queen Amina's sister Zaria who reigned after her, according to some versions of the historical account. Whereas Queen Amina's reign is well documented, her mother's reign is not so well reported and yet the latter's reign was almost as remarkable as her daughter's. Amina's mother, Bakwa Turunku (1536–1566), is believed to have succeeded her uncle and her reign was spectacular as it marked a new era by making the king's position more authoritative and effective. Her reign also became the period of the greatest expansion. Bakwa's daughter, Amina, consolidated her achievements from 1576 (Abubakr, 1992).

In the 17th century, a woman, Inkpi, also ruled the Igala people of Kogi state in the middlebelt area of Nigeria. This is not surprising since it is believed that the founder of the state was a woman. Another exemplary woman leader was Queen Kambasa of Bonny, who ruled successfully over the war-torn delta area of Nigeria around 1450. She consolidated and expanded international trade in Bonny as well as being a great warrior. Similar accounts of women rulers elsewhere in Africa contradict the image of inaction portrayed about African women. In Angola, Nzinga made a strong impact from 1581 to 1665. Around the same time, a woman regent, Orompoto, led Oyo people to fight off Nupe invaders of Oyo in southern Nigeria.

The 19th century was an outstanding period in African women's mobilization all over the continent. Nehada of Zimbabwe was another formidable woman while, in Ghana, Yaa Asantewa posed a threat to colonialists. Madam Yoko was another invincible leader who expanded the Mende kingdom of Sierra Leone. Madam Tinubu of Lagos was another thorn in the flesh to colonial administrators, and local kings had to have her approval to succeed.

Many of the great women leaders have received some attention by scholars, but the collective actions of ordinary women of Africa remain only tangentially charted. During the trans-Atlantic slavery, some of the greatest acts of resistance and tenacious fightbacks against slave traders were led by the women. The most striking example is the invincibility of the women amazons of Dahomey. They dominated king Agaja's army and it is on record that 8,000 amazon women fought against and resisted Beecroft in 1851.[3]

The 20th century has equally witnessed women's concerted resistance in various parts of the continent. Amina Mama has documented important roles played by women in resisting colonial incursion (Mama, 1984). In Uganda, women were prominent in the rebellion of 1928, in which the woman warrior Muhumusa played leading roles that made white colonialists dread her. Another Ugandan woman, Nyabingi, mobilized mediums against the whites. The role of women in Kenyan Mau Mau struggles are no less outstanding. One can see from these examples, and they are by no means exhaustive, that African women have been empowered in several ways before colonialism and the mediation of western canons of empowerment.

Several parts of the West African coast experienced unique enabling status before colonialism and some are still struggling to sustain women's influence. In Yorubaland, several women inevitably became power brokers, as was the case in Ibadan in the 19th century. Throughout this period and earlier, powerful women received the title of *Iyalode,* an exclusive female title of recognition and influence. One such Iyalode of Ibadan, Efunsetan Aniwura, became a terror to the men in 1887. She was a very prosperous businesswoman, a creditor, and so became a political bigwig and a member of Ibadan city council. She even had her own army! Similarly, Madam Tinubu became a powerful influence and supplied arms to Egba people in the 19th century. She was a visible influence on and exerted overt control over King Akintoye and Dosunmu of Lagos. Elsewhere in Yorubaland we have a catalogue of unwritten women leaders and warriors. These include Endei of Afin-Ifelodun in Kwara state, who mobilized women against male domination. She was a symbol of courage and bravery and was subsequently deified like Moremi. Aina Orosun from Ara near Ede in Osun state is another example of women's dynamic roles. She settled the dispute between Ogiyan, the king of Ejigbo and Alara of Ara and subsequently led her people in the war between Ara and Ilorin, the Nasamu war.[4] She also freed the men from taxation. These examples further confirmed the role of women as mobilizers even in small rural areas in the 19th and early 20th century in Yorubaland.

Like the Yorubas, Ijaw and Igbo women of southwest Nigeria had strong social spaces for women in pre-colonial society. Women were very independent and resourceful in these places. Trade guilds were strong points of female mobilization among the Yorubas just as Igbo women's cultural groups were sources of enablement and positive bonding. Among the Ijaws of the Niger delta, women in pre-colonial and traditional society were resourceful and Ijaw women's associations had intricate legal and democratic set-ups (Nancy Leis, 1973). These were used for self-assertion and socio-political influence.

Much of the documentation of Nigerian women's mobilization in pre-colonial and early colonial times comes from the *magnum opus* of Nigerian scholar Nina Mba, *Nigerian Women Mobilized*. This is the most encyclopedic and comprehensive historical account of the resilience and tenacity of Nigerian women's resistance and struggle. From her research, it is well established that Nigerian women were very visible before the 19th century and that they in fact lost some ground in terms of influence during the colonial rule. That this account focused on a mass movement of women proves that they were not isolated cases.

Among Edo people of the Benin area of Nigeria (not to be confused with the republic of Benin—another West African nation formerly called Dahomey), several women rulers were in power before the 12th century. When women did not rule directly, the queen mother or *iyaoba* was a powerful symbol of respect, counsel and authority. They were called *ogiso*. In neighbouring Itsekiri, women made dynamic contributions to every area of social life. An Itsekiri princess, Idolorusan, was at the head of the ruling council that took control during the political confusion of the last half of the 19th century.

The role of the Omu among the Igbo people signified strong economic and political influence. In some places, she was the head of a strong council of women that was a parallel leadership to men's leadership. With these overt visible roles and a high level of political awareness, subsequent revolts led by women against colonial administration that spread across eastern Nigeria between 1927 and 1930 are hardly surprising. They resisted the erosion of their traditional power by colonial regulations. They also took advantage of new economic opportunities and dominated some aspects of trade. They controlled the market economy and rioted against the imposition of tax and market tolls on women. The riots spread like a bushfire to Calabar, Oron, Aba, Lagos, Abeokuta and all along the coast of southern Nigeria. They fought against the undermining of their traditional influences and the new political and economic advantages for men.

These "historic women's wars" forced the colonial administration to change certain laws and abolish women's taxes. They even asked for a return to pre-colonial status quo while they broadened the bases of their grievances to include colonial interference on issues of marriage, bride price, as well as prostitution, social development, and legal matters:

> The *nwabiola* movement indicated a rejection of the new social system among the older women. They saw their social and moral order threatened by the political, social and economic innovation of colonialism.[5]

These women also attacked local chiefs who collaborated with colonialists and facilitated colonial oppression to show that they were resisting all forms of tyranny. The issues included not only those peculiar to women but touched on the people's welfare. Educational fees were resisted in certain places, especially among Ibibio women, who were mostly responsible for paying their children's fees (Mba, 1982). These uprisings were not labelled as ideological 'isms' by these women, but this fact did not deter from their invincibility and success. They were highly conscious and were motivated by innate convictions, not gender ideology as we know it now.

The women's mobilization was not limited to Eastern Nigeria, as identical simultaneous and spontaneous uprisings were recorded in the southwestern areas of Abeokuta and Lagos. Women like Funmilayo Ransome-Kuti were leading women against oppressive rules as well. She participated actively in pre-independence talks in London and subsequently played a leading political role in western Nigerian politics and women's mobilization.[6] The high political consciousness of Yoruba women caused a widespread wave of agitations and women's revolts that ultimately enhanced women's self-reliance and empowerment. Their economic dynamo aided this as they became a force that could not be ignored. Women's trade guilds became pressure groups as we see in the association of clothes dyers.

Several other coastal people along the southern parts of West Africa boast of revered roles of women especially in matrilineal societies among the Ewe and Asante of Togo and Ghana. Among the Asantes, many queen mothers founded dynasties, as we see in the examples of the Juban and Wenchi areas of Ghana. Ewe women are well known for their spectacular economic success. These women tower above men in economic achievement and this has motivated the stereotype of *Nana Benz* in Togo and Ghana. Mende women in Sierra Leone used women's cults as strong agents of enablement. The impact of Madam Yoko in building and expanding the Mende nation remains indelible in the history of this people. In the historic strike action across francophone West Africa in 1947/48, women played central roles in the demonstrations against African rail workers' exploitation and impoverishment. They motivated the subsequent march to Dakar. The women's action was a serious challenge to the French colonialists.

The tremendous power enjoyed by women in ancient Zimbabwe has become the focus of research in recent times. Although the important role of Nehanda has been reinscribed and is being fictionalized, hers is not an exception. During the early iron age, Zimbabwe was egalitarian and women enjoyed a high level of empowerment. Women in fact played dominant roles in the economy of that society. Power and wealth remained in the female line. Grains constituted the main food and women were in charge and were respected for feeding the community in addition to being mothers and wives. Men did the harder works such as digging and building. As recently as 800 to 500 years ago, Great Zimbabwe still thrived in political strength along this pattern. However, with the encroachment of male-dominated societies and protracted colonial rule, the set-up changed and the emphasis shifted to male domains such as herding, trading, metal working and fighting. This new kind of wealth from trading was passed on to children while women were "reduced to chores and pottery-making."[7] Even in recent times, some parts of Zimbabwe still have women in charge of sowing and harvesting the grains, toiling for the family's survival. In Mosoka, the women still do most of the work as they toil on arid land to provide food for the family and this picture is true of many other African societies.

WOMEN'S POSITIVE ACTIONS IN MODERN AFRICA

In more recent times, women's groups have continued to get mobilized to confront governments and the society for their needs and increased power. The conditions of women in the home and at work, gender inequality in law, differential remuneration or benefits, continue to be the focus of attention. In many places, bride prices are so outrageously high that the impression one gets is that girls are being sold off. In the eastern areas of Nigeria, bride price has lost the traditional significance as a symbolic gesture of appreciation and valuation of the girl and a means of insuring that some of the basic things that she needs to settle down to a married life are provided by the bridegroom. Some people need to take a loan to pay the bride price. No wonder some men take it out on the women after marriage. In Zimbabwe, bride price or *lobola* is being exploited. In the traditional society, *lobola* was a symbolic exchange of gifts, such as a hoe and a basket. This tradition has been perverted and women are like commodities as bride price becomes commercialized at the expense of the girls.

Women's wings of some trade unions have succeeded in improving women's conditions. Association of University Women in Nigeria as well as national women's groups like Women in Nigeria, among others, have become strong pressure groups. Many national women's groups and in some places mother's unions are avenues of positive women's mobilization. Professional women's groups are struggling against women's marginalization in diverse ways. There were strong women's groups in Ibadan in the '40s and '50s while Funmilayo Ransome-Kuti has headed a strong women's group since 1947. She liaised with the International Women's Federation and attended their conferences. Contemporary groups include AAWORD, an active research group across the continent. *Women In Nigeria* is an example of a national women's group that has carried men along, while the Senegalese women's group *Yewwu Yewwi* embraces all categories of women in an inclusive way. In Zimbabwe, women's clubs have been an important avenue of self-actualization and mobilization since pre-colonial days. Now under the influence of the Women's Commission and government funding, women's clubs continue to play an important role in Zimbabwe as women help each other, support the poor, needy, abused women and oppressed or deprived widows.

The level of consciousness revealed in the activity of these women is remarkable and these organisations cut across class. Generally, one sees the positive side of women's bonding. These women are not asking for a female utopia and the struggles do not threaten the family structure basically. In spite of this progress in women's awareness, struggle, revolt, and empowerment, gender inequality remains a major factor shaping women's status in Africa. The need for self-realization is therefore an on-going process. Africa is a vast continent and the level of women's consciousness varies. The documentation of women's visibility and power does not assume that a majority of African women have equal opportunities and are fulfilled. The myth that African women are free and need no struggle for self-esteem is as dangerous as the myth of African women's total effacement and invisibility. Cheikh Anta Diop's view is relevant here:

> Thanks to the matriarchal system, our ancestors prior
> to any foreign influence had given women a choice
> place. They saw her not as a sex object but as a mother.[8]

One needs to see African women's experience objectively and not emphasize one role at the expense of others. The place of women in matriarchal African societies transcended the mother image, as we see in formidable roles of women in public spheres as well.

Africa is a vast continent and the level of women's consciousness is mediated by numerous factors. Canons of women's marginalization such as tradition and religion in some places interact, while there is much room for full emancipation in other places. Many women are still contending with a situation in which many place a high premium on boys' education and when the resources can not stretch to all the children, the girls are denied education. In many rural places, the ratio of literate adult females to males is 1:5.[9]

Elsewhere, poverty levels have increased due to international economic monitoring, and the responsibility to feed the family rests heavily on women as families are dislocated. Many employment sectors still discriminate against women. But these are often highlighted without documenting attendant efforts to resist the feminization of poverty. One needs to avoid over-romanticization of African women's power that can jeopardize true self-knowledge. Black women are not static entities, but rather they influence their society and are influenced by it, particularly in ways that will improve the women's lot. Joyce Ladner, like many other sisters in the diaspora has underscored the Black woman's dynamic power of influence:

> Black people are involved in a dynamic relationship
> with their physical and cultural environment in that
> they both influence and are influenced by it. This reci-
> procal relationship allows them to exercise a consider-
> able amount of power over the environment.[10]

Believing very strongly in Black women's enablement, Angela Davis has condemned certain wrong notions of Black women in her thesis about the strong link between gender, race, and class. She also foregrounds the positive power and comfort that Black women derive from the family, their communal life, and even their reproductive role. Her contention about Afro-American women is a reflection of the power of Black women globally:

> The concept of empowerment is hardly new to Afro-
> American women. For almost a century, we have been
> organized in bodies that have sought collectively to
> develop strategies illuminating the way to economic and
> political power for ourselves and our communities.[11]

She traced the way Black women have resisted and countered racist groups through their concerted activities. But these facts are played down in feminist writings. Several other African-American women have reiterated this connection between gender, culture, and race. Recognizing the centrality of multiple and simultaneous identities, Audre Lorde emphasizes the impact of African women's power as a source of inspiration a motivation for the yearnings of Black Americans:

> We remember the old traditions of power and strength
> and nurturance found in the female bonding of African
> women. It is there to be tapped by all women who do
> not fear the revelation of connection to themselves.[12]

African women's traditional bonding is robust and positive as it is based on cultural, economic, political, and spiritual collective actions. African women, past and present have been social mobilizers and social actors shaping the world around them. Contrary to the historical facts about African women's social space, however, certain myths still persist about their docility. In the words of Molefi Asante, "Certain myths refuse to die long after the needs which created them have passed away."[13] After all, myths do have a productive as well as a destructive force.

AFRICAN GENDER MYTHS AND THE QUESTION OF EMPOWERMENT

The indices of African women's resistance and achievement have been heavily mediated by several myths, some of which are traditional while others are externally imposed. Although mythic imagination structures human thought and actions in many societies, it does shape lives and values more profoundly in Africa than in Western societies. Many critics emphasize myth as non-truths, pure fiction, fables, or unrealistic and illusory tales. Many Greek and other European myths fall into this category, as we see in the myth of Sisyphus—a paradigm of the negation of destiny. Other critics focus on the ritual origin of myth. Sigmund Freud emphasizes the psychoanalytical basis of myth while Jung relates it to the collective unconscious and this explains the similarity in the myths of different people. Like Levi-Straus, Northrope Frye explains myth in terms of structure as one of five modes of fictional expression. Frye further relates myths to culture. He defines it in terms of a broad cultural concept that relates people to social values :

> A mythology is ... a cultural model, expressing the way
> in which man wants to shape and reshape the civiliza-
> tion that he himself has made.[14]

In all these theories, scientific knowledge has made myth less central and often just an academic exercise. Using Nigeria as a paradigm, I intend to foreground the way mythoform impacts on women's space in a very pragmatic manner and how myth provides the *raison d'être* for male domination of the power structure. This is of course true of other parts of Africa, as Helen Nabasuta Mugambi observes in her research on some aspects of Baganda myths and the way the Kintu myth of origin subverts women's roles and has become an explanation for patriarchal domination in that society.[15] African myths are to a large extent paradigms that explain the reasons for the status quo and explicate the origin of certain actions, values, or social patterns. As a socializing phenomenon, mythoform validates and authenticates existing power patterns. The strong influence of oral traditions of folktales, proverbs, riddles, and anecdotes facilitate the transmission of certain myths about women and particularly legendary or historical women leaders. Many African societies were matriarchal and some still enjoy what I like to describe as middle-level matriarchal empowerment. But Africa is still largely patriarchal, and myths have been manipulated to vindicate women's disempowerment in vital public spheres. As a corollary, many women internalize such to entrench negative self-image and these internalized myths become an additional burden on women's backs that fosters self-negation as opposed to self-realization.

As in all societies, African myths are varied, but the strong communal culture encourages easy transmission and acceptance of myths as codes of morality if not of conduct. To many people in traditional African societies, myths are imbibed in such a near sacred way that they possess some factual values. This is not necessarily a historical position because many people still celebrate traditional life-styles and ethos. African literature, philosophy, religion and arts incorporate myths of gender that have tremendous influence on women's self-esteem. So one can see that mythology has both connotative and denotative impacts on Africans.

Concerning traditional women's self-evaluation, therefore, their emotions, intelligence and the way they respond to social or political stimuli are bound to be conditioned by some mythical canons. Myths become a tool for enforcing certain epistemological values. It is easy to graft gender fallacies into many areas of life and entrench gender bias, moral codes and behavior to normalize men's visibility on the power platform. I will attempt to analyze some categories of myths: some may be identical to categories elsewhere, but the function will address the African peculiarities.

Creation and analogical myths about human origin explain

how man came to be and how some African societies are where they are. This category sometimes elicits serious gender codes as they concentrate more on the supernatural creation of human societies. Men and women usually play specific roles in bringing the society into existence. Analogical myths explain the beginning of natural phenomena logically. Myths of origin explain the beginning of specific societies and in a majority of cases the founders are male. There are several African societies founded by women, however, and this is of special interest to this discourse. Even when the founder of a people is a man, there is often a woman playing an important role. On the contrary, myths as ritual highlight magical and supernatural status of human existence and this is one of the areas of empowerment of women. African women's visibility in ritual myths as priestesses and goddesses is well documented and will not occupy much space here.

Fictional myths are common to all societies, but African folktales are replete with gender myths that project negative values such as rivalry, jealousy, impatience, inconsistency, and unreliability. Yet African tales are usually moralistic and overtly didactic. Those myths that serve as legends and archetypes are very important because it is this category that brings out gender prejudices most vividly. There are many legends about women rulers and leaders who failed because of one feminine trait or the other. Such women are demonized and this provides fundamental reasons why women cannot subsequently be rulers.

In looking at specific examples of gender myths and the way they have facilitated women's empowerment, the collective and archetypal nature stand out. I will cite some examples from south-west Nigeria as paradigms. One can see clearly that myth has a basic role of structuring reality into acceptable patterns. In the African context, mythology plays a central role in transmitting values and instilling discipline. It enhances the understanding of human civilisation and shapes gender roles and socialisation. Mythoform is significant in the ongoing attempt to construct an African feminist theory for several other reasons. Myths of creation, origin, empowerment, motherhood, and the concept of heroism, all work together to determine gender delimitation, roles, and status in the society.

The internalization of values is relevant to the analysis of African woman's positioning. African myths, legends, encomiums, proverbs and folktale play prominent roles in shaping the woman's place. I agree that several kinds of proverbs have elicited negative images of women, as Mineke Schipper delineates in *The Source of All Evil.* Archetypes constitute an aspect of the modern equivalent of mythification in these writers' literature. One needs to evaluate traditional myths and the recreation of modern myths and archetypes by female writers. The study of myths is indeed a valuable tool for studying a people's culture, and literature in particular. Mythoform has always been central to African traditional oral literature. Among the Yoruba people, oral genres are very central to daily experience as well as more official transactions. Gender construction derives largely from mythic transmission from one generation to another. The anonymity of myths makes this genre a basic source of socialisation, identity construct, role sharing and self-perception. Yet, the anonymity enables myths to function without necessarily posing a threat. Myths of gender and femininity, among others, combine to shape gender roles through the imbibing of certain concepts.

Archetypal concepts do not always get projected as legendary tales or folktale. Often, archetypes are constructed through succinct anecdotes and proverbs. New myths and archetypes of gender are particularly so transmitted. A revision of existing myths and archetypes through diverse sources of orality is a valid method of evaluating women's images. Consequently, new myths of gender can enhance the current quest for positive female assertion. There are numerous instances of African myths and archetypes that shape women's self-evaluation: only a few will be selected to illustrate the theory that myths determine gender roles.

The example of the well known Baganda foundation myth is a paradigm. On a leisure trip to earth, Nnambi, the daughter of Ggulu the king of Heaven, met the only man on earth, primitive and uncultured Kintu. She decided to go back to heaven to ask for her father's permission to marry Kintu. Ggulu consented but warned that she should avoid meeting one of her two brothers, Walumbe (Death). Unfortunately she forgot to take millet for feeding her chicken and as she returned to do so, she and Kintu met her brother Walumbi (Death), who insisted on following her to the earth. Nnambi then becomes the metaphorical bringer of death to the earth and this provides the reason for women's relegation and patriarchal domination in Baganda. In several other myths of origin, heaven was near the earth and God was physically closer to men. The sky receded because women (not men) were pounding food and hitting the sky of heaven with their pestle, or rubbing oily hands on the sky. In all of these instances, women are to blame for certain primordial calamities.

The empowerment of women among the people of Ondo town in southwest Nigeria has some remarkable features that are also ambivalent. Among this people, the foundation myth reveals that a woman called Pupupu[16] founded the town of Ondo. Pupupu then became the first ruler of Ondo town. It is believed that she was blackmailed by men for giving much attention to her poultry farming and other domesticities. Subsequently, she was deposed by male chiefs. This forms the basis for not allowing females to rule in Ondo. Nonetheless, women still wield a strong political and economic influence. The male king must be crowned by a female chief, *Lobun.*

The king, Osemawe, and the *Lobun* must not reign together however, as one dies for another. This dramatizes the male-female tension in practical terms. For every male chief, there is a parallel female chieftaincy too:

Male	Female
Osemawe	Lobun
Lisa	Lisa-Lobun
Jomu	Jomu-Lobun
Sasere	Sasere-Lobun
Adafi	Adafi-Lobun
Ogede	Ogede-Lobun
Orangun	Orangun-Lobun

Each of the male Iwerefa or high chiefs has an equivalent female — *Opoji*. The Lobun is confined to the house while she is excluded from strenuous activities like the male king, *Osemawe*. According to C. O. Osungbohun, "The Lobun and her own chiefs looked after the interest of women but also contributed to matters of interest to both men and women, the organisation of festivals, the declaration of war and the imposition of curfews in the town." Her role is so central that she is indispensable in appointing new kings. The female leader, Lobun, also plays a judicial role as she participates in conflict resolution among male chiefs. She is at the centre in opening new markets, so much so that she is considered as the "economic priestess." No new market can be built without her permission. Women's visibility in the Ondo public sphere is not limited to the Lobun's role. According to Yetunde Togun, women's role is widespread:

> Apart from the important roles played by women in
> Ondo-Yoruba economic life, their influence is also felt,
> to some extent, in the political sphere. Though women
> do not participate in deciding succession to the throne,
> no Ondo *oba* is installed without the significant involve-
> ment of the *Lobun*. It is the Lobun that practically
> installs the king.[17]

However, the symbolic loss of power by Pupupu is still valid
as women no longer reign as rulers in Ondo but remain a
dynamic force.

The central role of women in traditional and modern Ondo
society is not as exceptional as it appears. Elsewhere in
Yorubaland, women as *Iyalode* play equally vital roles in con-
trolling the market and other economic matters. Simi Afonja
and Funmi Soetan have worked on the importance of the
women's guilds and the power wielded by them. In many
places, a woman has to formalize the coronation by placing
akoko leaves on the king's head. In the old Oyo kingdom,
women enjoyed eight chieftaincy titles that conferred vital
palace roles on them. These titles are: *Iya-aba, Iya kere, Iya
Naso, Iya Monari, Iya Lagbon, Orun Kumefun,* and *Are Orite.* The
highest of these titles is *Iya Kere,* the keeper of the king's trea-
sure. This is confirmed by Oshungbohun, "She wields the
greatest power in the palace. She is in custody of the kings
treasures. The royal insignia are in her keeping, and all the
paraphernalia used on state occasions. She has the power of
withholding them and thus preventing the holding of any state
reception to mark her displeasure with the king when she is
offended" (Oshungbohun, p. 62).

> In many parts of Yorubaland, roles of distinction are
> conferred on women.These include the role of Yeyeoba
> (honourary Queen leader), Eyemokan — the head of
> bead makers who also play advisory political roles.[18]

The mythic foundation in Ondo still places an emphasis on
women's indispensable power, in spite of the legendary demonization of the female founder and first ruler, Pupupu. In modern Ondo community, women are still central to the economy
and dictate the market perspectives and regulations. Ondo
has other unique values that encourage women's empowerment and freedom. For instance, an elderly woman can "retire"

from her husband, leaving the younger wives to take care of him. She then establishes a new home independently while maintaining a friendly relationship with the husband. Ondo's social set-up clearly disproves the myth of African women's invisibility, subjugation and disempowerment. However, many other parts of Africa do not sustain such viable gender role sharing as in Ondo

Although female rulers as executive queens are generally circumstantial and exceptional, female regents are common features in many parts of West Africa. Regents play the king's role when the heir is young or when there are trustees over the choice of a new king. In old Oyo kingdom, the wife of *Oba* Agaju Iyatun reigned as a regent after her husband's death until her son was older. According to Johnson, she wore the crown and other royal emblems (p. 156). Similarly, in Akure, the oldest daughter reigns as the regent until the funeral rites are concluded and a new choice is made for the throne. The 13th ruler of Akure, Deji was a woman according to Toyin Falola, although she did not wear a crown.

Often women earned a social status by their wealth and economic viability. Efunsetan Aniwura as *Iyalode* of Ibadan maintained a large personal army (Johnson, 1990: 83). In spite of these women giants, the patriarchal system still has inherent tools that put women in a relatively disadvantaged place in their contribution to socio-political matters. As Yetunde Togun affirms, sometimes these female roles are shrouded in mystery to give it necessary authority and respect. This is true of Moremi myth. Moremi, the wife of Oranmiyan, a king of Ile-Ife, was a woman of exceptional beauty. She offered herself as a captive to expose the secret behind the victory of Igbo raiders and gave privileged information to Ife later, causing the town's deliverance. She vowed to offer something precious to the deity of Esinminrin river if her mission succeeded. According to this myth, she had to offer her only son, Oluorogbo, on accomplishing her mission. This provides an explanation for deifying Moremi subsequently. Myths of gender sometimes provide a positive explanation of the reason for certain important social, political or religious traditions in Africa as elsewhere.

Instances of women's power and influence are not limited to the Yorubas. Among the Nupes of Nigeria, the women are known to be dynamic, resourceful, and pushy in economic matters. They travel to other parts of Nigeria and in these places dominate some aspects of trade such as smoked fish, peanuts, *guguru* (Nigerian pop-corn), *Kuli, aya,* and *donkwa.* They constitute a formidable economic force. To explain away this commercial drive and success of Nupe women, a myth exists that every Nupe woman or girl is a witch and this is the source of their success!

So, in many instances, women's dynamic power is *conferred* by myths. At other times, myths are deployed to derogate negative images to neutralize the visibility of women. These myths often etch negative images that encourage women's lack of self-assertion and self-fulfilment. Nonetheless, the myth of docility and passivity is further debunked by women's empowerment in some other parts of Africa. Among the Ewe people of Southern Togo and Ghana, the women dominate much of the commercial scene. Many women prosper and own luxurious cars, often to the discomfiture of apparently less visible males. This modern trend is an offshoot of the matrilocal cultural basis of Ewe people in the traditional set-up. Elsewhere, women dominate food processing and harvesting and this involvement creates a measure of economic independence. This is true of the Hausas of parts of West Africa, where women's role is more conservative.

In constructing gender myths, some theories are often informed by cultural biases and inadequate investigation of the same. Ironically, patriarchy sometimes exists side by side with matrilocal units, as among the Igbos of Southeastern Nigeria. Polygamy is considered a threat to the woman's influence. This is only partially true. On the other hand, it enhances matrilocal relationship. The father in such a set-up is a "universal" father, shared by many children. Each woman, therefore, has the privilege of a closer tie, influence, and empowerment as regards her interaction with her children. In many parts of Igboland, the set-up is matriarchal, and significantly, children bear the mother's name. Such matriarchal arrangements are well known in Ohafia and Idemili areas. Similarly, according to Professor Hassan Salah, in Northern Sudan, men bear their mother's name such as Salah Ibn Walad, Nafisa Fatima. In this subtle enjoyment of empowerment by these Sudanese women, men are identified by their mother's names in praise songs.[19] Similarly, in many parts of Malawi, male and female children take their mother's surnames and in case of a divorce, wives take the children.

Nancy Tanner brings out this strong link, "The mother-child tie is strong and persistent and is supposed to be that way. Igbo patrilineages segment along maternal lines."[20] The mother's centrality is, however, often underrated in the construction of myths of gender empowerment. Traditionally, African women do not lose the maiden name or adopt the husband's name. It is an acquired western practice. Women's economic resourcefulness among the Igbos, as in many other parts of Africa, creates political advantages:

> As in the other societies described above, the women have economic resources. They plant their own marketable garden crops on land adjacent to their houses and they are active traders. Indeed they control the local markets, while the men, for their part, engage in long distance trading.[21]

Mythology serves many functions in a given society. It may be less significant if equated with "fallacy, superstition and is associated with an escape from, rather than an immersion in reality"[22] (Molefi Asante, 1987). The anonymous origin of myths may play down their appropriation by individuals. But as Levi-Strauss observes, myth often influences and shapes imagination unconsciously, since it "operates without our knowledge." One therefore tends to agree with Molefi Asante that myths constitute "a productive force." Although Asante's observation relates to African Americans, it is equally true of any group which derives values from myths:

> ... myth becomes an explanation for the human condition and an answer to the problem of psychological existence in a recent society.[23]

Ile-Ife, the cradle of Yoruba civilization, has recorded the reign of some female chiefs in spite of the conservative status of this town. Among these female *Ooni,* Olowu towers above many of the historical kings. She reigned in the 12th century and is famous for designing indigenous building technology. She created the traditional potsherd device used for the construction of roads and terraces in Ile-Ife. Some replica of this artistic device can be found at the Ile-Ife museum while actual remnants still exist in several places in this ancient city. But, as usual, she was condemned for being a brutal slave driver who forced men to work strenuously to construct the potsherd terraces. Subsequently, according to legend, women are now disallowed from the throne of Ile-Ife.

The formidable role of women such as *Ooni* Olowu can be best apprehended if one understands the underlying philosophy of African power structure. More recent research confirms this, as Mikelle Smith Omari-Obayemi's recent field work into the power structure of women among the Yorubas shows. According to her, Yoruba women "maintained positions of great cultural power *(agbara)*, not only in the domestic arena, but in economics, ritual, religion, politics, and other social domains" (Omari-Obayemi, 1990/91).

Apart from myths and legends, several other modes enhance directive language uses. Affective use of language is dominant in folktale, panegyric, dirges and anecdotes. However, the impact of such on gender will be analyzed using proverbs as an illustration. Proverbs have been central to the inculcation of certain gender related values in the African set-up. As Mineke Schipper's work confirms, proverbs on women consist of a great deal of derogatory image depictions. Of course, several African proverbs present positive pictures of women as well. The level of adoption of these concepts determine girls' socialisation and women's acceptance or rejection of certain roles.

Matricentric proverbs usually exalt the women's role as mother, both literally and symbolically, especially along the coast of West Africa. Among the Yorubas, the mother is an artefact of respect, almost to be worshipped:

Iya ni wura	Mother is the gold
Baba ni digi	Father is the mirror

The implication is to adore the mother but look up to the father as a mirror, a reflection of the ideal way of life, a role model.

Among the Akan people in Ghana, the concept of the good woman, *Obeapa* is an important philosophy. Positive concepts and proverbs include:

Enapa ye	A mother is precious
Onyame Baatan Pa	A mother is god/divine
Asaase Yaa	Mother Earth

These attributes are taken seriously and women's centrality in Akan dirges confirms women as custodians of the deepest human emotions. No wonder Akan women played vital roles as queen mothers. The resistance of Yaa Asantewa to British rule is well known.

In Zimbabwe, the centrality of women as mothers is heightened through the proverb, *Musha mukadzi,* which translates as "Behind the successful family there is a woman."

Similarly, in Igbo cosmology, *Nneka,* "Mother is supreme," underlies the attitude of respectability, but it implies the woman's importance as an arbiter rather than as a custodian of authority. When the social edifice disintegrates, when a man is dishonored, disgraced, or exiled—like Okonkwo in *Things Fall Apart*—he takes refuge in his mother's home or village. As if to reinscribe an apologia, an afterthought, or an adjunct, the concept of *Nwayibuife*—"a female is also something"—is also central. In many instances, the mythification of the women is ambivalent. Many writers, male and female, have canonized the myth of Idemili as a source of women's empowerment. Flora Nwapa's heroines derive their experiences or predicament from their relationship to Idemili, the woman of the lake. However, Chinua Achebe's allusion to this myth in *Anthills of the Savannah* is the most profound and versatile:

> In the beginning Power rampaged through our world, naked. So the Almighty, looking at his creation . . . saw and pondered and finally decided to send his daughter, Idemili, to bear witness to the moral nature of authority by wrapping around Power's rude waist, a loincloth of peace and modesty. (Achebe, 1987: 102).

Consequently, any male seeking titles of empowerment in Igboland, such as *ozo,* consults Idemili before and after receiving the title, for approval. If Idemili considers him unfit for such power he dies before the end of three years unless he obeys her. He gets the title if all goes well and he is considered able to keep peace without breaking even a single fragile finger of peace. So, the woman mythically possesses the checks and balances of power. She is the moral eye who authorizes the man to handle the nexus of power by pulling the harness, "Such is Idemili's contempt for man's unquenchable thirst to sit in authority on his fellows." Ironically however, Idemili is not seen to involve women in identical wielding of power directly.

This myth shows the paradox of empowerment in certain instances in the traditional society. Power becomes even more elusive to the woman in the post-colonial context, in which she is marginalised. At best, she is an accessory of power, filling gaps in the power story which in modern African societies is essentially a male story. The woman punctuates the political landscape, often refusing to be scorched by the tropical sun and remaining resilient like the anthills of the burnt out savannah landscape of Achebe's novel. This will be further discussed in a subsequent chapter.

PROVERBS, GENDER, AND WOMEN'S DENIGRATION

In addition to myths, folktales also actively delimit specific images of women, especially through the co-wife tales. Women's rivalry, envy, triviality and selfishness are recurrent issues in African folktales. Proverbs, by their succinct pragmatic centrality in daily discourse, are equally deployed to validate several negative images of women. This is plausible since proverbs are male-dominated. Indeed, the attitude to the woman as reflected in many African proverbs is ambivalent. A Shona proverb from Zimbabwe sums up this attitude:

> *Mukadzi munaku kurega kuroya anoba*

> "A beautiful woman always has a blemish,
> if she is not a witch, she is a thief."

According to a Zimbabwean woman, Clarissa Dhliwayo, however, this proverb is not as negative as it appears when seen against the Shona philosophy that informs it. The underlying concept is the imperfection of human beings. These people believe that for a beautiful woman to be human and not supernatural, there has to be a pysical blemish or a moral flaw. So this ambivalence underlies this proverb. Significantly, another Shona proverb centers women's vital role in moulding the family and by extension, building the society: *Musha mukadzi*— "Behind a successful family there is a woman."

Several proverbs portray women as unreliable and inconsistent among the Yorubas. This is reinforced by Ifa corpus:

> *Obinrin L'eke, obinrin l'odale*

> "The woman is a false person,
> The woman is a traitor."

This excludes her from involvement in salient public offices since she is seen as unreliable and treacherous. Another Yoruba proverb is more categorical:

> *Obinrin o se finu han*

> "A woman cannot be trusted to keep
> Secrets/be a confidant."

Among the Luba of Zaire and the Somali, a proverb presents women in a similar tone:

> "A woman is like a shadow;
> Go to her, she flees,
> leave her, she follows you."

When these views are adopted, they cannot but create limited self-perception in some areas of life. Consequently, myths of gender have shaped modern archetypes constructed in many literary works by African writers as well. Early writers, being predominantly male, replicated the negative images found in African myths. However, many female writers attempt more positive depictions of the African woman, with varying degrees of success. By omission or commission, however, the strong dynamic woman is invisible in many female writers' works (Obioma Nnaemeka, 1992).

Some critics aver that the very act of writing is masculine, as seen in the necessity to feminize the art of writing through terms such as "female writer" or "female poet." Lee Gershumny strongly identifies gender myths that dominate Western literature:

> The sexist omissions and commissions of the English language, out of necessity, have been the cultural legacy of writers and poets. Their metaphors have echoed the stereotypes of western mythology....[24]

The Need for New Images and Women's Redefinition

Time now calls for a rethinking and recreation of new myths, legends, proverbs and other orature constructs to delineate an authentic image of the African women. Positive role models and other outstanding legendary women giants are closer to the reality of the African women's positioning. Several writers have identified madam Tinubu of Lagos, Efunsetan Aniwura of Ibadan, Queen Amina of Hausaland, Yaa Asantewa and Mumbi of Kenya as mythic-legendary or historical archetypal figures of stature and achievement. African feminine poetics needs a cultural matrix. Cheikh Anta Diop focused attention on certain aspects of African values that create gender conciliation, as opposed to gender dichotomy:

> Black Africa had its specific bicameralism, determined by sex. Far from interfering with national life by pitting men against women, it guaranteed the free flowering of

both. It is to the honour of our ancestors that they were
able to develop such a type of democracy.[25]

Many of the existing myths about the African woman are extraneous. Such myths are no longer valid, yet they live on. Gender
role, like culture, is evolving and is not static. The African
woman responds to changing social demands (Kolawole 1992).
Yet, many critics parade outdated myths of gender and the status of the African woman. Ironically, the African literary scene
is inundated with "motherhood literature" or "domestic literature." This gives the impression that the African woman is still
preoccupied with the private at the exclusion of the public
sphere. The truth is, she has emerged in both arenas while her
private role is more central than is appreciated. George
Lamming's contention at the conference on West Indian literature (1961) is very true, "Certain myths refuse to die long after
the needs which created them have passed away."

Finally, the African woman's spirituality is a central myth
that many writers have adopted. It is generally believed that
African women are more spiritual than men. The presentation
of the African woman along mythic dimensions therefore
includes the priestess image. The old woman is particularly to
be feared but respected. On the contrary, the younger woman
is dreaded for possible supernatural impact on men and on the
society. At other times, she is a potential Pandora with mystic
power. This underlies early literature by male and female, as
revealed in the Ihuoma, Efuru, and Selina types in the novel and
the Anowa type in drama. The Olurombi folktale of the Yorubas
dramatizes the predicament of the woman who sacrifices her
only daughter for wealth as if the woman cannot be fulfilled in
both the domestic and economic arenas simultaneously. These
issues will be further explored in subsequent chapters.

Since many myths are linked with religion and rituals, even
casual or secular myths sometimes assume a religious import.
People allow such myths to underpin and regulate certain soci-
etal behavioural patterns. The very nature of myths implies the
delineation and validation of values, norms, traditions, even
regulations, that are essential to the ways things are, and
ought to be. Ordinary rules and norms thus get encapsulated
in the mystic and the supernatural, to instill fear in the acceptance of the way things ought to be. Like the mask, the natural
becomes shrouded in the supernatural. This fact does shape
gender socialization and role sharing. Modern myths about

the African woman's role are as potent as the religious ritual-istic myths of the past in this regard.

The quest for the exotic and the unusual still leads to the creation of pseudo-myths about Africa and the African woman. Several scholars still perceive that which they preconceived about the African woman and her `passive subordination.' The robust, dynamic, pushful and resourceful African woman (even if she is in the minority) is often suppressed while the scarecrow or effigy of the true African woman is paraded in modern academia. One needs to transcend randomisation that concentrates on the divided self of the modern middle class African woman, who is often mistaken for the norm of African womanity.

Gender insularity is an aspect of the hangover of the gen-der asymmetry created by certain acquired western values and perception. Whereas tradition plays a central part in gen-der inequality, this is often underscored while the gaping gen-der gap created by colonial attitude to the place of women is ignored. It is a well documented fact that the Victorian English woman, like other 19th-century European women, was largely invisible in the public sphere. Consequently, women writers such as the Brontes had to adopt male names, to be accepted and read. This fact and the necessity to stay away from home for long hours created plausible invisibility in certain produc-tive spheres. The delay in girls' education heightened the prob-lem. Yet, these facts are often overlooked in creating myths of the African woman's effacement.

It is time to create and recreate lifelike representations of the African Everywoman. Exactitude has been sacrificed in the search for newness in Africa. The Roman writer, Pliny said, "There is always something new from Africa." This belief accounts for much of the distorted portraiture of the African woman. In addition, modern technology has undermined much of the traditional role of the African woman. Francis and Subhadra Abraham acknowldge that this is a side product of modernization:

> In the wake of modernisation, many of the traditional
> economic roles of women were eliminated or replaced
> by men or machines.[26]

The portrayal of the African woman has suffered from incom-plete, falsified or distorted theorizing. Like Africa, African peo-ple have continued to be debased through jaundiced accounts.

Many scholars still find gratification in presenting condescending portraits of the African woman. Cultural idiosyncrasy
pales to insignificance in these attempts. It is time to take cog-
nizance of the intersection between the African woman's reality and the experience of all Africans, all women, Third World,
all colonized, indeed, all liminal and undervalued groups everywhere. The invention of the African woman, like the invention
of Africa, needs to give way to reality and fidelity to actuality.
Myths have exacerbated women's marginalization, modern
myths can correct this. The predicament of the modernized
African woman is only a slice of the reality, not the norm of all
African women.

New myths need to focus on the dynamic "female genera-
tive force" of the African, like the *Sakti* of Tamil women. After
all, myths do possess a productive as well as a destructive
force. The African woman's status is protean. Any myth concerning her requires historical and cultural contextualization.
One cannot disregard the impact of what Eleanor Leacock
described as the "western male-biased gender structure" that
affected Africa's balance of power. Similarly, Christine Obbo's
observation that colonialism is a "male dominated system," is
valid. A basic question emerges from these observations, "Is
African women's passivity or invisibility a myth or a reality?"
As a corollary, one may ask, "Does the African woman contend with the same gender imbalance and is she struggling for
her rights or for autonomy?"

The emphasis here is the missing link. Much has been written concerning the invisibility of the African woman. This is
not the whole truth especially as the focus is on the westernised African woman. Much of the documentation of African
rural women's passivity emerges from lack of cultural contextualization. The concept of power and visibility are not universal but depend on cultural variables. On the other hand,
myths shape women's self-perception. Often, direct use of gendered language admires the same effect. Among the Igboho
Yoruba people of Northern Oyo, when food is deliciously hot
and steaming, the people remark, "*O s'okunrin,*" meaning "the
food is masculine." Yet the food is prepared by women. Myths
diminish women more.

The paradigmatic status of myth makes it vulnerable as it
is cited with authority. Women writers are now decoding existing myths to reconstruct new myths of gender. Archetypes of
powerful African women are being created in fiction. This

includes Mumbi as a formidable woman in Kenya and Nehada of Angola. History records many African, female warriors and leaders that were terrors to men, as we see in Queen Amina of Zaria in Nigeria, and Efunsetan Aniwura of Ibadan who was feared by men as an economically strong woman. Others are Yaa Asantewa and more recently Madam Ransome-Kuti of Abeokuta in Nigeria, a symbol of women's mobilization. African worldview is centred on a continuum between the past, the present and the future. The past is now being unfolded by women writers to explicate the present and chart new directions for the future. Many are creating plausible myths of gender to reveal the link between the private and the public, the personal and the collective, the specific and the universal.

I do agree with Alex Preminger that myths are implicitly symbolic of certain deep-lying aspects of human and transhuman existence. It is a specific mode of consciousness that occupies a central space in African thoughts. Contrary to Jungian concept, one can see that myth is not always created without our knowledge. Rather the role of myth is multiple and complex as Helen Chukwuma's analysis of Igbo myth reveals. Among this people, myth is:

> a stabiliser of social systems, a means of recreating past history or as a psychoanalytic insight into human behaviour motivation.[27]

In a similar way, Molefi Asante emphasises the productive force of myth:

> ...myth becomes an explanation for the human condition and an answer to the problem of psychological existence in a recent society.[28]

This is why African women writers and theorists are embarking on the process of demythification, unveiling the hidden gender codes that have enhanced male domination of power structures. This is an attempt to reorder ethical and moral consciousness. For too long, unverified reality has impinged on proximate reality for the African woman.

NOTES

1. Bolanle Awe, ed. *Nigerian Women in Historical Perspective* (Ibadan: Sancore/ Bookcraft, 1992), p. v.
2. Sa'ad Abubakr, "Queen Amina of Zaria" in Awe, op. cit., pp. 13ff.

3. Saburi Biobaku, *The Egbas and their Neighbours* (Oxford: Claredon, 1965).
4. Bisi Ogunsina, "Awon Akonibinrin Yoruba," University of Ilorin "nd Odujinrin Memorial Seminar," 4-6 April 1991.
5. Nina Emma Mba, *Nigerian Women Mobilized* (Berkeley: University of California Press, 1982), p. 72.
6. A new book on Funmilayo Ransome-Kuti as a giant in Nigerian women's mobilization by Emma Nina Mba is in press.
7. See Richard Wawman's video filming, "A Zimbabwean Trilogy," in Endangered World Series, Discovery Channel.
8. Cheikh Anta Diop, *Black Africa* (Trenton: Lawrence Hill, 1987), ch.6, p.33.
9. See statistics in the document, *Women In Nigeria: Conditions of Women in Nigeria and Policy recommendations to 2000 A.D.* (Zaria:Ahmadu Bello University Press, 1992), Chapter III.
10. Joyce Ladner, quoted in Humm, *op. cit.,* p. 125.
11. Angela Davis, *Gender, Race and Politics,* p.3.
12. Audre Lorde in "An Open Letter to Mary Daly" quoted in Humm, *op. cit.,* p. 138.
13. Molefi Kete Asante, *The Afro-centric Idea* (Philadelphia : Temple University Press 1987), p. 95.
14. Northrope Frye, *Spiritus Mundi,Essays on Literature, Myth and Society* (Bloomington: Indiana University Press, 1976), p.21.
15. Helen Mugambi, "Intersections: Gender, Orality, Text, and Female Space in Contemporary Kiganda Radio Songs," in *Research in African Literature* [Special Edition on Women as oral artists] Vol. 25, No. 3, (Fall 94): 51.
16. Pupupu is the legendary daughter of the founder of the Yoruba tribe, Oduduwa. She was a twin and her twin brother founded another town in Ijebuland of Southwest Nigeria called Odogbolu.
17. Yetunde Togun in an unpublished M.A. thesis at Obafemi Awolowo University, Ile-Ife.
18. Osungbohun, p. 62.
19. Information culled from my interview with a colleague, Professor Hassan Salah, a visiting professor at the Africana Studies and Research Center, Cornell University, Ithaca, N.Y., March 1992.
20. Nancy Tanner, "Matrifocality in Indonesia and Africa and among Black Americans," in Michelle Rosaldo et al., *op.cit.,* p. 1974, pp. 147/148.
21. *Ibid.*
22. Asante, *op. cit. ,* p. 95.
23. Asante, *op. cit.,* p. 98.
24. Lee Geshony, "Sexism in the Language of Literature," in Alleen Nilsen, et al., *Sexism in Language* (Urbana, Ill.: National Council of Teachers of English, 1977), p. 107.

25. Cheikh Anta Diop, *Black Africa* (Trenton: Lawrence Hills, 1987), p.33.
26. Francis and Subadra Abraham, *Women, Development and Change: The Third World Experience* (Bristol, Indiana: Wyndham Hall Press, 1988), p.1.
27. Helen Chukwuma,"Igbo Mythic Schema," in *Critical Theory & African Literature,* ed., Ernest Emeyonu (Ibadan: Heinemann, 1987), p. 100.
28. Asante, *op. cit.,* p. 98.

CHAPTER THREE

WOMEN'S ORAL GENRES AND AMBIVALENT LITERARY HEROINISM

In problematizing women's space in a modern African setting, orature is a domain of visibility and audibility, as scholars such as Carole Boyce-Davis and Molara Ogundipe–Leslie have remarked. In recent studies, scholars are highlighting areas of positive women's location. Contrary to some existing myths and theories, creativity in traditional African setting is not an exclusively male affair. Obioma Nnaemeka, Helen Nabatusa Mugabe, Grace Okereke, Chinyere Okafor, and Akosua Ayidoho have confirmed this. Even male scholars like Kofi Agovi, Ropo Sekoni, and Thomas Hale are unfolding oral genres that are tools of women's self-enhancement in African orature.

As in several spheres of life, role sharing is vivid in African orature. Many genres are women's genres but in certain places this is undermined or subverted. Ode Ogede makes this revelation with regard to the stifling and subversion of women's voices in the Igede area of Nigeria:

My primary interest is to explore some Igede female voices that persist in the face of opposition. One of the injustices in the experiences of the women in contemporary Igede society is the fact that many of the oral forms with which some Igede male artists are now associated were, in fact, first invented by women but strangely enough, Igede religious and social precepts no longer allow or have marginalised the participation of members of the female sex in many of those cultural practices.[1]

In many other places, however, women's voices remain audible, as we see in satirical songs and poetry which are women's domain. Egungun satirical songs among the Yoruba, Hausa women's court poetry, Nzema Maiden songs in Ghana, Impongo solo among the Ila and Tonga of Zambia, Akan dirges and Nnwonkoro in Ghana, Galla lampoons, Kamba grinding (work) songs, are specific female oral genres. A plethora of female genres exists among the Yorubas. These include Obitun Songs, Olori songs, Aremo songs, Ago-Oka, Gelede, Olele, and Alamo songs. The Fulani Bori songs in northern Nigeria consist of overt modes of self-expression and self-assertion for the women in this esoteric religious group. Other genres specifically dominated by women include Hausa women's court poetry, Igbo birthsongs, Ogori Ewere, many panegyric poems, and folktales, among others.

In addition to the historical evidence of African women's active impact on their society, traditional oral literature confirms their immense contributions. Contrary to some existing myths and theories also, African women have an immeasurable creative force. Many oral genres were and still are exclusively women's domains. The central role of women in sustaining and transmitting African culture in the diaspora during the slave trade has been a focal point of my on-going research (Kolawole, 1994). They are deconstructing old and existing myths to recreate new ones that reflect women's positive self-esteem.

Ali Mazrui believes that African indigenous culture has been endangered (Mazrui, 1991). But certain aspects of this culture have also been engendered, as we have seen, in the way myths have been manipulated to create disadvantages in women's social space. The documentation of matriachates in African history past and present raises important points about women's empowerment as well as the historic actions. Myths, legends, and history confirm the visibility of the African woman. Among several groups such as the Dogan, Ondo and Ewe people, women cannot be said to be effaced. The variables of power and cultural creativity in such societies reveal unique value structures. Other sources of women's empowerment and leadership come from diverse crafts (Afonja, 1986). African women's oral literature as a source of empowerment needs to be re-inscribed because several women writers derive inspiration from this.

ORAL GENRES AS A SOURCE OF WOMEN'S SELF-EXPRESSION

Their roles in cultural creativity have been undermined in the usual male/positive, female/negative attitude. In spite of extensive research into this region's orature, basic misconceptions remain. Certain critics maintain that African women are not artists; at best, they parrot communal oral pieces. As usual, women have been consigned to a secondary status in an attempt to overlook the diversity of creative role and their pragmatic functions. Many critics, including well-meaning ones, have adopted an essentialist perspective. Ruth Finnegan's *magnum opus, Oral Literature in Africa,* has made a profound contribution to the documentation of African oral genres. Yet, her attitude is sometimes ambivalent:

> Certain kinds of poetry are typically delivered or sung by women (particularly dirges, lullabies, mocking verses and songs to accompany women's ceremonies or work), and each culture is likely to have certain genres considered specially suitable for women. However, references to men seem to occur even more often and, with a few striking exceptions, men rather than women tend to be the bearers of the poetic tradition. (Finnegan, 1976: 98)

There are many instances of oral poetry by women all over Africa and Finnegan's observation reveals the basic problem of an outsider researching into African culture from a Western perspective. With the best of intentions, there are usually conspicuous absences.

One needs to go beyond glossing over the predominantly female genres that exist all over the continent. It is relevant to reiterate that Africa is not one small cultural entity. The study of African culture is at once the study of a part and a

whole. Cultural identity does not necessarily imply homo-
geneity. So much remains to be discovered about African
female oral genres and their creative worth. Critics who contend that African women are no artists but ululators or par-
roters are either only partially informed or else wholly
*mis*informed about the dynamic, complex, and varied scope of
this region's orature. A Yoruba proverb is relevant to this
issue, *Agbongbo tan ede, ija ni da*—"Incomplete understanding
or partial knowledge generates conflicts."

A keen appraisal of selected female genres of African orature reveals the wealth of original creativity. From Hausa Bori
songs to women's court poetry, this creative impulse is visible.
These oral genres are manifestations of collective women's
voices, dynamic group consciousness and a tool of eliciting
positive influence on the society. They are not passive texts.
From Akan dirges to Nzema satirical songs, the women are not
simply parroting communal texts. Among the Yorubas, dirges,
wedding chants, *rara,* satirical songs, and story-telling are areas
in which women excel in creativity, adaptation and manipulation of existing or new texts into contemporaneous situations.

Women's oral genres are a rich repertoire of literariness
and the exposition of semantic and linguistic innovation. In
some parts of the continent, orature is not a passive pastime.
Women's voices are effectively women's outcry as June
Goodwin observes in *Cry Amandla.* If these women's oral
pieces were mere parroting, there would be no sustained interest. The diversity of genres illustrates their prevalent roles.
Among the Yorubas alone, women's genres include: Obitun
songs (Ondo), Olori songs (Igede), wedding chants (Igbomina
and Oyo), Aremo songs, Ago, (Oka-Akoko), Gelede songs
(Egbado), Olele (Ijesa), Alamo songs (Ekiti) as well as pane-
gyrics.

In spontaneous performances such as Igbo birth songs or
solo performance as in the case of impango of the Tonga of
Zambia, creativity and originality are inevitable. What is often
overlooked is the functional womanist purpose of African orature which necessitates relevance and instant adaptations of
texts to the occasion. Oral genres are strong weapons of self-
assertion and Micere Mugo confirms this:

> Within the world of orature the woman had a lot of
> power. She spoke the word. She created the word. She

was instrumental to defining the ethics and aesthetics around which the world operated....[2]

The African woman as a transmitter and vector of cultural, spiritual, social and moral values implies the process of original creativity.

Among the Ogori people of Nigeria, some measure of primary orality is still maintained in spite of the impact of literacy. Orature still underlines much of the values of society and women play a cardinal role. *Ewere* is a predominantly female genre. Although this genre is largely composite (Kolawole, 1984), some scholars consider the poetic trait of Ewere as the most noticeable, (Olabayo, 1989). Ewere is only an instance of the individual talent, methodology and originality that women oral artists put into their performance. It is a vivid example of the way women use oral genres for self-expression, social castigation and rejection of oppressive laws. In many parts of Africa, folktales are dominated by women (Ojo, 1991). Akan story-telling with the famous intricate weaving of Anansi's web of stories is elderly women's domain. In addition, queen mothers interpret the rich poetry encapsulated in drum language. Women move from the original communal structure by adapting the oral genre to women's needs. Women use oral literature and exclusive female genres to condemn social problems, immorality, unfaithfulness, and idleness—and to make demands. Nzema maiden songs in Ghana are a good example of this. These values are expressed in rich poetic forms. Other aims of women's oral art include moral mediation and legalistic intervention as well as confrontation of and resistance to negative change and acculturation, as we see in Nzema satirical songs (Agovi, 1992). These texts reveal women's collective consciousness, composite voice, female bonding, unity, identity and positive eliciting and reassessment of womanhood and femininity. They act as a metaphor and a repository for the predicament, problems, hopes, aspirations, burdens, and ideals of womanhood:

> Nzema women appropriate a profound awareness of changes in the environment as a form of empowerment to undermine fixed perceptions of women and their seeming marginality in the social process.[3]

In many other parts of Africa, women use satirical songs to resist oppression and call for gender justice. All these are channels for enunciating women's self-healing and self-assertion. In Southern Sudan, Nuba women enjoy a level of equality that is exceptional, as they participate in all levels of activities except hunting. Here and in many parts of the Sudan, folktale is also women's genre. Indeed, in Central Sudan, the role of grandmothers in story-telling is so dominant that grandmothers, *Habboba*, are an institution. Satirical wedding songs or *"Aghani Al-Banat"* are a strong avenue of girls' self-expression too. They castigate men for suppressing women. Through this genre, girls also condemn social ills, negative values, and the move towards materialism while reinforcing positive values. Women folk poets are also common in the Sudan and praise songs as well as eulogies are dominated by women. Another popular genre is *hija,* a traditional defamatory Arabic poetic form that satirises people's moral laxity. *Hija* is exclusively a women's genre in northern Sudan. (Although this is not an exclusively female genre in the south; it is equally used by both women and men for self-expression. It is considered more serious, however, if women use *hija* to ridicule or castigate a man than if he is so satirized by a "fellow" man.)

African women's contribution to cultural creativity and their ability to use oral art for gender retrieval poses an important challenge to modern writers. Women writers are facing the challenge posed by traditional women who saw oral literary genres as avenues for self-enhancement. The role of literature and orature in fostering African women's relocation is vital to the womanist philosophy (Kolawole, 1992). Many female genres are sources of positive self-evaluation, society's well-being and positive self-retrieval. Abu Abari cites Birom women (Jos, Nigeria) as another group that manipulates oral literature to elicit its plight and fate as socially constructed, so as to transcend the same. Afam Ebeogu also highlights the vital role of Igbo birth songs:

> These birthsongs are an extremely convenient avenue for Igbo women to express their understanding of the norms and values of the Igbo society, and to comment on some of these norms and values.[4]

If through proverbs and other areas of folklore, the African woman has been demonised, female oral artists are still attempting self-retrieval and repositioning of their gender's social status and self-image. Through oral creative master-pieces, women writers as their gender mouthpieces are underscoring women as the source of virtue. They are analyzing myths, proverbs, folktales, and history and are recreating new myths and archetypes that strengthen positive images of women too. This is true of legends, myths, and folktales as well.

WOMEN'S LITERARY ARCHETYPES AND A PROGRESSION IN CONSCIOUSNESS

By omission or commission, most male writers in the early phase of African literature encouraged women's marginalization. It is true that "incomplete and one-sided understanding is distorted understanding" (Dube,1986). Since the breakthrough by Flora Nwapa and Ama Ata Aidoo in the mid-60s, African literature has been moved from a predominantly male domain. African women's literature has been a reflection and a refraction of reality in an overt and unapologetic way. These women's creative works have evolved in direct correlation with the level of awareness and this in turn has been shaped by socio-political exigency. Like the traditional women artists, these writers have tried to make literature a mode of gender self-expression. The initial naive portraits have given way to female archetypes that resist oppression and struggle to discard the image of women as victims. We see these women in social change responding to the demands of tradition and modernity, the personal and the collective, the productive and the reproductive roles. These dualities form the core of African literature about women.

The dilemma of the woman in a patriarchal society is a central preoccupation in the first phase of literature emerging about the African woman by male as well as female artists. She is often at the center of the tension created by tradition and modernity. At other times, she is at the cutting edge of social conflicts. Writers problematize these issues often without a resolution but rather leaving heroines in a tragic situation. The individual's desires rarely coincide with the collective ethos. The group's values are pitted against the individual's self-perception, creating ever-widening ripples in the irreconcilable pool. Sometimes the female protagonist and even secondary characters are caught between the image of the heroine and the anti-heroine.

This initial focus of African literature continued even in spite of a new level of awareness. Most male writers continued to fictionalize women as objects or minor characters that are vehicles for fostering a world of male heroism. At other times, women are objects of admiration. Art historian J.I.O. Ojo explains this attitude: "In a male-dominated society, the woman is an artefact." Jane Parpart and Kathleen Staudt corroborate this view: "The male-dominated state warps women's ability to make history on her own terms."[5] Major themes revolve around men confronting colonialism, struggling for independence, and attempting to manage the first generation of post-colonial Africans.

Elechi Amadi's novel *The Concubine* stands out as one of the limited instances in early African literature in which the fiction focuses on a heroine, Ihuoma. Generally, male heroes dominated the scene on the laudable attempt to reclaim the African past. Achebe's *Things Fall Apart* and *Arrow of God* are dramatizations of his people's heroic past and rich heritage in which women played no major role. Each of these focused on male protagonists, Okonkwo and Ezeulu. It is therefore a remarkable departure from this norm that Amadi's first novel focused on a woman. But the heroine is not fulfilled, being mythically and mystically tied to a sea-king that has destined her life to be a failure. Significantly, Amadi admits that he did not create such a heroine to identify with the women's plight but that he created women as he saw them in real life.

Much has been written about the warped vision or asymmetrical presentation of the African woman by writers male and female (Davies and Adams-Graves, 1986; Lloyd Brown, 1981). The naive categorization of women is equally well discussed. The sources of women's dilemma remain as pluralistic as the factors shaping and delimiting the modern African wo/man's realities. One reason is the fact that writers concentrated on these naive images of women in African literature in the early phase. In addition to peripheral roles, recurrent character types include mothers, wives, prostitutes, slaves, brides, witches, priestesses, vampires, ogres, simpletons, tempters, and mistresses (Adams-Graves and Boyce-Davies, 1986). Since the mid-60s, however, the emergence of women writers as their own voices transformed the depiction of femininity in African literature. Women as objects and marginal characters gave way to women as subject and positive protagonists. This breakthrough came with women writers such as Ama Ata Aidoo and Flora Nwapa as pioneers. One witnessed a new wave of awareness and the need to deconstruct existing stereotypes and reconstruct new image and role models.

African literature, by its highly pragmatic nature is an appropriate tool for measuring African women's level of consciousness. Since the mid-60s, when women emerged as their own voices, there has been a gradual progression in the consciousness of female writers in line with social change. Images of women depicted in women's literature have grown from characters with a naive passive outlook to more dynamic heroines confronting tradition and every socially constructed tool of subjugation and oppression. Women's dilemma being conceptualized in fiction includes the divided individual, divided loyalties, poverty, economic independence, and the struggle for survival. The strong space occupied by women in matriarchal societies is not reflected in many of these works, however. This situation has retarded the forstering of a positive and dynamic womanist consciousness.

WOMEN'S WRITERS' EARLY FICTIONAL HEROINES AS VICTIMS

The first archetypal category in women's literature is the presentation of the African woman as a victim in several ways. She is usually a mystery, an individual too supernatural to find fulfilment in the natural world. This is a replica of men's portrait, like Elechi Amadi's heroine Ihuoma in *The Concubine*. This category includes Nwapa's titular heroine Efuru, and Rebecca Njau's Selina in *Ripples in the Pool*. These characters' attempt to defy set limits creates ripples in the social pool. Anowa and Edufa also belong to this group. Others in the same category are caught between economic fulfilment and personal or family happiness.

This gives flesh to the Olurombi myth of prosperous women who seem to have opted for wealth at the expense of family happiness.[6] Economic hardship is a major predicament as the African woman confronts built-in philosophies and ideologies that pre-suppose that the woman's choice is between economic progress and domestic happiness. This is more of a myth than reality because women in many parts of Africa sustain a very high economic drive that carries with it some empowerment. Nonetheless, the myth that a woman who pursues economic prosperity will lose love, peace, and satisfaction in the home is a very common theme in early literature about African women. Flora Nwapa presents this in *Efuru,* while Rebecca Njau's heroine, Selina, is completely destroyed in *Ripples in the Pool* for identical reasons. Generally, these works depict pre-colonial or early colonial Africa. The heroines are tragic, failing to strike a balance between economic prosperity and domestic duties.

In overemphasizing Olurombi myth, many writers played down the reality of strong women in many African cultures. For instance, Aidoo's portrait of Anowa trivialises the status of Akan women who are historically very powerful and strong. Her perception of women's reality has been transformed, as we see in subsequent heroines in her works. The myth of Olurombi parodies this problem among the Yorubas of Nigeria. Every person made a vow to the Iroko tree concerning prosperous business on the market day. Olurombi vowed to give her only daughter to Iroko if she sold all her goods. She prospered and fulfiled this vow. Olurombi myth dramatizes the predicament of the economically ambitious woman. The aim of such a myth is to deter others from being so ambitious. The manipulation of culture and tradition to give women negative images is largely responsible for the persistence of docility where it does exist. The modern version of Olurombi myth is seen in women caught between two worlds, women struggling to overcome the important question of a chasm between women's productive and reproductive roles. The middle-class woman, professional, or even working-class woman, is often faced with the choice of striking a balance between domestic duties and her profession. In pre-colonial Africa, this was easier as the woman could combine her productive with her reproductive duties. Lovett, in fact, observes that:

> Prior to the imposition of capitalist production the distinction between productive and reproductive labour did not exist.[7]

There was complementary gender-role sharing and, since the woman's work involved self-employment, most of the time, she could strap the baby on her back while harvesting on the farm or working around the home or selling her wares at the market place, without any serious tension.

Another kind of tragic heroism consists of the Penelope image—women deserted by irresponsible husbands. They wait desperately and sometimes in a pitiable mood, for the return of their unheroic Odysseus. They are pitiable protagonists, often too faithful to tradition to take a plunge. This trend is exemplified in Efuru, and Nnu Ego in Emecheta's *The Joys of Motherhood*. Another prototype is the woman destroyed by the agony of barrenness — a central canon in much African women's fiction. Anowa, Efuru, and Idu are typical examples of characters who fall into this category.

Nwapa's *Efuru* is a paradigm of the predicament of the African woman in traditional society with minimal or no western influence. Nwapa claims in an interview that Efuru is a type, like many heroes of African literature and that her experience is representative of the determination and resourcefulness of women from her home town Oguta. *Efuru's* uniqueness and diligence undermine and overshadow her husband, Adizua:

> She was a remarkable woman, it was not only that she came from a distinguished family .... She was distinguished herself. Her husband was not known and people wondered why she married him. (Nwapa, 1966: 7).

Efuru's plight is that of an economically prosperous woman in a traditional society. She is barren for several years and this intensifies her problems. She is unfortunately caught in the web of traditional bigotry. Her child dies after she breaks the yoke of infertility and this complicates her problem. A second attempt at marriage ends on the rocks too. It is significant that she is admirable and well loved. Both Adizua and Gilbert love and dote on her initially. But her worth is tied to her motherhood value.

Efuru represents many traits that are common to women's portrait in early African literature. These plots usually resembled African folktales about women. Nwapa also creates the myth of the heroine with a mystic attribute in Efuru. This accounts for her childlessness as a priestess/worshipper of Uhamiri. *Efuru* is a typical example of several early women's novels, depicting the plight of the woman in a traditional society where self-realisation seems to elude the outgoing woman.

The second archetypal category is the self-conscious woman whose awareness is premature and aborted because she lacks the strength to change the society. Sometimes she is ahead of her time, at other times, she is a lone fighter and collective values stifle her iconoclastic position. Often these women are presented as victims or scape-goats of one social bigotry or another. This type is not a tragic heroine *per se.* Hers is the experience of the non-conformist and the women caught in the periphery of social change. This, again, is a vivid reflection of social reality at a particular point in African history. Miriama Ba's *So Long a Letter* and Zaynab Alkali's *The Stillborn* present such heroines. Even when these women do not fully impose their will on the society, they do assert themselves meaningfully. The unique nature of the problem of the African woman in an Islamic society is the focus of Zaynab Alkali's *The Stillborn,* Mariama Ba's *So Long a Letter,* and all of the works by Nawal El Saadawi.

This second phase depicts the African woman on the verge of social change. Her problems range from the choice of a husband, to infertility, desertion and the paradox of being economically successful at the expense of marital joy. So, the same themes of the ambivalence of the successful woman continue to occupy a central space. Motherhood, and the joy and woes of it, usually still constitutes a central dilemma. The heroine of this phase is still a divided individual, the pseudo-self, no longer at ease with tradition and not ready to acquiesce. Generally, the social milieu reveals an encroaching change. The male characters often overlook the need to strike a balance between the old and the new order. The woman becomes the scapegoat of social change and modernization.

Zaynab Alkali's novella *The Stillborn* illustrates the tension in the life of the woman who tries to embrace change within a society that still imposes traditional values on her. The heroine, Libira (Li), is caught in the middle and her dreams, hopes, aspirations are aborted by a combination of traditional and religious bigotry. Like her sister Awa, and friend Faku, marrying strangers instead of men chosen by their parents is at the root of their problems. However, urbanisation and encroaching modern values are the real causes of their tragic or semi-tragic lives.

These characters are types of the African woman unable to reconcile themselves to social change. Breaking the fetters of tradition is not easy. Yet, one cannot transplant old values into a changing social order. Li's husband, Habu Adams, a deserter and alcoholic, treats Li contemptuously. He keeps another wife in the city while Li waits for him in the village. His ultimate tragic end brings out the human qualities in Li, in contrast to his callousness. Here, even older characters recognise the inevitability of change. Remarkably, her grandmother is more sensitive to this than younger characters.

Alkali's heroines all attempt a halfway measure to come to terms with change. Faku becomes a social worker, deserting her husband and children in a struggle for survival. Li in turn abandons her daughter to train as a teacher. Her returning to her husband shows her dream as being only partially fulfilled.

These women find compromise in unconventional decisions but their liberation is abortive and partial. They cannot go the whole way to initiate radical self-actualization. This dramatises the reality of many African women. They desire change in their status within existing male-female structures, rather than insisting on autonomy.

The protagonists of Alkali's fictional works have a multiple burden—confronting patriarchy, tradition, and Islamic ideology, which all put the woman in a specific liminal place. Several of Nawal El Saadawi's heroines have identical predicaments, but this writer's radical vision creates stronger characters who are also rebels.

The Joys of Motherhood is more distanced from the auteurist personal experience. Here, memory plays a significant role since it is a castback into the colonial period of the 1940s. This is no coincidence; Emecheta was born in Lagos in 1944. It is a conceptualization of the impact of social change on the society and like most other novels by African women, it is equally a biographical fictionalization of a moment in the collective history and therefore a portrait of the artist's collective consciousness and predicament. It is a tale of two communities and the setting shunts between the author's home area of Ibuza and Lagos where she grew up.

The impact of cultural implosion is central to Nnu Ego's tragedy. Her belief in tradition sustains her through suffering and deprivation, convinced that, naked today, her children will clothe her tomorrow. Today's starvation will be compensated by tomorrow's plenty as the blessing will accrue from her children. This is a common African belief that sustains women suffering from poverty and/or marital neglect. The portrait of Nnaife, her husband, is the typical one that is a common feature of Emecheta's male characters—a lazy, good-for-nothing oppressor of his wife. This is a direct product of the author's biography. She is often condemned for this bleak pessimistic picture of the African man. Some critics even explain this trend as the consequence of her uprooting and long stay in the West. I consider her portrait of men as only a slice of life and not the whole story. Strong positive men who respect the female exist in real life and this includes writers such as Sembene Ousmane, Ngugi Wa Thiong'o, Driss Chraibi, and others. The African woman writer is generally not a hater of men, but a woman singing her song and the song of the society as she sees it. She may sing a dirge or a war song every now and then, but she sings songs of hope, love, redemption and the possibility of justice, coalition, self-respect, and empowerment for her gender as well.

The Joys of Motherhood is an ironic portrait of the artist as the conscience of her society. The story is one of Emecheta's strongest indictments of a woman clinging to marriage at all costs—which she detests, according to her interview with Marie Umeh: "Personally, I'd like to see the ideal, happy marriage. But if it doesn't work, for goodness sake, call it off." Emecheta's self-portrait is often contradictory and her picture of the collective consciousness is at times defective. She justifies critics, white and black, who claim that her perception is alienated because of her long stay in England. Her comments in the interview with Adeola James exposes this trend. In her reaction to Omolara Ogundipe-Leslie's call for a threefold commitment for the African woman, Emecheta has this to say:

> What does she mean by commitment as a woman? A writer is a writer, and writing is sexless. But you can write from a particular situation, for example, if you are a working-class person and you want to highlight the oppressed conditions of your class, or you want to write about women and men.[8]

Emecheta exalts her work as being sexless, colourless, and cultureless. This is self-effacement as a precedent to self-denial. On the question of the African writer's language and the impact of living in England on her work, she replies:

> Writing coming from Nigeria, from Africa (I know this because my son does the criticism) sounds quite tilted. After reading the first page you tell yourself you are plodding. But when you are reading the same thing written by an English person, or somebody who lives here you find you are enjoying yourself because the language is so academic, so perfect. Even if you remove the cover you can always say who is an African writer. But with some of my books you can't tell that easily any more because, I think, using the language everyday and staying in the culture my Africanness is, in a way, being diluted.[9]

She goes on to say that her publishers, Collins, no longer group her books as African literature. She further condemns "everything coming out of Africa" for being preoccupied with colonialism and "what the Englishman has done." This gives the impression that Emecheta is unaware of the large body of post-colonial disillusion literature that is largely inward-looking as well as those from Francophone and Portuguese-speaking African countries who are not concerned with what the English have done. Gendered writing with culture-specific orientation as well as the use of non-African languages by Africans has been vindicated for decades. Self-contradiction comes from the artist's obsession with self-exoneration at the expense of larger collective concerns. Her attempt to erase African identity from her work is an aspect of some writers' desire for Western canonization.

Emecheta refuses to be seen as a feminist writer and at best accepts being a feminist with a small 'f.' She is not alone in rejecting feminist perspective. Some western critics also decline an identification with feminist focus. Nina Aueberch opposes gynocriticism, "I have no nostalgia whatever for woman's separate sphere." Emecheta's claim is ambivalent, however, in view of the predominance of strong feminine—if not feminist—aesthetics in her works. The African woman writer is not always preoccupied with woman-centered epistemology at the exclusion of other considerations. Bessie Head's novels and short stories also reveal women as victims of their socio-political environment as much as ethnic, class and gender bigotry. She presents the meeting point between various aspects of the African woman's social problems.

Head provides a profound insight into the cross-currents of political, racial, ethnic, national, economic, class, gender, and cultural problems. She reveals the many-pronged monster that holds the woman down. It is hardly surprising that Bessie's major protagonists are women. The South African scenario was so politically charged that identity politics in one form or another became inevitable. In a *Question of Power,* the central figure, Elizabeth, is the victim of miscegenation (mixed blood), reminding one of the tragic mulatto with a drop of black blood in the literature of the diaspora. She dramatises the woman's search for self-knowledge and true identity in a multi-cultural apartheid setting. In a painful process of inner growth, Elizabeth discovers that sanity cannot be easily maintained, where the socio-political situation is stifling and self-effacing. Because reality in South Africa is repugnant, Elizabeth withdraws into herself through dreams, visions and a strange soul-searching relationship with two men, Sello and Dan. Insanity seems to be her inevitable plight and escape.

Some writers are more liberal and ideologically neutral. Ifeoma Okoye has elicited some womanist gender awareness although she prefers to be seen as a humanist. Her most recent novel, *Chimere* (Longman Drumbeat, 1992), presents the titular heroine's search for identity which can not be easily separated from a collective quest for self-knowledge by the African woman. She prefers to be seen as a humanist and de-emphasises a womanist perception. Her recent heroine, Chimere, hates men initially because she feels cheated by her father and boy friend. She reconciles with the men in her life at the end. She believes that men and women need to work together for a more humane society.

In tracing the growth in awareness revealed in African women's literature, therefore, one cannot fail to see a parallel between social changes and individual consciousness in a gradual way. In each phase, the African woman is searching for meaning, new identity, and reintegration; she is crying for just treatment. Her identification of femininity is not depicted by the erosion of female roles or the invisibility in the public sphere. Her quest is more fundamental and profound. She tries to deconstruct tradition by recreating new models and new yardsticks.

The female writer faces many challenges. Writers need to look into history for collective actions of women who caused social change. In an interview with a Nigerian male playwright, Akinwumi Ishola, he was asked why he focuses attention on historical female heroines such as Efusetan Aniwura and Madam Tinubu. He explained that the invisibility of women in existing literature motivated him and caused his interest. He then searched for historical accounts of women's special and spectacular roles in initiating socio/political changes. He discovered that many strong women exist in African history and has since written several plays centred on powerful women in Yoruba. These include *Efunsetan Aniwura, Iyalode Ibadan,* and *Madam Tinubu.* The cycle is now complete but writers have not sufficiently focused on great women of African history as the basis of their fiction. The recent fictionalization of Nehánda of Zimbabwe is a step forward. There is also the need to shift from individual heroines that are not representative. The grassroots have been fictionalized effectively by Ngugi wa Thiong'o, Ayi Kwei Armah, and Sembene Ousmane.

The impact of African women writer's development include the transformation of male writers' depiction of women. Writers who presented typical biased pictures of women in their early works began to show sensitivity to women's needs and recreated more positive depictions of female characters. Modern myths have been successfully used to cause a new awareness of the woman's reality. The initial emphasis of myth as ritual has given way to the secular depiction of myth. Helen Chukwuma has defined myth as used in Igbo beliefs and her delimitation is relevant to the African woman's cause. To her, myth is "a stabilizer of social system, a reflector of value systems, a means of recreating past history or as a psychoanalytic insight into human behaviour motivation." This is an appropriate interpretation of the way African women have used myth in a progressive and dynamic way.

Notes

1. Ode S. Ogede, "Counters to Male Domination: Images of Pain in Igede Women's Songs," *Research in African Literature,* Vol. 25, No.4 (Winter 94).

2. Micere Mugo, in James, loc. cit., p.93.

3. Kofi Agovi, "Women's discourse in Social Change in Nzema (Ghanaian) Maiden Songs," a paper presented at the African Studies Association Conference, St. Louis, Missouri, December, 1991.

4. Afam Abaogu, "Igbo Birthsongs," an unpublished seminar paper at the Folklore Society of Nigeria annual conference, Obafemi Awolowo University, Ile-Ife, Nigeria, 1984.

5. Jane Parpart & Kathleen Staudt, *Women and the State in Africa* (Boulder, Colorado: Lynne Rienner, 1989), p.1.

6. Olurombi in Yoruba myth is a classical exemplar of this tension and the same myth exists in many other parts of Africa with varying details.

7. Margot Lovett, in Parpart et. al., *op.cit.,* p. 25.

8. Emecheta, in James, *op. cit.,* p. 40.

9. *Ibid.*

PART TWO

THE MIRROR AND THE GOLD

CHAPTER FOUR

THROUGH THE LOOKING GLASS: IMAGES OF AFRICAN WOMEN IN MEN'S LITERATURE

The impact of social change on the growth in perception has gender implications but it also transcends gender lines. Whereas most female writers embody some aspects of feminine consciousness, others are not emphatically interested in projecting strong female awareness and viewpoint. It has been acknowledged that most early African literary luminaries are men who logically presented a world of male heroism. This trend continues and some male writers on the continent still maintain this attitude. However, there are some exceptions to this trend and the existence of male writers who are sympathetic to the women's cause is central to some of the issues raised by womanists. Some men have shown understanding and sincerity in the need to portray female characters as active heroines making meaningful contributions to their societies. Others have created a central space for women, making them visible

but not necessarily revealing their strength clearly. Such writers have presented women ambiguously. From Elechi Amadi's
pathetic portrait of Ihuoma in *The Concubine,* to more realistic
works by Ngugi Wa Thiong'o, Sembene Ousmane, Ola Rotimi,
Ayi Kwei Amah, Driss Chraibi, and Femi Osofisan, one identifies
male writers who are consistent in their positive attitudes to
women while others are rather ambivalent in depicting women.

Ngugi wa Thiong'o stands out as a writer who is fully aware
of the invincible role of mythic women like Mumbi as well as historic women leaders. From Ngugi's early works to his more revolutionary later works, he has been consistent in fictionalizing
strong African women. He is also persistent in acknowledging
the woman's strength, political inspiration and spirituality. His
depiction of women in his fiction reveals the indispensability of
women as opposed to their irrelevance in socio-political situations. From his early trilogy to more recent works, women are
treated with respectability whether as individuals or as a group.
From the mythic Mumbi to the collective women amazons in
Petals of Blood, Ngugi's objectification of women's experience
runs through his fiction. Women are not passive objects but
active dynamic centres of consciousness and action. Indeed,
the climax is revealed in portraits such as Wariinga, who is pitted against male cruelty, oppression, and suppression.

The works of Sembene Ousmane in English translation corroborate the position that some male writers reveal greater
fidelity in elevating the positive attributes of the African
woman. Ousmane's females are true to life and he does not fail
to focus on the social strictures and structures that delimit
women's role in his society where Islam and tradition combine to force women into the "socio-political harem." He further depicts women who struggle as individuals to reject
docility, as seen in his short story, *Her Three Days.* However,
the crux of Ousmane's concern for women is the collective
role as demonstrated by women in *God's Bits of Wood.* From
the young Ad'jibid'ji to the blind Maimouna, women play
diverse active roles just like in the historic strike action that
shook the entire francophone West Africa.

The height of women's active participation was their collective role as they joined the men in the revolt and march to
Dakar. But Ousmane does not just present mass women's
movement as one can see individual growth in consciousness
in several of the female characters to prove that the ultimate
march is not a mob action. Ramatoulaye rejects both class

and male oppression, by initiating her own solution to the problems of starvation and survival. The climax is seen when she kills the well-fed ram, Vendredi. Her reason shows her new awareness that the women can no longer leave bread-winning helplessly in the hands of the striking men:

> ... we were all too hungry for it to go on. The men know it too, but, they go away in the morning and don't come back until the night has come and they do not see. (Ousmane, 1970: 69)

This symbolic shift in role points to other areas in which women rise to action when the men are incapacitated.The attack on the hungry women by the police reveals that the myth of women's docility is over, as reality confronts the uniformed men. The women spontaneously take up sand-filled bottles. Like the self-sacrificing Ramatoulaye, the women show new strength in resisting authoritarian oppression. Mame Sofi, Bineta, and Houdia M'Baye led the attack, and the rest of the women followed, seizing upon anything that could be used as a weapon (75).

The women's battle and confrontation with the police precedes men's action. It is a brief fight but the women become mobilized, never again to retreat into passivity:

> The battle between the women and the policemen in the courtyard of N'Diayene was of short duration. Overcome by sheer weight of numbers, the police beat a hasty retreat, and after they had gone the crowd that had gathered in the compound also began to disperse. Some of the women, however, formed into little groups and began patrolling the streets of the neighbourhood, armed with bottles filled with sand. (109)

Women such as Mame Sofi become formidable threats to armed policemen using bottles and flaming sheaves. The grande finale of the women's active revolt is the march of the women from Thies to Dakar. Ousmane has gone further than many writers in the power of empathy and identification with the women's dilemma and in fictionalizing the dynamic role of women, not only fighting on behalf of their gender, but going further than the striking men to reject racial oppression and class deprivation.

AMBIGUITY IN WOMEN'S IMAGES

Men's attitude to women is not always clearly defined, as we see in the ambiguous female characters of Wole Soyinka's novels. Considering the background of this giant of African creativity, one would expect formidable women heroines that reflect the high level of consciousness of Abeokuta women, including Funmilayo Ransome-Kuti and Soyinka's own mother and several relatives. His various biographies show the strength of these women. Several of his plays also represent the strong points of African women's position, particularly in traditional societies. The central female protagonists of *The Lion and the Jewel, Death and the King's Horseman, and Madmen and Specialists* are illustrations of this. But the women in his novel are ambiguously treated. The Nobel prize winner, Wole Soyinka, is one of the most versatile as well as the most prolific male writers focusing attention on the female gender. His background as recorded in *Ake* justifies this. Women with an unusually high level of political consciousness from the first generation of educated African women surround Soyinka's childhood, and this inevitably shapes his consciousness. His catalogue of the activities, resourcefulness, diligence and socio-political awareness of Eniola Soyinka, his mother *(Wild Christian)*, underscores women's dynamism in a conservative society. Along with other sensitive but economically energetic women like Mrs. Ransome-Kuti, Mrs. Odufuwa, and even the nameless rural market women from Isara and Abeokuta, women's mobilization is an indelible aspect of Soyinka's childhood.

Quite naturally, Wole Soyinka's fictive world is a world of women portrayed in their diversities. Women play central roles in many of his plays, including *The Lion and the Jewel,* the Jero plays, *Death and the King's Horseman,* and several others. Women are portrayed as objects of admiration, indispensable to the male-dominated world. Old women are revered as the "dome" of religious mysticism, as seen in the symbols of Iya Agba and Iya Mate in *Madmen and Specialists.* Yet, given the formidable role of women in his biographical works, especially *Ake,* the stature of political awareness and involvement commensurate with real-life casts like *Wild Christian* is missing in his novels. Soyinka's portraits of women have been well documented by critics of Soyinka's plays. This chapter will not focus on this well researched area, but the place of women in his novels needs a close attention. His depiction of women reveals some remarkable paradigms and ambivalence.

Women are very visible in most of the creative production by Soyinka, and his novels are no exceptions. In *The Interpreters* and *Season of Anomy*, women occupy important spaces; some fit into the usual stereotypes while others are more problematic. A reappraisal of these fictive works reveals many female characters as caricatures and embodiments of certain conventional images of women that are not much of a departure from the usual stereotypes. Even Ofeyi, the heroine of *Season of Anomy*, falls short of the positive radical motivator of social change that she appears to be. The image of women in Soyinka's fictive narratives almost constitutes an apologia, a retreat from a full conviction about the place of these women. They are not presented as identical representations or true life replica of women activists. Even when they seek actualization, one observes an ambivalence in Soyinka's attitude.

Wole Soyinka's novels *The Interpreters* and *Season of Anomy* are good instances of certain trends in the attitude of male writers in portraying feminine images and consciousness. Several conventional female stereotypes are reiterated in Soyinka's novels. His depiction of women is not altogether negative in that he avoids popular portraits of timid, slavish, defeated individuals, beasts of burden in a 'man-made' world. However, these women are either marginalized or over-idealized without a sense of achievement. His male heroes are often depicted as the lion demonstrating his prowess and vitality; powerful, ready to pounce on the female who is a symbol of beauty, a jewel to be possessed at all cost.

In these novels, one observes the imbalance common to many African male writers in their depiction of male-female relationships. This ambivalence has been highlighted by Soyinka in the tension between male and female protagonists. Three dominant stereotypes in *The Interpreters* and *Season of Anomy* exemplify this trend. Female characters in these novels can be categorised into three, very much like Sagoe's observation of the conveniences at the radio station, "one masculine, one feminine, and one for the neuter board" (Soyinka, 1978: 249). The masculine group consists of radical domineering women playing the role of conquerors over the men around them. The second group includes idealised females who are feminine to the point of trivialisation of womanhood. The third group is made up of apologetics or subdued women who fall short of total achievement.

The radical women are repulsive in their physical outlook

or roles. We see Mrs. Faseyi in her domineering nature and this makes her a tyrant to her son, Ayo Faseyi. Her treatment of her son's male friends is equally dominating as she sends fear and intimidation into them. Having acquired her independence of a husband, she asserts:

> There is nothing mysterious in a broken home you know. I ought to know .... But I don't like unnecessary sentiment. (211)

She is as tough, as her actions reveal, and in her opinion all men are beasts! She overrules her son and expatriate daughter-in-law in major decisions even as she controls their lives. She is certainly not the picture of an ideal wife or mother but a rather despicable woman getting on everybody's nerves.

Mrs. Batoki of *Season of Anomy* is a twin picture of Mrs. Faseyi. She is troublesome, proud, and conceited as she takes over the husband's role in her home. She is a terror to both Chief Batoki and her daughter, Biye. Her portrait as a harridan is perfected in the war of words between her and her husband and Biye. Her husband is not safe under her intimidation and she tries to prove that she is an amazon in attacking her husband and daughter (Soyinka, 1973: 188).

The second category is made up of so-called heroines of these novels: Simi the notorious conquistador, seducer, tempter of men, and Iriyise the caged tigress, firebrand with mermaid attributes. This image of the legendary beautiful woman with a pandora box is frequent in Soyinka's works. In his plays, Sidi and Segi, among others, are manifestations of this preoccupation with the mythic beauty, the 'femme fatale', the object of men's quest and/or destruction. These protagonists are painted as bitches, goddess-like, ephemeral, and intangible. Simi is well known as the 'notorious, international courtesan.' Mrs. Faseyi, in her usual anti-male attitude, maintains that Simi's "little finger is worth 10 men put together outside this place and all the men in here at the moment" (249). Her role is hardly heroic:

> Even children knew of Simi! Wives knelt and prayed that their men might sin a hundred times with a hundred women, but may their erring feet never lead them to Simi .... For then men lost hope of salvation, their home and children became ghosts of a past illusion .... Simi broke men and friendship. (50)

The picture of Iriyise is a replica of that of Simi. Iriyise is depicted as a misty woman vanishing into vapour and resurfacing at intervals. As a member of the campaign team, she towers over the male members who "don't believe the sun is out until they see Celestial ...." (74). She wears the cloak of a goddess, princes, and "the Chrysalis of the cocoa grain." As the source of attraction to Aiyero, Ofeyi sees Iriyise as "the only brightness in a long progression of compromise" (58). Simi and Iriyise are, therefore, symbols and commodities for satisfying men's yearnings. Like Simi, Iriyise "accepted her habitual homage, continued to hush hotel foyers with her appearance and drove diplomats to indiscretions" (62). One therefore sees these heroines fitting neatly into the usual images as witches and/or seducers. Femaleness is being equated with cheap exploitation of beauty in these novels. The portrait of Owolebi, the dancer, sums up Soyinka's ambivalent treatment of women: "she wasn't a woman at all, she was just a matriarch symbol."

The third group reveals women as underdogs, as underdeveloped subdued individuals incapable of asserting positive influences. Failing to achieve meaningful female roles and lacking the strength of character needed for a reinscription of positive status and empowerment, they are like the third of the conveniences, the neuter group. This group consists of passive characters who are limited by one flaw or the other. This category includes the anonymous pregnant girl subdued by Egbo, Monica Faseyi and Mrs. Oguazor. Biye also falls short of real achievement. Mrs. Oguazor is a puppet; her role in advocating shallow morals is as unconvincing as her personality. She is ridiculous in spite of her social status as a professor's wife. Monica Faseyi could have been a voice of reason but she is completely engulfed and overwhelmed. She lacks the strength of character to make her views effective. Egbo's unnamed pregnant girl friend is another paradoxical symbol, a tool, she has an "unfeminine handwriting," yet she is frail and fragile. All these characters fall short of an ideal or achievement while their ostentatious feminine roles are undermined and neutralised by lack of positive impact or non-feminine qualities.

A few female characters fall outside these categories. Dehinwa could have been a positive character but she too is just an appendage in a 'man-made' world. Although the voice of reason during Egbo's drunkenness, she is merely a symbol,

a companion, a guide, sometimes a driver. Though realistic
and not over-idealised, she plays no dynamic positive role to
effect social change or at least advocate such, like the male
interpreters around her.

Taiila too could have been a positive cast. She could have
been more convincing but she makes no significant contribution in her own right. She is still an appendage to the men in
her attempt to make a mark in the society. Soyinka seems to
suggest that the time is not yet ripe for these women to activate their society and this is an irony when one looks at the
strength of character of African women in traditional society,
which is a central issue in *Death and the King's Horseman*. He,
nonetheless, carves a positive future role for Iriyise as regards
a dynamic social change:

> When the moment arrives, a woman like Iriyise becomes
> for them a chattel, a Deborah, torch and standard-
> bearer, supermistress of universal insurgence. To aban-
> don such a potential weapon in any struggle is to admit
> to a lack of foresight. (Soyinka, 1973: 219)

It is this hope of Iriyise's potentiality as a tool of social change
that prompts Ofeyi's speculation. However, by the time she is
found, she is an unconscious effigy, permanently incapacitated
and stifled, an illusion, a mirage.

Soyinka's ambiguous perception of women's status and
sensibility is clearly revealed in the images and roles of these
various categories of women—all stereotypes. One group of
women that Soyinka constantly exalts is the old and the spiritual. The image of Iya Agba, Iya Mate, and Iyaloja—the old
woman, the embodiment of traditional archetypal virtue and
the metaphysics, wielding power and influence—is missing in
these novels. In a passing reference, Bamidele refers to the
royal mothers of Benin as "old and immutable." In a philo-
sophical-metaphysical undertone, women are said to represent
the dome of religion. This is where Soyinka's real fidelity lies
and yet it takes a stammering voice to make this point in *The
Interpreters.* Woman representing the "D-d-dome of love . . . the
D-d-dome of Religion . . . the Universal D-d-dome" are either
not practically depicted or presented in an abortive effort, in
these novels.

Having avoided depicting women as the center of these
vital domes, most females are ambiguously treated, very much
like albinos. Like Usaye, the albino, these female characters are

short-sighted and freckled, explored and exploited—freaks or anomalies in the drive for social regeneration and self-appre-hension. They are simultaneously attractive and repulsive, like Usaye, objects of male curiosity, search, and research. It is paradoxical that Soyinka believes women to represent the body of religion as well as its roof, sacred and to be respected, yet he presents a collection of debunked, under-rated, over-idealized non-achievers in these novels.

Carole Boyce-Davis, one of the most versatile Africanists, has made a noteworthy observation on Soyinka's treatment of female characters. According to her, many male writers see lit-erature as a forum for projecting "negative attitudes and stereotypes of women." She maintains that this attitude on the part of African male writers is a heritage of western patriarchal mentality and prejudices. Boyce-Davis' stand is validated more in Soyinka's fictional novels. At least one male character declares himself a misogynist. In his newspaper column, Spyhole passes this comment on Iriyise in *Season of Anomy:*

> I despise women...it is my duty to despise women for what they are, but I finally met a woman that wasn't a woman.... (Soyinka, 1973: 62)

One is inclined to agree with Carole Boyce-Davis that Soyinka could present "women as neither victors nor victims but part-ners in struggle."[1]

Ngugi's Women as Symbols of Self-Reliance and Dynamic Power

Ngugi and Ousmane have made deliberate attempts to depict realistic female characters as active tools of social change. Traditional African women symbolize self-reliance and dili-gence. After analysing the various dimensions of oppression of African women as gender, class and tradition, Ngugi Wa Thiong'o makes this declaration:

> I would create a picture of a strong, determined woman with a will to resist and to struggle against the condi-tions of her present being.[2]

This is fulfilled in *Devil on the Cross* through the portrait of Wariinga. In an identical radical step, Sembene Ousmane has created heroines who reject retrogressive customs and tradi-tions in his novels and short stories. Such total women revo-lutionaries with positive achievements are lacking in Soyinka's two novels. Dehinwa misses the mark of real achievement. Taiila is one of the few positive females, as we see in her action, positive concern and pity for victims hidden in the grotto. She is a source of comfort to Ofeyi in time of agonizing search for Iriyise. One wonders why she is not an African but an Asian. Perhaps Soyinka wishes to broaden the basis of the struggle.

Soyinka's treatment of women is, therefore, one of a paradox in his novel. Believing women to be cardinal to religion and love, he successfully presents women as religious symbols in his plays. In the novel, there are only passing references to women's spiritual roles. Taiila desired to be a nun before her meaningful participation in retrieving and caring for the victims of the grotto. The radical female characters are dynamic in a negative way. They are tyrants, nags, and are repulsive in adopting a domineering attitude over men. Others are so feminine that they become caricatures of womanhood.

One can see that Soyinka's women in the two fictional novels are less successfully portrayed in terms of the representation of women and particularly the modern African woman on the cutting edge of social change. Soyinka's plays and non-fictional biographical works present stronger images of women. Ironically, even the women he depicts struggling for self-assertion in the traditional society are more dynamic than the apparently radical women of *The Interpreters* and *Season of Anomy*. At best, Soyinka's attitude is apologetic. His portrait of the "black immanent" is romantic and idealistic, not pragmatic; quite like his *abiku* image. Soyinka's women in these novels are caught between two worlds like the *abiku* child. They are hedged in between a radical life and a passive romantic existence.

Soyinka is usually more interested in the social space occupied by women and not a psychological probing of their lives and so they are types and embodiment of specific images. This is equally true of his plays as well as his novels. This also accounts for the stereotyped compartments of his females, which causes Carole Boyce-Davis to observe:

> In fact, a feminist reading of Soyinka reveals enough female stereotypes to suggest a definite sexist bias against women. Additionally, an examination of the characteristics of these women produces the distinct impression that the author is conjuring up the image of the same, ideal woman over and over again.[3]

WOMEN AS VICTIMS OF TRADITION

The Moroccan writer Driss Chraibi is another writer who presents women in a central space but his treatment is also ambiguous. Like Ousmane, Chraibi's society, which constitutes the fictional setting, is a conservative one where women's relegation is sometimes a matter of fact. Women's life and experience is a central theme in Chraibi's works, *Le Passe Simple, Succession Ouverte and La Civilisation, Ma Mere*. The latter presents a more predominant picture of the woman and in particular the mother. His treatment of women in *Succession Ouverte (Heirs to the Past)* is, however, ambivalent and this calls for a closer look. Few male writers are consistently positive in treating women as subjects. Others allow women a central position but a closer analysis reveals ambiguity in the attitude to the woman as a positive force in the socio-political set-up.

In *Heirs to the Past* (1972) Chraibi's preoccupation centers on the impact of colonization, civilization, and westernization on colonized people. His treatment of his father, 'Seigneur', and his mother reveals the paradox in post-colonial situation. Chraibi's idealization of the woman is not controversial. The strange Arab man's attitude to his wife is one of surrender and submission, the attitude of "a worshipper prepared to wipe out a whole tribe for love of a woman" (15). The author confesses his own attitude of submission when he met a woman on the very first day of his arrival in France, "I had looked at her as one would look at a mother. I was very willing to be protected, to be colonised, civilised, be given a certificate of existence" (15). His attitude to his wife, Isabelle, however reveals some ambivalence, "I had no desire to make a woman unhappy, but I got married .... My insomnia dates from that time. All my ability for loving was turned on Isabelle. And I had been reduced to loving a stone, a match, or a tooth brush." (20). This unromantic attraction to Isabelle is validated by Isabelle's physical description, "frail, decalcified by the war, but serene."

Chraibi's women occupy central positions in his works. They are presented as being at once attractive, repulsive, and inquisitive, but ignored or undermined. Bouchaib's wife is scared and "afraid to understand." Yet, she is the voice of conscience, more human and humane than Bouchaib. The latter prefers to show ignorance and incomprehension at his father's agonized cry for his son's attention and acknowledgement. The wife is perceptive as intuition gives her an insight into

Bouchaib's pretence. As Bouchaib brushes her aside, saying that he does not know what she is saying, the wife repeats, "I may not know what I'm saying, but I know what I'm feeling. And it is my impression that you're hiding something from me(25)."

Typically these passive women are presented as devoted mothers. Bouchaib's mother has had sleepless nights waiting for her son. Driss Ferdi's mother is another symbol of dedication and self-sacrifice. On Driss Ferdi's arrival, the mother's benumbing profound emotion is described, she feels "as though she was emerging from the mists and fogs of a very long dream." (34). As she approaches her sons, her description is equally expressive of a person isolated from reality. "She came straight towards us with the little stumbling steps of a sleep-walker, her eyes demented in their sleep sockets, she so small and thin as to be almost without substance." (34). When Driss embraces her, he likens the feel to "clutching a farmyard chicken all fluttering and shaking" (Ibid).

The author's description of Driss Ferdi's mother reveals several of the stereotypic descriptions common to female characters—frail, fragile and vulnerable:

> The flesh had gone from her face, the skin had shrunk and was stretched tight over the bones, a skin that was chalky and shrivelled—but that was not what made me ill at ease and ashamed. It was her eyes; they had no lashes: the lids were as thin as cigarette-paper, and the gaze was dreamy and distant. (Ibid.)

It is therefore paradoxical to see Driss Ferdi's reference to his mother's protective eyes even cutting across time and space to mysteriously oversee his interest. His ambivalent attitude is further drawn out in his description of her gay and lively disposition despite suffering. Nonetheless, she emerges from a dead past. She becomes so lively that Driss doubts if she has just lost her husband. She immediately assumed the position and role of a mother fully in control of the situation as she gives firm orders to her children. This is a radical shift from conventional portraits of Moroccan women acquiescing to a passive subordinate role without self-assertion or authority. Chraibi's "many-sided image" of Driss Ferdi's mother culminates in the portrait of a woman as an under-developed individual to be aided, assisted, protected and provided with essential requirements. Seigneur Ferdi's orders to the successor, Madini, clearly confirm this:

> You will not make an allowance to your mother, she
> would not know what to do with it. Money has never
> meant emancipation. You will act as though we were
> still alive ... you will provide her in our name with every-
> thing she needs. She has never known the daily strug-
> gle for what is called life, she has never known the value
> of a banknote and a good thing too. (75)

Driss Ferdi's mother is thus presented as a protected, ignorant
individual who will be destabilized by emancipation. "At her
age, emancipation, the idea of absolute freedom, would mean
nothing to her, if not a complete upset" (75). However, the
Seigneur makes room for social change and encourages Madini
to indulge her if she chooses to move with time and take
advantage of change. For the most part, Madini is to treat her
like the immature brother, Jaad.

Finally, from the horse's mouth, we get a picture of Mrs.
Ferdi's suffering and loneliness, we get to know of the toils of
motherhood and the price she pays:

> ... all my life I've done nothing but that—bear children,
> and have babies in napkins around me ....Everything
> was alright while I had children round me .... But now
> they are all grown men, and I'm left alone. (p. 99)

When Ferdi's mother finally speaks for herself, she opts for solitude and 'imprisonment' as opposed to change and freedom.
This attitude fits too neatly into conventional images of North
African women under the double burden of conservative Islamic
and traditional yokes. Chraibi's depiction of women here lacks
the radical stance of many of Sembene Ousmane's women who
have identical religious and cultural heritage. Seigneur's authoritarian rule has indeed killed something in her, permanently.

Ola Rotimi's play, *Our Husband Has Gone Mad Again,* is an
ironic satire that is full of subtleties. The central character
Rahman Lejoka-Brown, is portrayed as a phoney, insincere,
self-conscious individual. His pretentious wisdom in handling
his polygamous home breaks down on the arrival of his
American-educated wife, Liza. Mama Rashida, his wife through
a levirathian marriage, is the typical obedient unquestioning
wife until Liza's arrival. Sikira, the young daughter of the leader
of the National Union of Nigerian Market women, is the major's
wife for political advantages. Before Liza's arrival, she too is
obedient, although sharp enough to be on the defensive as the
need arises.

However, Liza is the motivator of both women as she begins to influence them through her more emancipated view of women. Ultimate self-awareness begins and Lejoka Brown's secure oligarchy becomes threatened to its foundation. The trio constitutes a formidable three-fold cord. Jointly, they begin to puncture Lejoka-Brown's masculine domination. It is significant that Liza is the instrument of awareness to the other two women. This process of self-definition leads to Sikira's rebellion and even Mama Rashida receives a slice of Liza's liberated attitude. Liza encourages Mama Rashida's trade and therefore self-sufficiency. By a simple economic theory, Liza teaches Mama Rashida a secret of prosperity. With this, a new female bonding, even sisterhood, emerges among the three wives. This is remarkable in view of the usual rancorous relationship that characterizes polygamy.

Sikira in turn opens up her heart to Liza, expressing her fear when she learns of Liza's inevitable return. Her initial feeling of insecurity towards Liza gives way to trust, mutual love, and encouragement. Liza makes a new set of clothing that transforms young Sikira. This external change then initiates an inward change. Sikira begins to ask questions, seeking to know more about western and westernised women. This is the beginning of Sikira's journey of awareness and rebellion as revealed in her discussion with Liza:

> You are a strong woman, with a strong, strong heart. Sometimes I wish I, too, had your kind of strong, strong heart so I could tell our husband to go to hell! (53)

Eventually, Sikira imbibes Liza's conviction that "men and women are all created equal." Immediately Sikira suggests forming a party of all Nigerian women. At least all married women, to participate actively in politics. She begins to agitate for freedom, "Everywhere there must be freedom .... [In] every house there must be freedom, freedom for mothers. Freedom for housemaids." Freedom becomes her watchword and her dictum. The journey of self-awareness and self-definition leads to Sikira's sensitisation and conscientisation. She will no longer be kicked around by their husband, Lejoka-Brown. The husband's prompt reaction is expected as he accuses Liza of wielding an unhealthy influence on the other wives. With biting sarcasm, he tells Liza:

> I am very happy too woman, very happy indeed to notice that you have become used to this "gas chamber"

house so much, that you have now begun a Communist manifesto class in it. (56)

At the end of her journey of self-discovery, Sikira deserts Lejoka-Brown for her home. In this ironic twist, the young girl, temporarily a wife to Lejoka-Brown for political gains, leaves him before he executes the plan to discard her after winning the elections. The wives turn out to add the last straw to his political loss and humiliation. Liza's appearance in swimsuit during a press conference infuriates her husband so much that his subsequent crazy treatment of the pressmen and his political colleagues is his undoing. The final touch to his political loss is the withdrawal of the market women's support because of his treatment of Sikira.

ROTIMI'S PORTRAIT OF WOMEN FIGHTING BACK

Ola Rotimi's female characters in *Our Husband Has Gone Mad Again* fill some ideological lacuna. Both Mama Rashida and Sikira are submissive and obedient, even naive, at the beginning of the play. Rotimi deploys the entrance of Liza into the home, to destabilize the existing male chauvinistic order in the home. At the end, none of the women is devoid of self-knowledge. The two wives become determined to claim freedom, which they use for economic and political purposes, respectively. The husband is the worse off as a result of the wives' emancipation. The male characters do not show the same level of growth in awareness that we see in the women. The strength of character revealed by the three wives make them a foil to the Lejoka-Brown in his phoney masculinity. He is portrayed as an absurd character in all his affectations and expectation of obedience through a combination of force and threats. It is amazing that the wives take him seriously as long as they do.

Rotimi's play no doubt presents a positive feminist purpose and to achieve this, the male characters have to be undermined. This play is a reflection of positive attitude in men's female characterization. Although Mama Rashida and Sikira are relatively simplistic at the start of the play, their process of transformation leads to a rejection of domination, subordination, and overt repression at the end.

In *Morontodun,* Femi Osofisan merges a sense of historicity with an acknowledgement of strength of character in the female gender. Deriving his plot from a historical heroine, Moremi (a sacrificial symbol), he logically creates several positive values in the fictional heroine, Titubi. The historical model, Moremi offers her life and herself to go to the enemies' camp and study the secret of their prowess and victory over her people of Ile-Ife. The incessant harassment and defeat of her people defy any plausible solution. Not only does this mythic heroine succeed in revealing the secret of the Igbo people's power to her people, she offers her only son, Oluorogbo, to the goddess of Isimiri river, according to her vow.

The contemporary setting of *Morountodun* is based on the farmer's revolt in western Nigeria between 1965 and 1967. Titubi, a pretty, rich, middle-class woman, ultimately designs some ploy to get herself into the peasants' camp and so learn the secret of their indefatigable attacks against the government and the rich. Pretending to be a prisoner awaiting death sentence for murdering her children, she gets released when the revolting peasants break through the prison to set their members free. She wins their sympathy, poses as a nurse, and becomes useful to the group. She plans to bring the Marshall, the leader of the farmers, to the police superintendent. She gets the police to arrange her capture and with the same determination as the legendary precursor, Moremi, she embarks on a precarious adventure to save her class from being destroyed by the rioting farmers. In the process, she risks her life, contrary to her mother's plea and dissuasion. She almost gets killed in an attack.

The play within a play brings out a recast of Moremi's legendary strength, courage, and determination. This throwback provides necessary strength and motivation for Titubi. Fearlessness is characteristic of both women, and here again we have a departure from the usual naive painting of women in African fiction. Moremi's virtues and heroic attributes are summed up by her husband, Oranmiyan. Explaining to her that he took other wives as tradition requires, he highlights her uniqueness:

> Kings are like Mother Bee. They must clothe themselves in people. The palace must fill its hives with the nectar of female voices. This is how our fathers made it. But your courage is strong, like our ancient rafters. Your name alone holds up with esteem the tottering roof of our besieged kingdom. (p. 36)

Just as Moremi refused to be discouraged by her husband's love and by the concern of her friend, Niniola, in the contemporary fictional version Titubi refuses to be dissuaded by her mother. Osofisan's play is deliberately derived from the historical account and his fidelity in presenting a legendary woman's strength of character is remarkable.

Several other male writers, such as Akinwumi Isola have dramatized the heroic exploits of historical, mythic, or legendary heroes, eliciting positive virtues in such female models. Akinwumi, like several others, has limited readership because his works are written in Yoruba language. Akinwumi has admitted that his interest in female heroism emanated from the under-representation of women heroic exploits in Yoruba oral tradition and written literature. He grew up to know the stories of great kings and warriors in oral genres like Ijala but great women's stories were hardly told. He then started investigating history, myths, and legends to identify the great women that constituted the eponymous heroines in his plays, *Madam Tinubu* and *Efunsetan Aniwura*. He then began to locate and explore modern intelligent outgoing and dynamic women as role models and as the source of plays like *Governor's Campus Queen*. The heroine, Banke, is a formidable challenge to a popular and feared campus thug. Her personality forces the society to recognize her.[4]

It is gratifying that these, among other male writers, have identified with the need to construct positive female models through literary creativity. It is significant that some male writers have either consistently, or in specific works, portrayed the female experience in affirmative ways. Even when the image is not overtly positive, these writers have moved the women from the periphery to the centre. Bode Sowande fictionalizes and justifies Olurombi in *Farewell to Babylon*. This is a shift from the normal position which demonizes Olurombi as a woman who gives economic success a priority over her domestic role and needs. So, men's fictionalization of women is as diverse as men's reactions in reality. This justifies the contention of several African womanists that one can not draw a battle-line between men and women as feminists do. Some African men have elevated women's status in literature more than some women writers who prefer to be gender-neutral. Looking at women through the eye of the men, who are considered the mirrors of the society in many parts of Africa, is to see the other side of the coin. It reveals an overlap in the

writer's commitment as some men are commited to women's
cause while others are ambivalent. This is a departure from the
predominant marginalization and invisibility of African women
in much of the literature by men, especially the early phase.

NOTES

1.   Carole Boyce-Davis & Ann Adams-Graves, *Ngambika* (Trenton:
      African World Press, 1986), p. 75 ff.
2.   Ngugi Wa Thiong'o, *Devil on the Cross* (London: Heinemann,
      1982), Introduction.
3.   Boyce-Davis & Adams-Graves, *loc.cit.*
4.   Akinwumi Isola is a well known Yoruba literary giant who has
      several of his works centred on women in a positive way. He
      confirmed this in my interview with him at Ile-Ife in June 1991.

CHAPTER FIVE

NWAYIBUIFE, A WOMAN ON THE ANTHILLS: RE-READING ACHEBE, RE-WRITING THE AFRICAN WOMAN

Chinua Achebe's treatment of women in his fictional works confirms the world of male chivalry and macho heroism in his early works. A conventional reading of Achebe gives this clear picture. Unlike writers such as Ngugi Wa Thiong'o, Sembene Ousmane or Driss Chraibi, Achebe makes no pretensions about women playing prominent roles in the earliest works. Achebe's world in *Things Fall Apart* and *Arrow of God* is the world of ostentatious male heroism, patriarchy and patrimony. Achebe's literary debut is largely a dramatization of macho heroism in which women have a liminal defined role. Okonkwo's individual quest coincides with the society's collective ethos on success and achievement. *Arrow of God* is even more so. A world preoccupied with male titles and female kettles gives way to the milieu where male heroes and antiheroes still dominate the scene in spite of social change. Women punctuate the men's stories but remain in the periphery of social impact.

A re-reading of Achebe's early works, however, reveals a gradual progression in the role allocated to women. In spite of the failure to delineate a dominant role for women in the public domain, there is a budding attempt to give women some visibility in *No Longer at Ease* and *A Man of the People*. Going beyond a conventional reading and giving these works a revisionist reading highlights this. *Things Falls Fall Apart* presents a world where the women's role remains relatively static while the men confront the cultural disintegration brought about by the coming of the whites. Women are essentially objects and causative agents, as we see in the imminent war between Umofia and Mbaino. A woman's death is the reason for the inter-communal conflict. Even in this, women are mere symbols for executing traditional rites, as the dead woman—Ogbuefi Udo's wife—is to be replaced by the ransom, an innocent girl from Mbaino.

ACHEBE'S EARLY WOMEN AS VICTIMS

We see in Achebe's world wives bowed and terrified by the iron hands of men like Okonkwo. Among other factors, the toughness in dealing with their wives is a measure of male prowess and masculine invincibility. Okonkwo dares to break the week of peace as he threatens his wife Ojiugo. Okonkwo's second wife, Ekwefi, is almost shot dead for cutting banana leaves. Because Abame and Aninta men help their wives with some aspects of domestic chores, especially to pound *foofoo,* Umofia men lament that customs are turned upside down there. Wives drink only after the men have finished drinking. Apart from the dignity of motherhood, the number of wives is the mark of wealth as seen in Nwakibe's harem. The only exception is typically the respect enjoyed by women as priestesses. Women are even feared as priestesses and this is exemplified by Chielo, the priestess of Agbala. At critical times, the philosophy of *Nneka* ("Mother is supreme") comes in handy. Okonkwo, who eventually seeks protection and exile in his motherland of Mbanta, wishes Ezinma were a boy because of her outstanding potential. Men who betray tradition by joining the missionaries are considered effeminate, as Okonkwo warns his other sons, "If any one of you prefers to be a woman, let him follow Nwoye now while I am alive so that I can curse him" (p. 122).

Arrow of God is even more chauvinistic and patriarchal than its predecessor. Ezeulu's story has little room for femininity. Women fill gaps while the key actors in the male show of strength dominate the spiritual, social and political lives. Women are, at best, tangential to male actions and intra-gender clashes. Women are, most often, voices, eyes, and ears: "voices of women returning from the stream broke into Ezeulu's thoughts." Matefi, Obiageli, Ojiugo, Ateneke, and other females are interjections in the storyline. Dr. Mary Savage is described as "severe and unfeminine." We see women and girls as story tellers but for the rest, this novel is a celebration of patriarchy and masculine strength and rivalry.

A re-reading of *No Longer at Ease,* however, reveals Achebe's increasing preoccupation with women. Clara's position in the story is not liminal or peripheral. Her story is intricately interwoven into Obi Okonkwo's experience and a relatively positive strength of character is revealed in her. One observes some measure of self-esteem, which is a preamble to self-definition in Clara. She refuses to be a pitiable appendage to Obi's dream. In spite of her love for Obi, she is sincere from the start about her status as an *osu,* an alienated caste without self-pity. Although we see much of her in terms of her relationship with Obi, we also see her as a professional who possesses self-pride and integrity. She refuses to be presumptuous even after accepting Obi's marriage proposal. She carefully reassesses subsequent developments. She is always ready to back out rather than take advantage of Obi's love and patronage. She reacts to condescension and rejection by friends, relations and the community equally.

Achebe's depiction of Clara elicits some positive status in contrast to Obi's disintegration. While the latter is bent double by the economic burden, Clara's economic status is buoyant. Yet, she reacts promptly to Obi's refusal to let her bail him out of the economic abyss. In contrast to her selfless move, Obi's self-pride and pride of manhood are posited. Her refusal to exploit her pregnancy or blackmail Obi into marriage brings out her selflessness even at the risk of her life.

Obi's mother is also a woman who makes her points and contributes to on-going issues on the strength of her convictions. On the question of marrying Clara, an *Osu,* she firmly declares to Obi:

> If you want to marry this girl, you must wait until I am
> no more. If God hears my prayers, you will not wait long
> .... But if you do the thing while I am alive, you will have
> my blood on your head, because I shall kill myself. (123)

Ultimately, it is Obi's mother's threat, more than his father's or anybody else's aspersion, that stings Obi's heart and leaves a permanent impression on him. It is not the validity of her conviction but the impact it has as the first threat that really penetrates Obi's stony heart. He had disdained Joseph's pleas and the interference of Umofia Progressive Union, his sponsors. But his mother's emotional but firm threat almost breaks his resistance.

So, in Clara and in Obi's mother, we have women who have moved from the initial social space and traditional conditioning created by Achebe. Significantly, the strong outgoing Igbo woman that was the mark of pre-colonial Igbo society is completely missing in Achebe's early works. His representation of Clara and Obi's mother is closer to a slice of reality. Most of the other females, however, play peripheral roles. The Irish girls, Joseph's and Christopher's girl friends, Marie Tomlinson, Obi's colleague, and Mr. Green's secretary are deployed to highlight some issues of general principles from Obi and to monitor his emotions and temperament. Others are tools, girls seeking scholarship at all cost, exploited and degraded. But their exploitation goes beyond gender the question as an aspect of social malaise which has its parallel in the bribes received from male candidates. The emphasis is still on women's domestic roles as there is no central focus on the public role or contribution to socio-political change in an effective manner. In fact, Clara's relationship with Obi undermines her personality.

A Man of the People shows a kind of progression in Achebe's focus on women as protagonists. In this novel, we see a shift from women's myopic role to more broad-based activation of events in the life of the chief characters. The narrator-hero's experience and predicament cannot be divorced from his treatment of and attitude to women. Right from the start, Chief Nanga's political escapade is designed to use women as aids to his political campaign. Mrs. John's comic interjections at the beginning are not negligible but she raises vital questions about the personality of the political stalwart, Nanga. However, she is more of a physical showpiece as "her massive royal beads were worth hundreds of pounds according to the whisper circulating in the room while she talked" (p. 15).

Mrs. Eleanor John's biography does raise some curious interest in its portrayal of her as a self-made woman. Her "merchant princess" status has a long history of deprivation and poverty. But for the trivialized role she plays in Nanga's entourage, she could have been a woman symbolizing strength of character and resourcefulness, an exemplar of many women achievers along the coast of West Africa in real life. We are given a glimpse into her background that shows Okonkwo's kind of motivation and determination:

> Poor beginning ... an orphan, I believe ... no school education plenty of good looks and an iron determination, both of which she put to good account; beginning as a street hawker, rising to a small trader, and then to a big one. At present, they said, she presided over the entire trade in imported second-hand clothing worth hundreds of thousands. (15)

The portrait of Mrs. John is a departure from most female characters in the early novels ... usually flat, one-dimensional presentation. She is, in her own right, an acme of feminine achievement, but this is largely undermined by the ludicrous role assigned to her. Her warning about Nanga's corrupting, even destructive influence on Odili, though offered humorously, turns out to be prophetic. A Yoruba proverb upholds the words of a drunken man as being the substance of the hidden truths which he would not have the courage to say in sober moments. As Eleanor John teases Nanga, some hidden home truths are revealed in the discussion: "I done talk say na only for election time woman de get equality for dis country" (p. 19). Her allegation that women are treated as important people with equal rights only during elections to win their votes is profound.

Generally, women in Achebe's works are revered and honored as mothers. This is not strange in Igbo culture and most African traditions. Indeed, the inability to concede any other positive role to women beyond the "mother is gold" and "mother is supreme" ideology is at the heart of the allegation of male chauvinism as a dominant trend in many men's literary creativity, and Achebe is no exception. Mrs. Nanga largely fits into the prototypic image of the complacent wife-mother with no ambition or resourcefulness, accepting relegation and subjugation with grace and tranquility. She does speak out to show her repressed loneliness and anguish, nonetheless. She confesses that being a minister's wife is a curse. She admits her outdatedness and ironically vindicates Nanga's need of a modern young 'parlour wife' to fill the gap and play the social role that she is too old to play. Yet, her solitude reveals a hidden sense of rejection and a regret of her alienation. Moreover, we see her as a cultural apostle who will sacrifice the glamour of Lagos to acculturate her children and prevent them from being otherwise uprooted. She is a kind of gender scapegoat.

Like *No Longer at Ease,* the modern setting of *A Man of the People* makes inevitable the depiction of some women professionals who are successful in their own right. But they usually constitute an aspect of the main story which focuses on men. Mrs. Agnes Akilo, the barrister, is depicted rather briefly, to keep Nanga's story going. Nonetheless, her beautiful and sophisticated outlook enhances her success as a lawyer jointly owning a private firm of solicitors with her husband. Remarkably, Odili feels cowed and bowed before Agnes Akilo because of her personality, "I must confess to a certain feeling of awkwardness before her sophisticated assured manner" (47). Her dignity and self-assurance are pitted against Nanga's crudity when she declines his offer and refuses to stay in his wife's bedroom. She opts for a lodging at the Hotel International instead. Her imposing personality makes Nanga admit that she is "SHE, who must be obeyed." But such a character is mentioned with the brevity of an inconsequential participator. Achebe's apologia seems to be aimed at proving his condescension to women, from time to time. Odili, his narrator-authorial voice, therefore confesses:

> .... Chief Nanga and I having already swooped many tales of conquest, I felt somehow compelled to speak in derogatory terms about women in general. (59)

Consequently, several female characters are treated with similar condescension by both Odili and Nanga. Jean, the Irish girls, Elsie, and (to an extent) Edna are like properties to be exploited, even exchanged as the need arises. For the most part, Odili manipulates female characters like pawns on his psychological and political chessboard. They are tools of revenge to heal his wounded ego and fan the embers of his political ambition. Odili's attempt at working on Mrs. Nanga fails ultimately but his interaction with her and with Edna is significant. Nonetheless, Odili is instrumental to awakening

Edna's consciousness. The latter's budding political awareness is like a peephole into the female's dynamic role that
reaches maturation in *Anthills of the Savannah.*
Achebe's women in the first four novels are active inside
the cells of the anthill, with specified roles and rigid demarca-
tion of labor. *Girls At War* consists of short stories that reiterate these fixed roles and symbology. The configuration of
women's role continues to be limited to the private and domestic areas. At other times, Achebe repeats the earlier myths and
taboos through female characters while using them to enhance
his personal objections to certain aspects of traditions and
modernist encroachment. We see the wife-mother role and the
exploitation of girls which is heightened at war times.
In some of the stories such as *The Madman,* women as
wives are depicted to fill in the storyline and re-emphasize
men's quest for honor, tainted by personal or collective traditional excesses. Nwibe the protagonist only needs the wives
to initiate the irony of madness. In *Marriage is a Private Affair*
a young woman, Nene, succeeds where her husband fails to
break the fetters of ethnic prejudice in marriage. Her success
in breaking the stony heart of Nnaemeka's father is significant.
The story *Akueke* also vindicates the eponymous heroine
above moribund traditions and bigotry against a girl with an
independent mind.
It is the titular story, *Girls At War,* that redeems, to an
extent, the undermining of female roles. Here, the heroine,
Gladys, moves from moral purity as she gets corrupted by the
men at war. The final episode, however, retrieves her lost glory
as she becomes a sacrificial symbol. While Reginald Nwakwo
turns deaf ears to the cry of a maimed soldier in a bombing
raid, Gladys risks her life as she tries to save the soldier. She
gets caught by explosions in this humanitarian action and dies,
burnt and charred beyond retrieval alongside the one-legged
soldier. Her bravery and heroic death are poised against
Nwankwo's cowardice and self-seeking quest for personal survival. Here, Achebe's heroine pays the price of dedication to
humanity. This is a departure from the inertia and static role
of women with limited areas of influence and impact on the
society. Gladys' role is not peripheral or liminal, but a pointer
and a preamble to the more central roles played by women in
Anthills of the Savannah.

ACHEBE'S RE-VISION OF WOMEN

Whereas a re-reading of Achebe's earlier works reveals some efforts to focus on the female, he does not give women a definitive meaningful role until *Anthills*. His attitude remains ambiguous, sometimes ambivalent and ironic before this novel. As Ben Okri rightly judges, this novel is Achebe's "most complex and his wisest book to date."1 Elleke Boehmer's assessment of the versatile nature of this novel is remarkable:

> ... Achebe's view of that elite and its politics in the wider African context has become more uncompromising and ... at least theoretically ... more attuned to *gender* and populist ideas.2

In spite of the more obvious focus on gender issues, one needs to re-read critically Achebe's attitude to women to ascertain whether or not he has re-written the African woman in *Anthills*. Achebe, like Odili, no longer finds it convenient to arrogate derogatory roles to women. He is no longer at ease in his creation of women with limited roles. The walls of the harem confining women have fallen apart and Achebe can no longer hold on to the peripheral role that is contrary to the reality of the African woman in a changing modern society. Women are therefore seen participating dynamically in and activating social change. Beatrice is the fulcrum of social change right in the nucleus of socio-political schema. For once, we see women who emerge from the hard cells of the anthill. At certain times, they stand out, conspicuous, invincible and resilient against the burnt-out landscape of the savannah. At other times, Beatrice stands right on top of the anthill of change, like the mythic Idemili, playing a central role in shaping and mediating the realms of power.

Beatrice Okoh is depicted as a shaper and sharpener of consciousness in her relationship to Ikem Osodi and Christopher Oriko. She is a source of motivation, inspiration, and encouragement to Ikem, the artist and social conscience, and to Chris, the political conscience. Although unacknowledged, she is also a motivator of the head of the state of Kangan to some extent. Achebe creates in Beatrice a conservative but extremely intelligent girl. Chris describes her accurately as "beautiful without being glamorous. Peaceful but very strong. Very, very strong." Her strength of character and genius give her an indispensable central role. Even the head of state's comment reveals the inevitable truth:

Beatrice Okoh... the only person in the service, male or female, with a first class honours in English. And not from a local university but from Queen Mary College, University of London. Our Beatrice beat the English to their game. We're proud of her. (75)

Despite the head of state's ostentatious exhibition of a talented girl, he will not tolerate her independence of character and boldness. Nonetheless, her rebuff of Lou Cranford, the American journalist, points to her principled self. Her humility and self-effacement strengthens her formidable role, "Throughout my life, I have never sought attention: not even as a child" (84). Rather, as a child, she was "wrapped up in her own little world ...." But she comes out into the public focus without any pretentious ambition or individualism. As her awareness grows, she becomes alert to the changing situation around her and becomes sensitive to the need to change the social order along with Ikem and Chris. She lives true to her name, *Nwayibuife* ... "a girl is also something." Significantly, she has always done things considered 'unfeminine in the traditional context'.

Beatrice is presented as a rebel rejecting all traditions that delimit women's role:

> I was determined from the very beginning to put my career first and, if need be, last. That every woman wants a man to complete her is a piece of male chauvinist bullshit I had completely rejected before I knew there was anything like Women's Lib. (88)

In Beatrice, Achebe has successfully re-inscribed the African woman. In her, he creates a woman who defies certain gender conventions that have been taken for granted previously. Through her monologues, Achebe tells us that women's liberation is not western or strange to Africa:

> You often hear people say: But that's something you picked up in England. Absolute rubbish! There was enough male chauvinism in my fathers' house to last me seven reincarnations! (88)

More significantly, Beatrice is the ignition key to Ikem's thoughts and she shows an ultimate concern for womanhood. Ikem, Achebe's mouth-piece, becomes aware of his chauvinism through Beatrice's probing and prodding and we are told he is at first quite ignorant of a "chink in his armoury of brilliant and original ideas." Beatrice's allegation that Ikem has no clear definitive role for women in his political thoughts sparked off his change of attitude. This might well pass for a chink in Achebe's ideological reservoir until *Anthills*. Even in *No Longer at Ease* and *A Man of the People,* where women's role is more visible than in the first two works, one cannot consider their role clearly delineated. They are to a large extent adjuncts to men's stories. *Anthills* is unquestionably Achebe's positive response to a gap in his political thought in many ways. The woman accepting the challenges of a protean modern society is underscored here, not only in Beatrice the elite but in Elewa the salesgirl. This reinforces the womanist position that gender and class struggles are inseparable.

The women now emerge unto the modern scene rather than the anomalous portrait of the modern woman enveloped in traditional restrictions and conventions. Beatrice's comment on women's role in Ikem's novel might as well be a replica of critics' assessment of Achebe's earlier works:

> .. giving women today the same role which traditional society gave them of intervening only when everything else has failed is not enough, you know, like the women in the Sembene film who pick up the spears abandoned by their defeated menfolk. It is not enough that women should be the court of last resort....(p.91)

That Achebe's heroine launches this profound attack on the role assigned to women by several writers is some kind of self-critique.

It is curious that Ikem respects three kinds of women: peasants, market women, and intellectual women. He shifts ground from a cavalier and reactionary poise on the role of the modern woman. He confesses to an intellectual and philosophical metamorphosis as he elucidates his new found consciousness. Ikem's thought takes off from the demonization of women and stretches to the exaltation of the woman's supremacy, 'Nneka.' In the latter role, she is available to intervene in crisis situations, receive the exile son or retrieve the prodigal one. Ikem eventually admits that he has no clue about the modern woman's role since women should define their role for themselves. Believing women to be "the biggest single group of oppressed people in the world," and the oldest, Ikem posits a theory that brings all oppressed people together, cutting across class, race, and gender. He upholds the coalition of all victims of political, religious, ethnic, racial, and caste oppression all over the world. Highlighting the cumbersome nature of such heterogeneity, he decries the absence of a "universal conglomerate of the oppressed." He then recommends reforming the individual psyche to reform the society including re-ordering gender problems.

In *Anthills,* one identifies Achebe's use of three character blocks to elucidate his anti-orthodoxy and reformist theory. Achebe's works in general revolve round heroes, antiheroes and obligate heroes. Many of his *heroes* and *antiheroes* are also *obligate heroes* as regards their interaction with women. Obi Okonkwo's story can hardly stand alone. Although Clara's role is not significantly defined, Obi's tragic experience is encapsulated in his relation to women among other factors. His story is incomplete without his reactions to and interaction with women. Obi's self-pride and refusal of Clara's attempt to get him out of his financial dilemma deepens the crisis until he ultimately sinks. Odili Samalu and Chief Nanga also have their experience hinged largely on women's role. We have seen how Mrs. Eleanor John's role is subsumed in her relationship with Nanga. This undermines her attributes and economic resourcefulness. Her political role is trivialized, but one cannot but see that Nanga exploits the relationship to his political advantage. She could have been given a clearer role in her own right. Even Mrs. Nanga's inactivity elicits a subtle protest against her oppression and marginalization.

Odili's political awareness, which is inseparable from a quest for vengeance, is almost cloyed by an excessive, even inchoate drive for power. That he is fixated on snatching Edna from Nanga can hardly be described as an act of true love and he too is an obligate hero. His ultimate achievement rests partially on motivating Edna's political awareness but he exploits this to his advantage by marrying her.

In his earlier works Achebe's women are tangential to the actual social-political process to a large extent. But the male characters often depend on the females to move on. Like the parasite, some of them use the women as their hosts to survive. The women would be better off as their own mouthpieces and should speak for themselves, as Achebe asserts through Ikem. But Achebe did not give them such an opportunity in the early works. He fails to create such outspoken females sufficiently mobilized to speak for their gender in the earlier works before his creation of Beatrice. One can see clearly the turn-

ing point in his attitude to gender in *Anthills*. His portrait of
Beatrice could even be seen as an act of restitution. Beatrice
and Elewa play a formidable role in mobilizing opposition to
the corruption and chicanery of Kangan government, a paradigm of many post-colonial African states. Beatrice liaises with
Ikem and Chris to confront, at first ideologically and later
overtly, the dome of corruption and oppression. Beatrice is the
nexus of much of the action. She exhumes an incandescent
quality that is unique in the image of women in African literature. She is also the axis of the men's political thoughts, perception and awareness.

Both Ikem and Chris owe the inspiration, formulation, illu-
mination, and testing of their ideology to Beatrice. She is intelligent and not gullible; she critiques the budding thoughts of
Ikem the artist and social critic and Chris the political ideologue. Both mould their thoughts through the crucible of her
critical mind. Like her mythic equivalent, Idemili, accepting
Beatrice's counsel provides acceptability for their thoughts
and authenticates their search for involvement in a new power
base. Ironically, the refusal of the head of Kangan state to
accede to her counsel is instrumental to his fall. Significantly,
the ultimate sacrificial death of both Chris and Ikem brings
out the best of Beatrice's thoughts and actions.

As if accepting Ikem's challenging view that women are to
blame for non-involvement and non-commitment, the two
men's deaths spark off a dynamo in her. Even before their
death, her participation during Chris's hiding, and her reaction
to the elimination of both men unveils her latent zeal and
resilience. Her special bonding with Ikem's girl, Elewa, despite
the class disparity underscores the need to stretch gender
struggle to other oppressed groups across class frontiers. The
special role she plays in nursing Elewa's pregnancy is
enhanced by the new coalition with the student leader,
Emmanuel Obete, the taxi-drivers' union leader, Buraimoh,
captain Abdul and the girl Adamma (for whom Chris dies) and
to an extent the housekeeper Agatha, confirming the new unit
being forged among various marginalized groups. Beatrice's
positive action is enriched by a touch of femininity and humanity reflected in the way she nurses Elewa through pregnancy
and childbirth. She lives up to her name, 'Nwayibuife.'

The collaboration with the downtrodden from Abazon and
the Taxi Drivers' Union reveals the formation of a group that
cuts across different kinds of dividing lines. Beatrice's actions

are in line with the position of many African womanists; that building a wall around oneself to shut off the male gender is not the thrust of African womanist aesthetics. Here lies the strength of Achebe's new theory of social transformation. Moreover, for a change, Achebe's women are not on the periphery, nor on the fence but at the vanguard of social transformation. Ikem's relationship with Elewa reinforces Achebe's position. A salesgirl, a semi-illiterate and the daughter of a low-class market woman becomes the mother of the baby girl born posthumously to him. Beatrice's humility and self-effacement is a step to self-definition before a meaningful women's bonding and collective role can effectively take place. Beatrice is a clear re-writing of the African woman.

That Elewa's baby, born to Ikem, is a girl is Achebe's further reiteration of future hope which lies as much in the regeneration of the female as in any other consideration. The baby's radical new start is remarkable. Beatrice's reform of the traditional naming ceremony, shifting the name from the male to the female, is as significant as the given name—a boy's name, *Amaechina*—because of the spectacular meaning: "may the path never close/overgrow." Like the anthills standing out noticeably on the scorched savannah landscape, Beatrice is a woman re-presented, a woman who opts to stand out among other downtrodden women, playing ostentatiously the "men's role." She is as determined to transform obsolete traditions as she is eager to change the modern social-political decadent society. She gives the baby a boy's name since there is no equivalent female name to translate her thoughts or create the positive identity and personality expressive of the baby's status—a symbol of continuity and a regenerative force.

This optimistic note is a paradigm of the artist's role as a transformer of individual conscience and the society's collective consciousness. Achebe's women emerge from the compartments of the anthill; they stand on top of the socio-political anthill, creating new roles that will not delimit women's contribution and participation in social change. The anthills' cells symbolize rigid division of labor. Beatrice not only emerges from such compartments, she is as tough and resistant as the savannah anthills that refuse to be destroyed with the general landscape. She makes herself visible in the sparse, burnt-out political setting.

Elleke Boehmer considers Ikem and Chris as the novel's two main heroes. I believe Beatrice to be one of the three

heroes, with similar heroic qualities and sometimes exceptional traits that enhance and complement the thoughts of her
friends. Her physical attributes are augmented by her spiritual-
mythic depiction. Her transposition into Idemili is symbolic
and significant. Ikem calls her a recluse. This shields her from
maximum involvement in the social gatherings and moral
degeneracy as well as the political dissipation of energy in
Kangan. Her relative aloneness provides the needed sober
moments for insight and revelation of deep-rooted truths.

In Beatrice's legendary capacity as a priestess-prophetess
according to Achebe, she confesses experiencing apocalyptic
moments. Her exposition during such a moment of prefigure-
ment is profound as she warns Chris:

> As a matter of fact I do sometimes feel like Chielo in the
> novel, the priestess and prophetess of the Hills and the
> Caves .... Yes, it's on now. And I see trouble building up
> for us. It will get to Ikem first. No joking, Chris .... But
> after him it will be you. We are all in it, Ikem, you, me and
> even him. (p 114)

Ironically, one still perceives an underlying reiteration of certain stereotypic images of women in Beatrice's portrait. In
addition to the priestess image, which sometimes diverts
attention from reality by emphasizing the ephemeral,
Beatrice's major role rests on the portrait of the "woman as
inspirer and spiritual guide." Her initial bold attempt to stretch
her practical participation beyond the confines of her platonic
and romantic male friends respectively, results in disgrace by
the head of state and her march of shame out of the party.

There is an ultimate tone of divine justice as the head of
state gets destroyed as if paying a price for ignoring Idemili's
advice and daring to disgrace her. Beatrice attempts to play
the mythic role of bearing "witness to the moral nature of
authority by wrapping around Power's rude waist a loin cloth
of peace and modesty" (p. 102). His excellency invites her to
his party and insults her, reversing the tradition of men seeking power who are supposed to consult Idemili and seek her
approval. To further desecrate the moral order, he disobeys
her. Since he fails to get her approval, the mantle of authority
is ultimately removed from him. The citadel of empowerment
disintegrates due to the excesses of individualism and insensi-
tivity to communal ethos. Here then, we see that the woman
as a source of empowerment is entrenched. But ironically it

remains largely at the mythic and ideological levels. Beatrice's new coalition does not embrace a large group of women but a few individuals—Elewa, her mother, Adamma, and (to a limited extent) Agatha. The novel ends without any overt public participation in the new order by the coalition. Beyond re-ordering traditional naming rituals, one would have expected some collective conscientisation of women at a larger level for Achebe to have gone the whole way.

Nonetheless, Achebe has gone further than many writers, even some female African writers, in repossessing lost ground on behalf of the African woman. The hope lies in the open path into the future through a baby girl. As David Richards suggests, the repossession of time is an integral part of the artist's goal.[3] According to Derek Walcott, time is the dictator's enemy. One might as well add that time is an asset in the hands of women seeking proper involvement and recognition and empowerment. At the end of *Anthills,* Beatrice and her group are in possession of time, but they need to possess space.

Notes

1.   Ben Okri in Kriesten Holst Petersen and Anna Rutherford, *Chinua Achebe, A Celebration* (London: Heinemann, 1990), p. 102.
2.   Elleke Boehmer, "Of Godesses and Stories: Gender and a New Politics in *Anthills of the Savannah,*" Petersen and Rutherford, *op. cit.,* pp. 130-138.
3.   David Richard, "Repossessing Time: Chinua Achebe's *Anthills of the Savannah,*" in Peterson and Rutherford, *op. cit.,* pp. 130-138.

PART THREE

AFRICAN WOMEN WRITERS AND THE SEARCH FOR GENDER IDEOLOGY

Chapter Six

Women's Voices, Poetic Voices: Testimonies of Exile and Transformation

The interdependence of politics, culture, and gender has become a major focus in African women's creative and cultural production. Many African writers from the continent have emphasized this strong link in their womanist theory as well as in literary works. Yet, some critics treat African women writers as apolitical, with no ideological inclination. One needs to look back at the traditional African women who demonstrated overt levels of political consciousness to show that African women's literature can not be truly representative without being informed by social and political realities. Since indigenous political awareness was an aspect of women's oral literature in Africa, many writers have opted for occasional and relevant creative works. They have proved that consciousness-raising is not imported from outside of Africa. Traditional prose, drama, and poetry have always been utilitarian in this direction. Women's oral genres embrace satirical, overt political and cultural activism that depict women's predicament and collective ethos as well as tools for castigating built-in social strictures.

Considering the large body of novels by African women, one observes that in drama and poetry, African women writers are not prolific. Poetry is the most neglected genre, as dramatists such as Ama Ata Aidoo, Zulu Sofola, Micere Mugo, and Tess Onwueme have elevated drama next to the novel. Some of these writers have written poetry as a secondary genre while their focus is the novel or drama. However, this relative paucity does not undermine strong political viewpoints even through preoccupations that look like cultural activation *per se.* Themes designed to reinscribe African womanhood and self-esteem are as recurrent in drama and poetry as in African women writers' novel genres. Reconstructing her gender's self-perception and recreating a forum of enablement is reiterated in art as the woman emerges over the years as her own mouthpiece.

In looking at the outstanding functions of African women's traditional genres, most of the self-restoration comes from oral poetry and drama. Several women's genres confirm this—Ghanaian Nzema and Ayaboma maiden songs and Akan dirges, Yoruba women's satirical songs, Gelede songs, Igbo birth songs, Ballijja and Omwaami songs of East Africa. A close study of these artistic categories elicits a strong political voice that questions pictures of passivity. Whereas primary orality is being constantly eroded by literacy, many paradigms of female struggle for survival and empowerment are still embodied in oral poetry and drama. Modern women's drama and poetry are not intertexts to African male or western female literature. The woman poet and dramatist responds to the needs of her gender.

WOMEN'S POETRY OF SELF-RESTORATION

Molara Ogundipe-Leslie is a dynamic ideologue who has combined literary criticism with poetic creativity. Her collection of poetry, *Sew The Old Days,* is a versatile collection that encapsulates this genius' ideological zeal with a unique sense of cultural revitalization and consciousness-raising. This critic-poet is categorical and definitive about her triple preoccupation as an African, a woman, and a Marxist. She upholds the cognitive as well as the functional role of art. In her own words, one cannot excise art from history, past and present:

> ... I have been concerned with our pre-colonial past and
> what made it possible for us to be colonised; our colo-
> nial experience and its ravages on our land and our psy-
> che... the quality of life of our people as individuals and
> the condition of life of the woman in Africa. (James,
> 1990:67)

This writer has put her theory into practice not only by direct
participation in peace movements but also her involvement
with several groups that aim at enhancing the status of the
African woman. Consequently, her poetic imagination vividly
reflects her ideological convictions. She recaptures the past in
the poem *To a Jane Austen Class at Ibadan University.* Borrowing
her epigraph from Kofi Awoonor's poem, she advocates:

> .. Sew the old days
> Sew the old days that we may wear them
> ...to dance through coming storms
> our steps detoning. (3)

She recaptures the past, not in an elusive romantic tone, but cel-
ebrating the vibrant aspect of the past as an encouragement for
the present. She touches on colonial exploitation of resources
from Africa as well as other Third World regions. She upholds
the past as an incentive to the present, not as a lament for a
moribund past. Her preoccupation with the destruction of the
psyche in post-colonial Africa is as significant as her record of
the physical devastation. She alludes to the agony and alienation caused by slavery and colonization, but the ultimate tone
is of hope, not despair.

Several poems in the collection concentrate on the pas-
sage of time and an attempt to recapture the past. These
include *Africa of the Seventies,* which reiterates the need to
"pluck the days \ from transfixed clocks \ now the corridors
recede \ into conference rooms \ where bandits lurk." One
can see in this poem the harsh tones that often emphasize her
strong political commitment. Yet, her concern with the past is
not a call for sheer romanticisation of history. She rejects a
blind adoption of myths and legends which could be diver-
sionary to a bold confrontation of current problems. *On
Reading an Archaeological Article* is an allusion to the legend
of the reign of the Egyptian queen, Nefertiti. She captures the
ambivalent attitude to women rulers:

How long shall we speak to them
Of the goldness of mother, of difference
without bane

How long shall we say another world lives
Not spined on the axis of maleness
But rounded and whole, charting through
Its many runnels its justice distributive?
O Nefertiti . . . . (19)

This poet's refusal to hold on to archaeological relics of women's rule is predicated on the conviction that even in matrilinies, the ruling females did not necessarily enhance the condition of the ordinary women.[1] She also decries the honorifics of Motherhood that are not always matched with the trust of responsibility and public influence, and this comes out clearly in this poem. Ogundipe-Leslie is one of the most vocal on the strictures and restrictions as well as the problems confronting the African woman in general and the female writer in particular. On the society's expectations regarding her role, she presents the uniquely multivalent levels of predicament.

> Because of the definitely patriarchal arrangements of the society, publicly and privately, most women bear a double workload, if not a triple one .... African Society may welcome women writers. But it would certainly be shocked if they handled certain subjects on which western writers have now gained freedom to be vocal.[2]

According to Ogundipe-Leslie, because of the status of motherhood, she is probably expected to prove her loyalty to this role by writing children's or motherhood literature:

> She is falsely grandified with this task while all around she is discriminated against, excluded from real power, exploited at all levels and derided most of the time in the society. She is also usually seen as the cause of whatever happens negatively in the country. The national scapegoat. The cause of the nation's decline.[3]

This poet deliberates on the artistic creative self-consciousness; the purpose, responsiveness, vision, and mission of the artist in *Lunchtime and Questions to the Creative Self*. Here, and elsewhere, she laments the search for an audience. *Letter to a Loved Comrade* is a strong protest against the marginalization of the African female writer and the patriarchal traits in art:

Said a poet once: 'poetry is the sense of a man's action in the world.' And I say, little action, big action.

... Always in you is the lurking fear of woman bringing things down. Stymying them. Bringing things down in you. Not only with her demonic monthly river of life, as they used to fear, but with her demonic hidden strengths couched in silences and foreknowledge, her uncanny perceptions . . . her correctness. (25)

Ogundipe-Leslie rejects masculine shows of strength while elevating the woman's sensitivity to life as opposed to destruction of life for ideological reasons. This poem is one of the most ideologically charged of the collection. It clearly reveals the strong political and ideological voice of the radical African woman as a writer and conscience of her gender, race, class and indeed, of all oppressed. This poet has repeatedly called for the African woman's commitment as an African, a woman, and a Third World citizen. Her concern cuts across gender and class, as seen in her castigation of the middle-class in *Song of the African Middle Class.* Her focus is on the alienation of the middle-class from the suffering wretcheds of the earth ... citizens of the "Fourth World." She wonders why they are not sufficiently sensitive to their people's needs.

Many of the poems in *Sew the Old Days* are harsh castigations of social decadence, gender asymmetry, and bigotry. Others are optimistic that one can still learn positive lessons from the past without superfluous romanticization or mythologizing. This poet's conclusion is that hope and beauty will yet be born. In *A Harsh Beauty Must be Born Today,* designed as a rejoinder to Ayi Kwei Armah's novel, *The Beautyful Ones Are Not Yet Born,* she declares, "sister, there can be beauty today." This beauty is to be found in unusual places, "in the waste places\in the debris for the flowers." It rests in positive affirmation of life by the poor, "the loved ones." However, there can be no future without a past, as revealed in her poems to African Americans. Ogundipe-Leslie is more volatile in her political commitment than many male and most female writers. Her writing conveys the convergence between the personal, the collective and the ideological, which according to her are indivisible. In this, she is a paradigm of the African woman writer as a mouthpiece for her gender, culture, and race.

AIDOO'S VOICE OF EXILE

Ama Ata Aidoo, the pioneer of women's artistic voice in the African region, is better known as a dramatist and a prose fiction writer. Her concerns cut across genres, however, as she also writes poetry from time to time. Her poems dedicated to Achebe speak to our contention that the African woman is also a cultural and political voice through poetic creativity. Like Molara Ogundipe-Leslie, Aidoo uses poetry to celebrate some aspects of the past and as a critique of the present. We see the personal and the collective expressions of love, anguish, hope, despair, and the deep-rooted feelings of a throbbing heart. We hear some of Aidoo's most polemic cry and outcry. In *Questions ... For Us: Today's African Leadership,* Aidoo's posers are profound and inward-looking.

> They say
> all beings
> fight to live:
> the mole
> the lion and
> the crow.
> they say
> all creatures
> must fight to be .... conquer
> kill
> consume
> who will have us be human in a world
> of cruel beasts
> and even more cruel men?[4]

She identifies self-interest as an underlying factor that raises further queries about the motive for much of the bloody struggles for power in Africa. "Put quite simply, \ in whose name do we ever act?\ Whose tomorrow do we sell?" The issue of power and the misuse of it underlie some of Aidoo's other works. But in these poems, we see her most succinct expression of disappointment at the tussle for power by self-seeking individuals. The second poem, *Modern African Stories,* is a poignant exposure of political tyranny and intrigues based on her personal experience. It is very explicit and unambiguous, a bold critique of political intrigue:

> Yes,
> strange as it may sound,
> it is true.

> I got deported this morning from
> my home, my village, my country and the land which
> my forefathers and foremothers bled for, and tilled
> from the beginning of time.[5]

From the personal the poetic panorama shifts to the collective plight ... a tale of intimidation, treachery, and deprivation that is characteristic of post-colonial and post-independence African literature:

> ... a land where former freedom fighters are vagrants, or buy respectability only by guarding the property for those they mortgaged their youths to fight against... (ibid.)

The third poem, *New in Africa,* is a recast of the ubiquitous colonial past, a period

> when time closed in on itself and Europe closed in on us, and the only new things we served ourselves and our enemies dished to us were very old portions. (ibid.)

Aidoo's political voice merges with her cultural nationalism. She laments the physical, mental, psychological, and emotional violation and abuse of the continent as well as current tussle that gives the sense of an unending predicament:

> As for Africa herself, conquered, raped, reconquered, re-raped,
>
> She wriggles still; just like Snake before Ananse finished him. (75)

She concludes in an optimistic tone as the hope for social regeneration is not lost. The penchant mood of betrayal is commensurate with this writer's new level of awareness. Cultural nationalism and political commitment are still manifest but the political voice now predominates:

> So we also struggle on
> ... clear eyed or blind ...
> sometimes with song,
> often with dance,
> and always, with prayers on our lips. (Ibid)

The need for self-recovery as Africans, and also as women, is at the heart of the political cry in these poems. They are representative of the general call for African women's self-esteem as a step to full empowerment. The plight of the woman writer in this region, as a threat to the rulers, is an aspect of the plight of many writers. Aidoo captures the pitiable predicament of a writer in exile with the integrity of a person prepared for self-sacrifice in spite of the inevitable sense of loss and alienation from loved ones and a loved home and country. The issues are objective reflections of reality and her personal experiences. The relevance of the writer's experience with the communal reality makes these poems at once occasional and transcendental as well as timeless. These poems also reveal a movement from the tragic vision and lack of self-actualization of Anowa. Her voice becomes more openly political and her ideological vision is more radical.

BUSIA'S YEARNINGS FROM EXILE

Abena Busia's recent collection of poems, *Testimonies of Exile,* is the sum total of the centrality of the testimony genre in African women's self-expression. Abena Busia uses the lyric quality and the closer link between the poet and the literary work to reveal certain innermost ideas that are representative of the yearnings of many African women writers and critics. Written during her years of exile from Ghana and as a victim of political upheavals in that country, her collection derives largely from real-life experience. Many other African women writers are physical exiles, as we see in the realities of Micere Mugo who now lives in Zimbabwe in exile from Kenya for her vocality and activism. Ama Ata Aidoo, like Abena Busia, has been an exile from Ghana. She too now lives in Zimbabwe. Others in forced or voluntary physical or psychological exile include the Egyptian writer Nawal El Saadawi and Werewere Liking, the Cameroonian writer. The latter now lives in Ivory Coast in an artists' village. Many more are voluntary exiles in Europe or North America. Others still are psychological exiles, alienated and uprooted from African consciousness and culture. This issue of exile is therefore profoundly fundamental to African women.

The major feature of Busia's *Testimonies of Exile* is the currency and topicality of her preoccupations. It is no doubt a collection of personal testimonies during her years of exile.[6] However, the personal merges into the public, the individual into the collective as she touches on issues that are relevant to proximate African reality. The opening poem, *Caliban,* sets the landscape as she problematizes the language of exile in

African literature, "I speak this dispossesion/in the language of the master" (3). This heightens the sense of alienation of the exile, the sense of inevitable rooting. The scene then shifts and right from the beginning the gender of the exile is inscribed into the poem, "a woman ravished and naked/ chanting the words of a little girl lost/treading the edge of the waves"(5). The image of the virgin suggests innocence but the virgin's song is "a song of home" and this sets the tone of nostalgia. Other poems giving expression to the author's feminist identity include *Liberation* and *Mawu/Mawo*.

These poems and many others in the collection are affirmations of African women's poetic voices as cultural as well as political-ideological voices. Using personal testimonies intensifies the validity of the issues raised, "I am a Black man's child, still stranded on the shores of saxon seas." This alludes to a contemporary reality and dilemma of African intellectuals. Many are exiles from Africa trying to recapture African culture and experience from across the seas. This is a lyric that gives expression to the shift in borders and progressive movement of the center of African intellectual activities that is a very current issue of debate. Busia's testimonies therefore transcend the personal scope. She touches on the problem of migration and hybridisation and the impact on African scholars' consciousness. Kwame Anthony Appiah, like many others, is interrogating this issue of singing African songs from "the belly of the beast." The poem *Migrations* vividly underscores this reality:

> We have lived that moment of the scattering
> of the people—
> Immigrant, Migrant, Emigrant, Exile,
> Where do the birds gather?
> That in other nations, other lives, other places has become:
> The gathering of last warriors on lost frontiers,
> The gathering of lost refugees on lasting border-camps
> The gathering of the indentured on the side-walks
> of strange cities,
> The gathering of emigrés on the margins of foreign cultures. (8)

Memory plays an important role as a tool in these recollections and in the attempt to relive the past: "We relive the past in rituals of revival,/Unravelling memories in slow time; gathering the present" (p.9). Memory, personal and collective, is an important literary tool that enables writers to probe the past to comprehend the present and create conditions for future social change. Gayle Greene identifies the important place of memory in literature:

> All writers are concerned with memory, since all writing is a remembrance of things past; mine it as a quarry. Memory is especially important to anyone who cares about change ....[7]

Busia testifies to the multicultural and transcultural reality of her experience in exile and the fact that her experience coincides with others': "All my friends are exiles/born in one place, we live in another/we have everywhere to go,/ but home" (p.11). To her, self-writing becomes collective self-inscription. The sense of self-identity is as strong as the gender signature and the African consciousness. All these levels of awareness are condensed into one. Consequently the scene is often kaleidoscopic, as she shifts to larger issues like apartheid; Sharpeville and Soweto specifically resonate through the compact lines of the poem, *Freedom Rides Quiz.*

The sense of the divided self and the disharmony that comes from the attempt to negotiate the poet's multiple identity and plural consciousness comes out vividly in *At Last Rites,* which is a kind of dirge that is a prognosis into the future. Much of the poetry brings out the Akan woman's trait in Abena Busia. She elicits a strong poetic drive and often the tone is as powerful as in Akan dirges. Her hybrid Ghanaian background is significant. Her father is from the Akan Asante ethnic group, while her mother is a Ga. This has enriched Busia's consciousness to neutralize the alienation caused by her western education and orientation. This comes out aptly in the Mawu poems.

Testimony as a mode of literary representation is becoming increasingly popular among African women writers. This comes out in other genres besides poetry, as we see in Miriama Ba's *So Long a Letter,* Ellen Kuzwayo's autobiography, *Call Me Woman,* Bessie Head's works, Nawal El Saadawi's fiction, and some of the writings of Buchi Emecheta. The testimonies are both personal and collective. They give expression to African women's innermost emotions and self-consciousness. This enhances the process of self-assertion and gender transformation advocated by writers like Ogundipe-Leslie. Self-transformation becomes social transformation in an inextricable way. Self-conscious writing is an effective way of constructing identity and negotiating African women's space. Testimonies, however, transcend self-writing as they become tools of collective self-inscription for African women.

NOTES

1. Kolawole, M.E.M., "Women Work and War: Paradigms of Empowerment in African Literature," in Ann Adams, ed. *Gender, Politics and Cultural Production* (forthcoming).
2. Adeola James, *In Their Own Voices* (London: Heinemann, 1990), p. 67.
3. *Ibid.*
4. Ama Ata Aidoo, "Three Poems for Achebe," in *Chinua Achebe, A Celebration,* ed. Kirsten Holst Peterson and Anna Rutherford (London: Heinemann Dangaroo Press, 1990), pp. 71–75.
5. *Ibid.*
6. Abena Busia is no longer an exile as a result of a more liberal political atmosphere. She is on sabbatical at the University of Ghana in Legon/Accra at the time of the completion of this manuscipt.
7. Gayle Greene, "Feminism, Fiction and the Uses of Memory," *Signs,* Vol. 16, No. 2 (Winter 1991), p. 291.

CHAPTER SEVEN

DRAMA OF SELF-DEFINITION ACROSS TWO GENERATIONS– ZULU SOFOLA AND TESS ONWUEME

From ambivalent creation of heroines, many African dramas and novels now portray women's self-definition as a progressive development. This is as much an evidence of the growth in consciousness of the writer as of the epistemological changes in the reality of African women's experience. The older generation of women writers of the continent now present women not only as symbols of social change: their heroines are more radical. A re-writing of the African woman is visible in their recent works. Ama Ata Aidoo's recent heroine, Esi, is more determined to confront the forces limiting women in a changing society. Zulu Sofola has become more overtly vocal in creating women in the process of social change in her most recent plays. The younger writers like Tessie Onwueme and Tsitsi Dangarembga have the advantage of looking at the silences and absences of early literature about women and by women and they are poised for a more radical feminine commitment right from the start. The younger generation of writers also have the benefit of the restless spirit of the modern age and started off by creating heroes who are impatient with tradition and eager to change the nervous conditions and the social set-up.

SOFOLA'S SHIFT FROM TRADITIONAL TO MODERN HEROINES

Zulu Sofola and Tessie Onwueme represent the two generations and both are easily the most prolific African playwrights. They both come from the same part of Nigeria, the western Igbo, but their vision transcends a local commitment. Both women are cultural agents, as we see in their plays a conscious attept to recreate positive African cultural value even as they create characters that reject repressive traditions. They both represent the African woman writer as a cultural mouthpiece as well and the progressive radical commitment is visible in Sofola's canons, while Onmueme's womanist aesthetic emerges overtly from her first play, *A Hen Too Soon.*

Nwazulu Sofola is the first Nigerian playwright/dramatist and she is acclaimed both nationally and internationally. She is basically a musicologist, and this gives her plays a unique tone. Her global recognition is commensurate with her achievement. With no less than 12 plays to her credit over a period of some 20 years, she is a giant who should be cited on any honor roll of African playwrights. Zulu Sofola is a playwright whose positive self-consciousness towers above many others. Her works give vivid expression to her recognition of the multiple levels of commitment, as a Black, an African, a Third World writer, and a woman. These multivalent tiers of awareness are revealed in a balanced depiction as she concentrates on specific thematic preoccupations in a versatile manner.

Along with writers such as Bessie Head, Flora Nwapa, Miriama ba, Buchi Emecheta, and Tessie Onwueme, Sofola's canonization is vindicated as her preoccupations embrace the traditional and the modern, the local and the universal, as well as individual and collective predicaments. She focuses on a tragic theory in giving expression to the African woman's situation and African people's global human condition. Sofola has made her mark in a cross-section of other dramatic modes beside the tragic, not only in Africa, but Western academia.

Zulu Sofola is an outstanding cultural and political voice in African drama. She admits that her literary production is motivated by her questioning mind and her desire to probe various ideological and political 'isms': "You will find that most of my writing questions the 'isms' that have been superimposed on African people."[1] A reading of her plays confirms her inquisitive challenging of traditional, modern, indigenous and imported values. While women play important roles in her works, they are not always the center of the action. However, many of her works reveal a definitive role for women and the writer's conscious effort to be a spokesperson for her gender. Such works include *Wedlock of the Gods, The Sweet Trap, Queen Omu-Ako of Oligbo,* and *Songs of a Maiden.* These works bear the signature of Sofola's evolving definitive but well-balanced womanist consciousness. Her works are well-rooted in African world-view and this coincides with her husband's view as a sociologist who upholds the exaltation of African cultural values. She maintains Simone Weil's philosophy, "To be rooted is perhaps the most important and least recognised need of the Human soul."[2] She feels and fills this gap in her works, especially the more recent ones, which are not only culturally rooted, but give expression to a sound moral and spiritual sense of judgement.

Wedlock of the Gods conceptualizes the predicament and fate of a woman who puts personal love above collective ethos. Ogwoma's tragedy stems from her being liberated ahead of her time. Her true love for Uloko is thwarted because her parents need a lot of money to care for her sick brother. She is forced to marry a richer man since Uloko is too poor to pay a huge bride price. The death of Ogwoma's husband shortly after the marriage gives Ogwoma and Uloko a chance to attain their dream. However, tradition becomes an obstacle. She is expected to enter into a Leviathan union with a brother-in-law. To avoid this, Uloko begins to visit her before the end of the three months mourning period. This is considered an abomination by the society and Ogwoma's mother-in-law avenges her son by destroying Ogwoma. In a multiple tragic situation, Uloko kills the latter and commits suicide.

Sofola believes in taking the best from tradition and resisting the society when necessary. The tragedy in this play is that of the individual confronting the society, which is larger than that individual. Sofola is of the view that Uloko and Ogwoma should have been more decisive in preventing the forced marriage. She says the fight should not have been fought alone. She does not reject tradition, as she explains:

> I have always said that the only way the African woman of today, with her European orientation which we call education, can be liberated is to study the traditional system and the place of the woman as defined by it. There was no area of human endeavour in the traditional system where the woman did not have a role to play. She was very strong and very active.[3]

Ogwoma's tragic dilemma was common in pre-colonial, early colonial, and in many rural parts of Africa that have not been much influenced by modernism. It is not limited to Igbo culture and so such an issue deserves the attention given to it by Zulu Sofola. One cannot but decry tradition when it stifles the individual's legitimate personal desire and destroys self-realization.

Sofola believes that the European value system that accompanied the colonial experience had no positive role for women, "In the European system there is absolutely no place for the woman. In the traditional system, the roles are clearly demarcated."[4] Consequently, several of her plays reflect this definition of the woman's role. This as well as her positive political leadership come out in the play, *Queen Omu-Ako of Oligbo.* This play is not only based on historical facts, Sofola knew Omu Ako in real life, and her grandmother was also an Omu. The strong role of this queen and the high level of participation of women in the Nigerian civil war are realities. Other writers like Chinua Achebe and Flora Nwapa have fictionalized these Igbo women's strength of character during the Nigerian civil war as well. We see the women playing very dynamic roles for the society's survival. They also provide the human touch to a tragic situation. The women decry murderous actions on both sides and advise the men about the futility of the civil war. Queen Omu highlights the strong African woman who is often made invisible in much of the literature that focuses on the intimidated and subdued woman.

In *The Sweet Trap,* the focus is on modern women who have sheepishly imbibed foreign values to the point of becoming ridiculous. This play dramatizes gender conflicts very vividly to show that this writer rejects indiscriminate adoption of values. The women take over authority from the men in an absurd manner. Unlike queen Omu, whose authority is inherent, the women in *The Sweet Trap* seize power and authority in a phoney manner. Clara Sotubo's insistence on having a birthday celebration creates tension in her home as her husband, a doctor, insists that they can not have the birthday party for economic reasons. Clara's personal problem becomes the concern of the circle of friends who take it up as a gender war. They agree to defy the men by shifting the venue of the party to the home of Fatima Oyegunle. The party becomes a disaster because of the intrusion of ruffians and this creates conflicts between the men and the women. Sofola's commentary on this play is explicit and she clearly underscores her aim as the fictionalization of gender problems within the modern setting:

> ... I was handling women who were affected by the European superimposition; women who did not know who they were and where they were going. They were absolutely irrelevant and they were fighting the kind of fight that was almost like the chasing of a shadow.[5]

The struggle by women here is from a cultural void and so the women look ridiculous, like the academics in another play, *Song of a Maiden*. Sofola believes that the struggle against women's marginalization should be contextualized and purposeful. Her political voice and cultural nationalism are balanced as she critiques various forms of extremities. Womanist consciousness no doubt pervades the works of this writer, whose themes are diverse. Her heroes/heroines are usually poised against conventions. Many of these protagonists get engulfed because theirs is the lone voice in the wilderness. As her method of recommending positive change, she shocks the society with the way individuals are circumscribed.

Zulu Sofola's versatility has its origin in her being a musician as well as a dramatist and a stage director. She has indeed proved her accomplishment as an interpreter of "African cultural values to the Africans for the latter's self-knowledge, self-realisation and self-appreciation in dignity for meaningful self-emancipated life and living in post-colonial Africa."[6] Her plays are often expressions of strong political and ideological viewpoints. She is not apologetic about this, as she sets out to create art that enhances inward-looking efforts to solve the African wo/man's problems. Her *raison d'être* is derived from her inquisitive mind as well as a quest for roots inspired by her father, as she tells Adeola James. She recognizes the multiple burdens of the African woman writer working against "plenty of odds" while transcending these odds by her staggering accomplishment.

Sofola also stands out as a writer who is not carried away by the desire for strangeness and dissimilarity by outsiders. The need to be canonized by Western academia motivates some African writers to celebrate issues and values that are not rooted in the African personality or culture. Perhaps this is one of the strongest marks of her achievement. She decries the distorted image of the African woman as a result of colonized mentality:

> With European exposure the African educated person has been led to believe that the female is an afterthought, a wall-flower, and the man is heaven-sent, the controller of everything. When you look in our literature you find that this is how women are portrayed. Even where it is a woman in her own right within the traditional setting, she is going to be portrayed half-way her strength.[7]

Sofola upholds aspects of tradition that are not self-effacing or self-depleting. Whereas she rejects retrogressive tradition in *Wedlock of the Gods,* she is convinced that order and decorum could be sustained by tradition. In *Old Wines Are Tasty,* the hero gets into trouble because of his disregard for tradition. Several of her plays do not address specific women's problems, but rather the overall human condition. Others confirm the view that women's voices are indeed ideological voices in a definitive way.

Sofola's plays, *The Showers* and *Lost Dreams* are more overt womanist presentations that come out more clearly as ideologically charged, literary pieces.[8] The two have identical themes, setting and casts. They provide more direct commentaries on the modern African woman's condition than any of her other plays.

From the opening scene of *The Showers,* a gender battle-line is drawn. The remark of the female nurse, Nurse Odigie, against the men, reveals this tension when a woman in labor is brought into the Shasha hospital under emergency conditions,

> "They always do.
> It is always when their wives need them most
> that they are conveniently absent." (3)

The risk of childbirth and the exploitation involved in bride price and bride wealth are some of the other issues raised by

Sofola in this play. A young girl, Obinna, rebels against tradition by rejecting parental exploitation of their daughters' worth as brides. She has her way at the end. The female professionals, Magistrate Demola and Dr. Essien, also use their influence to cause awareness and social change in the course of the play. Their direct involvement in women's activism is embodied in the volatile group, 'Feminique Internationale.' Dr. Essien declares the war of the sexes:

> I am sure that if men were to lay their lives on the line for new lives to be ushered into this world the way women have to undergo this natural but dangerous function, all services would have been at their beck and call. Is it not more exciting to get a new wife than to save a used one? (17)

The male characters are equally poised to defend their sex, while Dr. Okezie queries Dr. Essien's position, "Must everything be seen through the lenses of gender warfare?" What makes this play remarkable is that in spite of Sofola's more overt gender commitment, the play is not a polemical gender manifesto *per se* as larger issues and social problems are presented. The question of avoidable death caused by inadequate medical facilities is a major concern. We also have a satire that brings out the reversal of roles in Mrs. Ogiame's pregnancy controversy. Her husband doubts his fatherhood since two other marriages have failed to produce the fruit of the womb. When his third wife gets pregnant, there is a dilemma. This is a departure from the predicament of women like Efuru whose domestic crisis is the result of the woman's infertility. This quest for the verification of his fatherhood becomes a major preoccupation for Mr. Ogiame. That men need to prove their manhood is the reversal of the 'femme fatale' whose tragedy usually comes from the failure to prove her womanhood through motherhood. Yet, it is a veritable slice of African life that many writers have ignored.

The theme of social change is focused on an improvement of the women's condition, as we see in the greater involvement of women in the core of the public sphere. Again, the theme of unhappy marriage becomes gendered because in this play it is a man, Mr. Adebekun, described as being of "a special breed of men," that is nervous about his marriage, having been thoroughly intimidated by his bitter experience with his former wife, Agnes. He now goes out of his way to please and do the will of his present wife. The Olurombi theme, the dilemma of a woman who sacrifices her only child in fulfilment of a vow for economic prosperity, comes up here in a different version. The issue is that Mrs. Adebekun has a medical condition, Psychogenia, that necessitates doctors' advice that she must stop her vigorous economic pursuits to avoid stress and get pregnant successfully. To give a mythic quality to this situation, she is also told by traditional consultants that "she chose in her destiny material wealth in the place of children" (22). This is a dramatization of the productive-reproductive tension, but Sofola allows the problem to be resolved, as Mrs. Adebekun eventually has a baby after consulting prophets. It is remarkable that the common African attitude to child-bearing, the joy of motherhood, still features here in Mr. Adebekun's comment, "She always wished to be survived by a child even if she has to lose her life in the process" (22).

Sofola treats other themes that range from the traditional (the killing of twins), to the modern, such as the indictment of men who keep late nights at dubious meetings. The indifference of male rulers to women's predicaments is reiterated here as well. The ultimate womanist message of this play comes out in a direct comment:

> The action must be precise and decisive. We must hold *The Showers* for the three categories of women who are suffering untold cruelty from the system. 'Feminique Internationale' must eradicate the system that dehumanises womanhood. (30)

Sofola has come out clearly on the side of African women as she advocates the eradication of any existing tradition that oppresses, degrades, exploits or endangers women. The shower of change is the crux of her call for a transformation of the women's condition.

ONWUEME'S VISION: NEW GENERATION AND REGENERATION

Tess Akaeke Onwueme is one of the most prolific African playwrights of the new generation. From her autobiographical debut, *A Hen Too Soon,* to *Go Tell It To Women,* Tess Onwueme has revealed a consistent womanist stand. Her creative canon is diverse; ranging from the traditional touch to a fictionalization of the modern African woman in a changing society. Some of her plays are motivated by her personal experience, others derive from her response to the communal ethos that shapes the reality of the traditional or modern, rural or urban African woman's sensibility. Onwueme's plays reveal a keen understanding of the issues of importance, problems and prospects, needs and self-retrieval of African women, and her stay abroad has not alienated this young artist from the demands on the African woman writer and the need for relevance. Consistently, hers has been a cultural voice, a political voice, but always a mouthpiece for her gender.

Onwueme's *The Reign of Wazobia* is a composite metaphor of African women's condition. This play could be seen as one of the most explosive and revolutionary fictionalizations of the quest for African women's self-realization. The very first lines present the author's unalloyed gender position. The play starts with a battle cry:

> Arise Women!
> They say your feet are feeble
> Show them those feet carry the burden of the womb!
> They say your hands are frail!
> Show them those hands have claws!
> Show them those hands are heavy!
> Wake up, Women!
> Arise, Women! (2)

This cry by the woman regent, Wazobia, sets the tone of the overt ideological content of this play. The root of the outcry is the dramatization of the tension between the male and the female in an unusual tussle for power. Wazobia refuses to relinquish power to a regular male king at the end of the three seasons ... the maximum time that tradition allows before another king is installed. Initially, she is unsure of the measure of support she would receive as she wonders:

> So they want Wazobia to step down
> so they can rig ... elect a male king.
> Should I or not?
> Perhaps I should ....
> It's the voice of the people ... the
> people ... people. (3)

But she changes her mind and resolves to hold onto the throne, rallying the women around her. She is determined to decorate the throne with her feminine fingers:

I, Wazobia have come with these
fingers to embroider it,
to knit your world together. Accept,
men, Men accept. (5)

Quite logically, the men resist her move and begin to conspire
against her, working for her removal, exile, or death.
Disregarding the threat, conspiracy and revolt of the men, she
affirms her readiness and determination to eliminate female
oppression and exploitation:

For ages, you have been dancing to the eyes of licen-
tious men and visiting generals
Dance no more!
What good has the gyration brought you?(6)

Onwueme clearly draws the gender line and most men react
with shock at their wounded ego, "Since when have women
become the pillar of the state?" Not even the Omu, 'the king
among women', will the men respect for being important in her
own right, as the priest of Ani remarks, "King of women but
woman all the same." Onwueme raises significant issues that
touch women convincingly. Such themes include improved
education, equal opportunity, inheritance, and inhuman discriminatory funeral rites that widows go through in many parts
of Igboland. Others are wife battering, women's oppression,
and inequalities. Wazobia incites the women to face these
aspects of tradition and challenge them:

Women, that is the task before you
To set the hand of the clock aright
To move time, not allow time to move you It's our
time to till. It's our time to tend
That we may be planted on firm soil ....
(23)

Quite expectedly, she is resisted vehemently by male chiefs
like Iyase and Idehen who reject a woman's reign:

Can you imagine
What foul air oozes from the mouths of our wives...
wives spreading such slogans as WOMEN
LIBERATION?
Women EMANCIPATION! (28)

Yet, one is not deceived that there is absolute consensus
among all the women about women's freedom or Wazobia's

desire to reign. The female leader, Omu, is as opposed to such as male chiefs initially. She is on the side of tradition. But her character evolves as she becomes liberated and resolves to rally the women around Wazobia by opposing the men's move to depose her. Like Wazobia, the Omu becomes vocal and authoritative. On the other hand, the struggle has its problems, as some women traitors collaborate with the men to expose their envy and self-centredness, as we see in the treacherous roles of Wa and Anehe. Onwueme's success, however, lies in using gender preoccupation to raise more general political issues. She condemns men's hold onto power, military dictatorship and misrule while advocating greater involvement of women and youths in political matters. Her portrait of the conflict is convincing.

The Reign of Wazobia is therefore one of the most effective political and ideological works by an African woman. The fact that Wazobia is only between 20 and 30 years old is significant. Tessie Onwueme herself is one of the new breed of Africans who have known nothing but misrule since independence. Most African states became independent about 30 years before the time that the play was written (1988). It is an indictment of the misrule in place since around 1960. The specific locale of Anioma kingdom is a type of the modern African state. Wazobia is a symbolic name: Wa, Zo and Bia— "come" in three major Nigerian languages—Yoruba, Hausa, and Igbo, respectively. The word is a well-known hybrid name that denotes unity in Nigeria. Onwueme's message seems to be a call for African women to come together in a progressive move to emancipate them from retrogressive traditions.

The support for the women's struggle by men like Ozoma and the priests heightens the effect of Onwueme's play, making it go beyond gender boundaries, lifting the struggle to a human level. The ultimate message is a profound one:

> Now hear our manifesto. Henceforth the symbol of our Kingdom shall be the palm-tree which from top to bottom has all and produces all from fruit, to wine, to oil, to kernel ....
>
> ... Each part its own value and yet interdependent on all other parts. We all, man woman and child must be schooled. To actualise these potentials for full benefit. For all with none posing an obstacle to another ....

Henceforth women will have equal representation in rulership. (33)

Wazobia's agenda embraces equality of opportunity, consciousness-raising, and elimination of enslavement, "man and woman decreed as partners in progress, not antagonists." Tess Onwueme's versatility cuts across the young and the old. Her themes are diverse, her vision is progressive. This play reveals her voice as a political voice. Several other plays by this writer focus on vital social issues, as we see in *Mirror for Campus* and *Go Tell it to Women.* The latter, like *The Reign of Wazobia,* is a treatise on African womanism.

These writers have clearly used literature for self- restoration for their gender and race. African culture is vividly brought to life in the styles of these dramatic works, while the poetry of women like Ogundipe-Leslie becomes lyrics of African values and pipe organs for Black people's collective yearnings. Sofola's works present women's reality in a more conventional way initially. Some of these women are even more vocal as political voices, as we see in the poignant castigation of the ruling class by Aidoo and Ogundipe-Leslie. Sofola's versatile artistic skill cuts across the traditional and the modern as her works are instances of African womanist self-expression. Onwueme's call for women's togetherness is an overt channel for African women's self-actualization in a dynamic way. Although Onwueme celebrates African womanhod right from her first play, *A Hen Too Soon,* a largely autobiographical play, one can still identify a growth in awareness and commitment in more recent plays like *Go Tell it to Women* and *Parable for a Season.*

NOTES

1. Adeola James, *op. cit.,* p. 143.
2. Quoted in J.A. Sofola, *African Culture and African Personality* (Ibadan: African Resources Publishers, 1978).
3. Zulu Sofola in an interview with Adeola James, *op. cit.,* p. 150.
4. *Ibid.*
5. James, *op. cit.,* p. 148.
6. J.A. Sofola, *op. cit.,* "Dedication."
7. James, *op. cit.,* p. 145.
8. Zulu Sofola's plays *The Showers* and *Lost Dreams* are in press. The manuscripts were made available with special permission by the author, to cite or critique these plays.

Chapter Eight

Women as Agency of Culture and Agency of Change

Much of African women's literature has been concerned with change, overtly or covertly. Indeed, the very process of literary creativity as an aspect of African women's cultural production is about change. Many of the writers have confessed that they are motivated to write by the impulse to change the status quo, interrogate partriarchy, imperialism and western feminism. This is closely related to the desire to liberate African women, change their consciousness and recreate a positive self-perception to enhance progress. African women are aware that change cannot take place *in vacuo,* but within a dynamic cultural crucible. Consequently, many have recreated women in their literature as agencies not only of culture but also of active socio-political change. Tsitsi Dangarembga's *Nervous Conditions,* Ama Ata Aidoo's *Changes,* and Flora Nwapa's *Women Are Different* and *One Is Enough* exemplify this trend. These writers confirm the position of Gayle Greene:

> In a sense, all narrative is concerned with change; there
> is something in the impulse to narrate that is related to
> the impulse to liberate.... Narrative recollects in order
> for there to be an escape from representation, in order
> for there to be change or progress.[1]

The dynamic young Zimbabwean writer, Tsitsi Dangerembga,
has restructured the direction of African heroines by presenting women who confront tradition by forcing changes in
her novella, *Nervous Conditions*. The film, *Neria,* based on her
story *Tessie* is a beautiful dramatization of the predicament of
widows in many parts of Africa, and the resolution confirms
the determination by writers to represent women as instru-
ments of change and the struggle this involves. *Nervous
Conditions* is a revolutionary novel that is difficult to fit into a
category. The women characters here show a very radical
change in awareness although they are unable to transform
their situations completely. Set in the Rhodesia of the 1960s,
Dangarembga's portrait of Tambu presents this problem.
Restless, full of dreams and hope, she is eager to pull out of the
circle of poverty. She sees education as a means of self-realization. Here we have the meeting point of economic and gender problems. Tambu's education is stopped by her parents
so they can rather educate her brother and so her dreams
appear thwarted. She receives inspiration from her cousin
Nyasha, who has a rebellious spirit and rejects parental control and distasteful traditions. Tambu also becomes rebellious
and assertive, clearly showing the impending social change
that is inevitable.

   This author makes very salient points about men that
clearly reveal her strong gender inclination and ideology. She
bitterly attacks a system that indiscriminately elevates the
importance of boys and encourages the inferiorization of girls.
Her portraits of male characters reveal this, as we see in the
despicable image of Nhamo, Tambu's brother:

> He did not like travelling by bus because he said it was
> too slow. Moreover, the women smelt of unhealthy
> reproductive odours, the children were inclined to
> relieve their upset bowels on the floor, and the men
> gave off strong aromas of productive labour. (1)

Nhamo represents gender and class bigotry. We see most
other men as repugnant individuals resisting change when it
involves women's freedom.

Tambu and Nyasha represent women who are sufficiently aware of their oppression and are ready to resist it. They want to probe their social space to redefine it. Unfortunately, when Tambu forces her way into the educational arena, she discovers that education, like colonialism and westernization, demands a price from her. Dangarembga therefore reveals a womanist consciousness in relating gender problems to the larger issues of class and race (colonialism and post-coloniality). Literature, to her, is as much a vehicle for collective cultural restoration as it is a channel for gender realization, and both are inseparable. Tambu has her education delayed initially because of poverty and insufficient resources, and this brings class into Tambu's multiple struggle. Her bitterness shows that her plight is not unique but an aspect of gender injustice:

> The needs and sensibilities of women in my family were not considered a priority, or even legitimate. That was why I was in Standard Three in the year that Nhamo died instead of in Standard Five as I should have been by that age. In those days I felt the injustice of my situation every time I thought about it. (12)

Tambu sees her story as an escape from the entrapment of her mother and other women. It is also the story of a girl's growth in self-consciousness. Although this story is set in the '60s, the author makes very succinct points about African women's realities. When Tambu's education is stopped, her father raises certain issues that typify the attitude of many men and even women that undermined women's education (in addition to the gap created by colonialists' establishment of male schools only for decades). Tambu's father asks, "Can you cook books and feed them to your husband? Stay at home with your mother. Learn to cook and clean. Grow vegetables" (p. 15).

At the end, many of the female characters have evolved from a passive awareness. Tambu's mother accepts the women's plight at first, but she is sufficiently aware to teach Tambu history not found in textbooks and she relates the women's problems to the larger predicament of race and class: "This business of womanhood is a heavy burden.... And these days it is worse with the poverty of blackness on one side and the weight of womanhood on the other" (16). At the end of the story, nonetheless, many of the women have evolved from a passive awareness of their social space and are

questioning the *status quo*. These include Nyasha's mother,
Maiguru, and Lucia. Tambu has been fully emancipated and
can no longer accept subjugation.

This young writer is aware that true self-realization by the
woman can only come when there is a concerted effort and not
through individual struggle. So, most of the female characters
in *Nervous Conditions* prove that women must take certain radical actions to move out of the zero degree status. Nyasha's
rebellion is encouraged by her travels and contact with western education. Her mother's is surprising, however, because
she is at first a passive, self-effacing submissive wife who has
accepted her role quietly. She later begins to assert herself
and resist her husband's cruelty. She refuses to be trapped any
further. Maiguru's unexpected rebellion is an indication of a
gradual disintegration of traditional values. The message
seems to be that one cannot transpose old traditions to a
changing situation. Education brings some profound awareness to Tambu, however, that women's victimization "was universal. It didn't depend on poverty, on lack of education or on
tradition. It didn't depend on any of the things I had thought
it depended on. Men took it everywhere with them" (15).
Nevertheless, these women have gone through a change in
their consciousness, a process which the heroine-narrator and
authorial mouthpiece describes as "the process of expansion"
at the end.

Dangarembga's declared intentions come out clearly right
from the first paragraph as the story of certain women's
entrapment, escape, and rebellion. At the end, the author's
metafictional device enables a kind of epilogue, a commentary
on the very process of this fiction. She makes Tambu, her
mouthpiece, declare, "Quietly, unobtrusively, and extremely
fitfully, something in my mind began to assert itself, to question things and refuse to be brainwashed, bringing me to this
time when I can set down this story. It was a long and painful
process for me, that process of expansion" (204). Tambu (or
the author) further declares that the story is her own story.
This close relationship between the story, the protagonist,
and the writer is enhanced by the choice of names.

Many of the names are deliberately contrived to heighten
the gender preoccupation. Consequently, names have positive or negative meanings according to their connotation and
roles. Tambudzai means "struggle" or being disturbed . . . to
corroborate the attributes of this restless girl struggling to

probe and escape from a society that puts a ceiling on girls' self-actualization. As she struggles with her subaltern position, her brother, Nhamo, is a major hurdle. Nhamo means "problem," "continuous problem" or, in a fuller version— *Nhamo inesu*—"problems are with us." Similarly, Tambu's sister's names are significant. Netsai can be translated as "give me problems but I will overcome in future" and Rambanai means "animosity" or "enmity," which is a prevalent feature in this home. It is not surprising that Nyasha means "Kindness," considering Tambu's evaluation of her predicament and sympathetic love towards her cousin. Chido's name is related to his ability to pluck himself free from their father's control and live a life of relative independence and fulfillment, as his name means "innermost wish" or "fulfillment of desire." The new male child born to Tambu's family is significantly named Shingai—"Resilience." Dangarembda's success in presenting Tambu as an agent of change makes *Nervous Conditions* one of the most effective gendered literary works from Africa.

Dangarembga's story, which produced the movie *Neria,* recreates a theme that is common in women's reality in many parts of Africa, but is unfortunately ignored by many women. The plight of widows in many parts of Africa is an example of cruel tradition carried out by men and women in the conviction that they are tools of keeping tradition alive. Patrick and Neria Kazande are a very happy couple who have worked hard to bring up a modern family and build an enviable home. In a very typical way, Patrick's mother and one of his brothers, Phinehas, detest the happiness and progress of this couple and quite logically pose a threat to the family's happiness. When Patrick suddenly dies in an accident, the reality that many widows confront in different parts of Africa is unfolded.

Patrick's relations share out his personal belongings among the extended family, including items of special nostalgic significance to Neria. Patrick's greedy and insensitive brother takes possession of his dead brother's car, furniture, and bank savings book, as the family suffers and the children are sent out of school for failure to pay their fees. He is about to possess the house, which is the only hope for Neria and her two children. The height of Neria's suffering is Phinehas' kidnapping of the two children. As he takes them back to the village, neglect almost causes the death of Neria's daughter, Mavis, because Phinehas has no time to take her to the hospital. Immediate intervention by Neria and an emergency surgery for appendicitis saves the daughter's life. After initial sorrow and silence and debt, Neria's friend advises her to go to court. Through this court action, Neria gains custody over her children and repossesses the property which she has worked very hard to acquire jointly with her husband. Neria is not presented as rejecting every tradition, but rather she respects positive aspects of tradition. So she refuses to burn the bridge at the end but remains cordial in her interaction with her mother-in law and other relatives. She still performs the traditional transfer of her husband's heritage and leadership to her son, Shingai, during the traditional ceremony, *Kurova gura,* or the transfer of leadership by handing over the symbolic calabash to her son. By this she also formally rejects the possibility of a leviratic marriage.

It is significant that Neria rejects a leviratic arrangement and continues to work hard to keep herself and her children happy. The role of the women's club where Neria works, and the support of her coworkers in her time of grief, is very significant. They encourage her to seek legal intervention. We see these women firmly behind Neria in the courtroom and we see them singing songs of encouragement and ululations after her victory. According to a young Zimbabwean woman, Mabel Machingambi, women's clubs have always played important roles in women's bonding in Zimbabwe: "There were women's clubs even before Independence. They are avenues for women to team up according to their profession or crafts. They work together for economic survival. But they also share family problems, problems of women's abuse and any other problems confronting the women. Some involve religious bonding like the Women Aglow, an international Christian group that meets regularly to share members' problems by counselling and praying about the problem."[2] Dangarembga's story has presented the widow's reality as close to life as possible. Her usual dynamic vision of women as agents of change comes out clearly in this story as well as in *Nervous Conditions.*

The modern African woman's dilemma often emanates from modern work ethics that take her away from home for long hours. This is central to Ama Ata Aidoo's latest novel, *Changes.* Her heroine Esi Sekyi is torn between her successful career and meeting the demands of a husband who wants more of her time and attention. She prefers her career and at the end she is forced to accept a polygamous marriage as her means of relocating herself within the new social environment. Ama Ata

Aidoo's early heroine, Anowa, is an undetermined woman, like many of the female protagonists of the first phase of African women's literature. She is quite different from the strong female characters of many Ghanaian societies. Unlike the domineering queen mother figure such as the Yaa Asantewa, Anowa is a tragic picture. Aidoo's heroine is a departure from the Naana image of the matriarchal society that informs her background. However, her change in awareness is clearly revealed in her latest novel, *Changes*. The heroine, Esi Sekhi, is a woman who struggles to come to terms with social change under her own terms. Esi is a determined woman who will not allow any obstacle to her self-determination. She comes to terms with the new challenges facing women in the public sphere. Aidoo's heroine is a typical middle-class African woman who is successful in her profession. Esi Sekhi is a modern African professional who struggles for self realisation. Her demanding job as a statistics consultant involves travelling away from home on her own and this causes conflict with her husband, Oko. She rejects him and opts to concentrate on her career.

However, her involvement with Ali Konde, and a second marriage into a polygamous home, create a new dilemma. Can she expect absolute love and devotion in a polygamous situation? Can she modernize this traditional type of marriage and strike a balance? Ultimately, the truth is revealed. Ali still loves his wife and family and cannot give her the needed attention. He substitutes expensive gifts and a car for love and attention and this creates a serious mental anguish for Esi. The moment of truth comes with Esi's crisis when both husbands clash. She then redefines her needs and relationship with Ali. She adjusts herself to this new situation and finds partial consolation. This compromise is the ultimate mark of her acceptance of change.

Nwapa's Expression of a New Reality

Nwapa's *One Is Enough* and *Women Are Different* dramatize this new reality. The dilemma of the westernized African woman, which has often created a divided self, is a major preoccupation in more recent novels. The existing conflict is, however, now being resolved. This category of African women's literary creative works reveals that many writers have shifted the emphasis from tragic heroism to women actively making their marks and asserting themselves. This category of literary production pins down the inevitable change in African women's experience.

In this third phase we see women refusing to be scapegoats of social change, plucking themselves from attendant fetters, breaking loose and looking for new ways of relocation. The characters depicted in modern African settings have turned the wheel of change around to suit their new dispensation. These writers are not just writing feminine works; an overt feminist ideological statement is visible. The thrust is the search for self-respect, dignity, self-assertion, and new moral values in a new quest for redefinition and self-esteem.

The settings in Nwapa's novels reveal that the hiatus created by earlier male education will no longer be a major force that limits women's achievement. The portrayals of jaundiced female stereotypes are being contested and rejected by both Amaka in *One Is Enough* and the more liberated Esi in *Changes*. In Nwapa's novel *One Is Enough*, Amaka's relationship with her husband is at first one of ideal love, devotion, and mutual respect, but she is barren. The mother-in-law, playing the role of a queen mother or an ogre, disrupts the peace as she pilots the life of her son, Obiora. She becomes a demagogue as she encourages the woman who has born children for Obi to move in. In the height of violence, Amaka retreats and re-evaluates her ideals about marriage and motherhood. Nwapa's heroine begins a journey of self-awareness as she questions traditional values and attitude to motherhood.

In her new beginning, Amaka decides to seek self-realisation outside marriage, and by pursuing economic success. This unconventional radical attitude marks a change in consciousness which also coincides with a change in her fortune. In Lagos, she is one of the women contractors and becomes rich. Incidentally, the villagers begin to explore this good fortune, and see her as a heroine. Initially, Amaka simply desires self-realisation. In this quest, she needs the help of a Rev. Father with military connections. Her motive is purely commercial initially. But she gets entangled in a relationship with Father McLaid and gives birth to male twins. In spite of pressures from the Reverend Father, who is ready to marry her and quit the priesthood, she maintains her freedom and determines not to marry again. Amaka's search for a new identity is successful as her search for freedom and success is crowned by motherhood. But she achieves this outside conventional codes of morality and by rebellion.

The myth that a woman can't be wealthy, successful and

happy in the domestic domain has therefore been debunked by Nwapa. In creating Amaka, Nwapa creates a new prototype that is not uncommon in the modern African scene. Several other characters fit this image. Amaka's sister Ayo has children without a conventional marriage and cuts her own path to economic success under her own set of values. The heroine's friend, Adaobi also pulls out of the conventional norm as she seeks economic emancipation without her husband's knowledge. The decision is justified when her husband, Mike, loses his job and their government house. The bungalow that she built secretly becomes their consolation and escape from embarrassment. Nwapa is not preoccupied with morality or propriety in creating new images of women's emancipation. Her portrait of these apostates is a true reflection of a slice of modern African urban setting. Again, a gap remains—the portrait of normal happy conventional women who are successful in their profession or business without having their marriage or homes in jeopardy.

Some understanding of Oguta's set-up and tradition enables one to appreciate Nwapa's heroines in a more profound way. The Oguta area of Igboland is a place where women were and still are at the vanguard of economic drive. The women travelled down the Niger and traded with the whites during the colonial period. So, women who towered above their husbands like Efuru because they were more prosperous than their husbands were common in Oguta. The choice of names like Efuru and Idu proves that such personalities were the norm and not the exception. According to A. C. Izuagba, who has carried out a lot of original work on Oguta lifestyle and traditions, Onyefuru is a common name in almost every Oguta family. This critic further confirms the establishment of the United African Company in Oguta in 1785 as having brought some advantages to the women who prospered more from this contact:

> The trade with the U.A.C. flourished and it favoured women, they bought and sold goods like palm kernels, biscuits, gunpowder .... Oguta men were reluctant to join the trade until much later.[3]

It is well documented that Oguta men did not like strenuous work and were engaged in fishing or farming while the women travelled, had an edge over the men and used their prosperity to elevate their husbands:

> These women worked so hard while their men remained
> at home. They were happy to make the money and were
> satisfied seeing their husbands enjoy the money they
> made.[4]

One can then see a close correlation between Oguta women's
reality and Nwapa's fictional heroines such as Efuru, Idu,
Amaka and others. She is focusing on the economic drive that
is still common to Igbo women today.

Nwapa's works continue to underscore the ambivalent
position of the African woman in a changing society. Like the
author, the heroines of her later novels begin to ask questions
about their identity and the social space created for them.
Conflict comes from the tension between the female role and
the desire for prosperity. Nwapa definitely sees the African
woman's economic problem as the core of her dilemma:

> I think the crux of these problem is economic. If the
> Black woman is economically independent, she and her
> children will suffer less. (James, 1990:112)

Women Are Different is an evidence of Nwapa's more radical
stance in fictionalizing the woman's problem. The heroines,
"the three musketeers," are precocious right from their school
days at Elelenwa. Like amazons, they trek from the nearby
boys' school to their's at night. The marathon walk is symbolic and the journey motif is recurrent in the novel. The lives
of the three heroines—Rose, Dora, and Agnes—reflect the
quest, the journey of self-discovery, only after moving from
the innocent urban setting to the corrupting influences and
experience of Lagos. Social change is a preoccupation in this
novel and it corroborates the change in awareness of the heroines. Each of the three musketeers—foot soldiers—has one
problem or another in the quest for a happy home and married
life. But unlike Nwapa's early heroines, Efuru and Idu, they
assert themselves in a more radical manner and force respect
from the society through their achievement.

Women Are Different is an overt statement on the African
woman's changing condition. Nwapa has created new images,
new symbols, new metaphors of womanhood. She has
depicted new archetypes as her own ideological commitment
increases. Critics often accuse Nwapa of concentrating on
motherhood literature, like several other female writers of the
region. She shifts from this position in *Women Are Different* and
Never Again as she presents several other themes that elicit

women's survival, change, self-retrieval, and positive female bonding. The three women represent three centers of consciousness as regards their experience and attitude to their dilemma. Agnes is a victim of a forced marriage which temporarily hinders her career. But through personal efforts, she achieves her educational dreams. Dora's marriage to Chris is initially happy as she prospers and shares her wealth and plans with him. But her husband deserts her after squandering her wealth and goes abroad where he gets involved with a German woman. Rose remains single after being deserted by Ernest and devotes her attention to her profession.

In producing these prototypes of resilience and determination, Nwapa's message is clearly enunciated in her interview with Adeola James:

> I think the message is, and it has always been, that whatever happens, in a woman's life . . . marriage is not the end of their world, childlessness is not the end of everything. You must survive one way or the other, and there are a hundred and one other things to make you happy apart from marriage and children. (114)

The portrait of defeated pitiable women, the "femme fatale," gives way to more assertive women responding to social change by rejecting strictures that militate against women's self-restoration. Her novel *Never Again* and her collection of short stories, *Women At War,* highlight women's active roles in the public sphere and particularly during the Nigerian civil war.

In her lifetime, Flora Nwapa preferred to be called a womanist, not a feminist. This accounts for her focus on family and its impact on women's social location. She created women's myths with the collective ethos in mind. Her later heroines struggle and achieved relocation. Nwapa's women characters are no longer the stereotypes of the early novels. She allows them to reconstruct new codes of moral values that are often contrary to convention, to achieve the goal of arousing and recreating feminine consciousness through fiction.

In *One Is Enough,* Amaka, Ayo Adaobi, Madame Onyei, and the nameless female contractors work together and help each other. Amaka's mother is exceptional as far as her awareness is depicted. She gives radical advice to achieve her daughter's dreams. In Aidoo's novel *Changes,* Esi and Opokuya show the same trend. Esi's strength at the end comes from the refusal to succumb to the advances by Opokuya's husband, Kubi. She refuses to betray Opokuya in spite of her own solitude.

Not all female protagonists are positively depicted by woman writers. However, generally, a new positive trend has emerged although it comes often from a travesty of conventional moral values and norms. Women are portrayed as agents of change, sometimes forcing the society to accept the imminence of change. These female writers are attempting to untangle the past, bring out relevant essence for the present, and identify new myths and archetypes as role models for the future. Aidoo's message is that productive and reproductive roles of the woman need not be mutually exclusive.

A new feminine aesthetic is emerging as African women writers are acting as their own mouthpieces. According to Sheila Rowbotham, "when the conception of change is beyond the limits of the possible, there are no words to articulate discontent so it is sometimes held not to exist."[5] Change is a major factor shaping women's lives and writers cannot pretend that it does not exist, as some feminists do. Social change is a reality in Africa, and the woman's adaptation to it is no longer a myth but a reality. So, women writers have debunked the claim of silence and invisibility. They are acting in line with a Yoruba proverb, *Owo are eni la fi n tun iwa ara eni se*—"You must be prepared to redefine your self-respect for yourself." There is, therefore, a shift from the kind of stereotypes being created by African women writers in their early works. They have become more overt, more convinced, even more revolutionary in their depiction of women. The new group of heroines being created by African women writers show compassion and a new positive ideology. Characters like Amaka and Esi would have been portrayed as tragic heroines in the earliest phases. A new form of woman's bonding is also revealed.

Notes

1. Gayle Greene, *op. cit.,* p. 291.
2. In my interview with Mabel Machingambi-St. Germaine on "Women's Bonding and Mobilisation in Zimbabwe," at Canterbury, Kent, May 1995.
3. A. C. Izuagha, "Oguta and the Novels of Flora Nwapa: A Biographical Approach," a paper presented at the 13th Annual International Conference on African Literature and the English

Language, University of Calabar, Nigeria, May 1994, p.2.
4.   *Ibid.*
5.   Sheila Robowtham, *Woman's Consciousness, Men's World*
      (London: Penguin, 1973), Introduction.

CHAPTER NINE

METAFICTION, AUTOBIOGRAPHY AND SELF-INSCRIPTION

Fiction as a tool of self-consciousness is not unique to African women's writing. In recreating reality, women writers have not adopted a disinterested attitude or neutrality. To many African women, writing is not a synonym for elusive fiction but a source of self-actualization. This is why African women's writing is largely biographical. In most cases one observes a direct correlation between fiction and actuality either at a personal or a communal level. Many are not apologetic about this biographical trend. In fact, the writer draws attention to the very process of fiction itself to reveal the thin line between fiction and reality. Some African women writers have used metafiction to declare overtly a direct correlation between the fictional process and the reality of their experience. Literature becomes useful as its own metalanguage and this is useful for declaring the writer's ideological position. These women writers do not conceal their active relationship to the fiction. This self-referential process is therapeutic, as it allows direct self-commentary by unveiling temporarily the veil of fiction. This authenticates the African woman's reality that is being depicted and validates any emergent theoretical position. This is central to the process of self-definition and self-healing. Metafiction therefore enhances self-awareness and self-definition, both being part of the integral aim of women's writing. Whereas western women writers can afford the luxury of fiction qua fiction, African women often have an urgent message and this precludes self-effacement. Given the pressing need for gender redemption, Buchi Emecheta, Bessie Head, and Nawaal El Saadawi stand out among women of the continent who have used literature for overt ideological ends.

African women writers are concerned with the process of fiction and attendant problems because the obstacles confronting them in the attempt to write and get published are inseparable from the problems of being women and being African. Emecheta, Head, and Saadawi represent various levels of the quest for self-expression against a background of gender and other related forms of oppresion. The African writer's predicament is an offshoot of her role initiating inevitable changes in her society. The prevalence of the biographical mode in African women's writing confirms the desire for personal as well as collective self-inscription. This accounts for the tendency to metafiction as well as the use of memory. Outside Africa, many other women writers often use memory as a tool of liberation. We see this in the works of Toni Morrison, Doris Lessing, Margaret Drabble, and Margaret Atwood. It is indeed true memory prevents history from becoming dormant. The words of Yvonne Vera, the author of the novel *Nehanda,* highlight this: "Forgetting is not easy for those who travel in both directions of time."[1]

SELF-INSCRIPTION AND THE INTERSECTION OF GENDER AND CULTURE

Metafiction has become popular with women writers because it highlights the struggles and the painful process of recreating oneself. The struggle to be a writer carries a special burden for the African woman who tries to negotiate a space in a hostile environment as she tries to tread on a male domain (modern literature has been a male domain for a long time). Nonetheless metafiction is a popular tool of women's self-expression. Gayle Greene explains this:

> It is a powerful tool of feminist critique, for, to draw attention to the structures of fiction is also to draw attention to the conventionality of the codes that govern human behaviour.[1]

Metafiction as the device that draws attention to the process of fiction enables African writers to recreate the way certain values have been deployed to promote or delimit gender roles. Patricia Waugh observes that metafiction unveils "how the meanings and values of the world have been constructed and how, therefore, they can be challenged or changed." These writers are therefore not interested in Joycean self-effacement, nor are they keen on standing outside the work biting their fingernails. Disinterestedness is not a feature of the biographical works by these African writers.

Gendered literature is an aspect of the constant search for African aesthetics that fosters self-knowledge without indiscriminate separatism. To borrow Maya Angelou's words, "image-making is very important for every human being." It is even more so for African women writers who need to confront multiple levels of otherness ... racial, cultural, regional, religious, third world, and post-colonial. Like other Black writers, to change her world is an imperative. Toni Morrison's view supports this:

> We are the subjects of our own narrative, witnesses to and participants in our own experience, and in no way coincidentally, in the experiences of those with whom we have come in contact ....And to read imaginative literature by and about us is to choose to examine centers of the self and to have the opportunity to compare these centers with the 'raceless' one with which we are all of us, most familiar.[2]

The process of writing oneself is also the process of re-writing the collective self. So, the communal values that inform the unconscious also emerge in the literary production. This is true of the works of Buchi Emecheta. This writer, like Ama Ata Aidoo, has rejected the tag, 'feminist writer.' Yet, personal experience, which is at the center of her story, is a redemptive act. In Emecheta's novel *Second Class Citizen,* dream and memory play important roles in the world of the heroines, both as vision and as hope. Emecheta's protagonist, Adah, is representative of the author's experience, personal and communal. Her birth at a time when a baby boy is expected is considered a personal, familial, and collective tragedy. It highlights the way traditional attitude entrenched into the society encourages gender differentiation.

> One clear demographic indicator of the relative value
> placed on males and females in a society is the extent
> to which parents show a marked preference for chil-
> dren of a particular sex. (9)

This profound cultural world-view forms the foundation of the
heroine's tragic life and experience:

> She was a girl who arrived when everyone was expect-
> ing and predicting a boy. So since she was such a dis-
> appointment to her parents, to her immediate family, to
> her tribe, nobody thought of recording her birth. (7)

This story is one of the most profound depictions of gender
bias in African societies in the fictional production of African
women. Emecheta shows with a keen sense of familiarity how
this often has a devastating effect in psychological and practical terms on the growing consciousness of young girls.
Consequently, the heroine's life is predicated on this archetypal disadvantaged status cut out for women in the Igbo society that she grew up to know, a paradigm of the experience of
girls in many other parts of Africa. Adah becomes disobedient,
rebellious and despondent as the reality is presented to her,
that although education is of a paramount importance among
the Ibos, she is to be excluded from it because she happens to
belong to the wrong gender: "School—the Ibos never played
with that! They were realising that one's saviour from poverty
and disease was education. Every Ibo family saw to it that their
children attended school. Boys were usually given preference,
though"(9). This directly threatens Adah's dreams. She is presented as a determined ambitious girl whose consciousness is
advanced for her age. One might even call her a genius, as we
see later in the story. The family can not afford to send two
children to school and their decision to send Boy to school as
the wise solution to the problem elicits fundamental gender
problems: "Even if she went to school, it was very doubtful
whether it would be wise to let her stay long. A year or two
would do, as long as she can write her name and count. Then
she will learn to sew" (9).

Adah refuses to be daunted and forces her agenda on the
family blueprint by running off to school and forcing her parents to keep her there with the help of a neighbor who teaches
in a nearby school, Mr. Cole. Adah's dream is aborted by her
father's death, her mother's leviratic marriage to her late husband's brother, and the family's decision to send Adah to a

maternal uncle to be the latter's servant. Subsequent decisions and the reasons motivating them are equally important in revealing the heroine's gender humiliation and degradation:

> It was decided that the money in the family, a hundred pounds or two, would be spent on Boy's education. So Boy was cut out for a bright future, with grammar school education and all that. Adah's schooling would have been stopped, but somebody pointed out that the longer she stayed in school, the bigger the dowry her future husband would pay for her. After all she was too young for marriage at the age of nine or so and moreover, the extra money she would fetch would tide Boy over. (18)

Adah is allowed to stay in school for such an absurd reason but she takes advantage, excels, and forces her way into the secondary school, earning a full scholarship by her exceptional performance. The rest of Adah's story is a reiteration of a self-made woman struggling against ethnic, gender, and race bigotry. What is so spectacular about Adah's story is the close affinity between the heroine's experience and Emecheta's own background, life, and experience. In spite of some fictional devices that mediate the story initially, there is a keen resemblance to Emecheta's childhood in Lagos until her departure for England. Adah's unhappy marriage to Francis, his wickedness, indolence, as well as his callous treatment, sadistic brutalization, and abuse of his wife bear a closer link between the author's life and the protagonist's.

In the account of Adah's tortuous marital relationship, the veil of fiction is removed. Auteurist mediation becomes maximal and Emecheta's biography melts into Adah's story with an almost one-to-one correlation. Autobiography is often the most effective way of presenting the author's voice and many African women writers are not apologetic about this dispensation. It is a deliberate attempt to inscribe the writer's experience as a mode of collective writing or re-writing of African women's reality. One can clearly see Emecheta's story intruding on the fiction, and in this process she highlights issues of collective concern, as we see in the question of exploitative bride price. This is a recurrent theme in Igbo women's literature because, in reality, it is a major problem in this part of Nigeria. The attitude to women and child-bearing is also prominent. Being prolific in child-bearing is so highly valued that the woman can easily be reduced to this worth. Among the Ibos Emecheta observes that it is "the greatest asset a woman can have. A woman can be forgiven everything as long as she produced children" (29).

The interference of relatives in the affairs of a family and the devastating effects on a young family occupies a central place in Emecheta's pre-occupations. In this we see Francis reduced to a puppet, "most of the decisions about their own lives had to be referred to Big Pa, Francis's father, then to his mother, then discussed among the bothers of the family, before Adah was referred to." Yet Adah is to finance such plans and when Francis is far apart from these family consultants, the Nigerian neighbors become his consultants and counsellors (29). In all these, personal experience is inseparable from larger problems confronting African women and in particular the peculiar problems of second-class citizens in Britain. The intersection of personal problems, communal dilemmas, ethnicity, race, class, and gender problems is remarkably underscored in this novel.

Second-Class Citizen as an autobiographical novel comes out most vividly as a metafiction and this unfolds the self-conscious self-inscription of Emecheta in an incontrovertible way. Any mask that the writer may have put on the real identity of Francis, the leech and indolent oppressive opportunist, is unveiled through metafiction. Adah becomes totally effaced and Buchi Emecheta comes out visibly and audibly in the last part of this novel. Emecheta's comment on the very process of fiction, the search for reviewers and the search for a publisher become overtly autobiographical. The turning point in Adah's ordeal is the possibility of working at home and writing the book, *The Bride Price.* The problems confronting Black women writers are unfolded here and Emecheta has reiterated these problems in interviews and in several of her writings. To Emecheta, like Adah, the most painful aspect is the rejection by her husband, who believes that a Black woman's dream of becoming a writer is a false dream. His narrow-minded and jaundiced vision is heightened by his reason for burning her manuscript: ". . . my family would never be happy if a wife of mine was permitted to write a book like that" (187).

The details may vary but many African women writers have admitted facing similar obstacles and rejection by individuals or publishers. Adah's comments on the process of writing are profound; it is the first thing that brings a glimmer of hope and happiness into her bleak life:

> It was in that mood that she went....and started to scribble down *The Bride Price*. The more she wrote, the more she knew she could write and the more she enjoyed writing. She was feeling this urge: *Write; go on and do it, you can write.* When she finished it and read it all through, she knew she had no message with a capital 'M' to tell the world....The story was over-romanticized. Adah had put everything lacking in her marriage into it. (180)

To Emecheta and to several African women writers, writing as the brainchild of the author entails self-inscription as well as writing the collective identity for self-fulfillment. Memory and dream therefore play central roles in the process of fiction as recollection and as an idealization of the collective consciousness. *In The Ditch* takes off the story line from the end of *Second-class Citizen* in a similar autobiographical and partly metafictional mode. Like Tsitsi Dangarembga's heroine, the sense of gender injustice motivates and validates the heroine's sense of inequality and gendered consciousness. One can therefore not separate Adah's primary experience from the collective consciousness. It is the second half of the novel that brings out more vividly a direct link between the fictional process and reality. Adah is unmistakably the auterist mouthpiece and a living proof of Emecheta's predicament and how she confronts the problem. The metafictional aspect reinforces Emecheta's real life experience. Adah's attempt to write creative work is consistently thwarted by her irresponsible, indolent, and parasitic husband, Francis. The destruction of Adah's manuscript unveils reality and merges it with fiction. Her experience is a replica of the experience of Emecheta and many female writers. Some experience a psychological or sociological, even political opposition and/or censorship. Ama Ata Aidoo is an exile from her country, Ghana, like Micere Mugo. Nawal El Saadawi is a permanent political suspect in her own country too. They are victims of politics and exiles of conscience.

Emecheta is obviously speaking for several African women, and others like Ama Ata Aidoo have a similar song to sing. Aidoo confesses, "while all African writers have many constraints to deal with, African women writers have a double

problem of being women and being African."[3] The portrait of
many of the fictional heroines is therefore a portrait of the
artist as a woman of Africa trying to unload the double, often
multiple yoke on her back. Through the artistic medium, she
cries out for help. Like the average African woman whose
dilemma she often fictionalizes, she is calling for help to balance her load, like her rural or traditional sister. Apart from
domestic discouragement, Emecheta confesses the rejection
of her manuscripts many times:

> ...we marry very early in my own area, so by the time I
> was 22 I already had five children and the marriage had
> broken up [sic]... the only thing I could do was to write.
> After several years of failure and rejections my work
> was accepted for publication. (37)

It is generally accepted that African literature is largely biographical either at the personal or collective levels and Bessie
Head exemplifies this trend in unique way. One needs to take
a quick look at her works as an avenue for self-writing in a
deliberate way and as a manifestation of the writer's concern
for all categories of oppressed people across race, ethnic, cultural, and gender lines. The South African milieu that motivates her writings is unique for amplifying various levels of
oppression. As a half-caste and product of a multi-cultural society, Head's protagonists represent a search for self-knowledge,
freedom, self-esteem, and identity within such a pluralistic setting.

  Bessie Head's fiction appeals to the West for obvious reasons, as Susan Gardener believes:

> Head received a westernized education, acknowledged
> Brecht and Lawrence as significant literary influences,
> lived in exile and never spoke an African language. What
> distinguishes her is how she attempted to become an
> African writer, through decades of living in a Botswanan
> village ... and producing, in between tormenting mental
> breakdowns, a body of work that increasingly con-
> cerned itself with the restoration of Botswanan history
> in fictional form.[4]

THE HYBRID CONSCIOUSNESS AND AMBIGUOUS LOCATION

A Question of Power has been exalted in the West because,
among other reasons, it presents themes that are attractive

there. The preoccupation with the theme of madness in this novel is typical and there is a close link between Head's experience and the solitary conditions of her heroines. The predominance of solitude and alienation is, however, not only identical to the auteurist experience but is welcome by readers in the West. This work is much more profoundly philosophical than most other works by African women and even Bessie's other works. In her mind, the heroine, Elizabeth, sees Botswana as a place where, "mentally, the normal and the abnormal blended completely" (15). Her traumatic childhood and her solitude as an adult are close to Bessie Head's predicament. In an interview with Tseja Mmopi, a former student of the Serowe school where Head taught, it is confirmed that she was never fully integrated into African cultural life and was very lonely.[5] In *Maru,* the heroine, Margaret Cadmore, is another portrait of solitude like the author, but this time her solitude springs from cultural-ethnic segregation. As a Masarwa, she lives with this stigma in the periphery of social existence and is exploited both as a victim of a caste system— an outcast—and as a woman by Maru.

Some of Bessie's works, however, probe larger issues that are of relevance to Africans. In *When Rain Clouds Gather,* freedom and the illusion of it are explored. Makhaya's quest for freedom transcends a concern with race. He shows his gender bias when he asks a woman at the border, "Are women of your country taught to shout at men?" (12). Head identifies the problem of Botswana as one of different levels of bigotry. The symbol of rain punctuating the drought of this wasteland goes beyond gender levels. Like her hybrid self, Head's works present multiple consciousness. Critics like Gardener see Head's works, especially *A Question of Power,* because of its introspective nature, as lacking African qualities. One can see Gardener's contention as a valid one when she asserts that the themes are "foreign to African fiction... madness, sexuality, guilt. In its concern with these ideas, A *Question of Power* bears closer affinity to works by Doris Lessing than to those of Ms. Head's African contemporaries" (*Ibid.*). Although Head occupies an ambiguous position as an African writer, the issues raised and her portrait of women *are* expressive of African values, and the biographical status of her works fits her into the category of women writers on the continent who are concerned with multiple levels of African women's oppression. Head's heroines are alienated. Many African writers are alienated for various reasons—gender, ethnicity, national problems, religious conservative values, tradition, and race (both ways).

Nawal El Saadawi is an African writer. This affirmation is essential because I've seen some colleagues in western and oriental academia raise eyebrows when this writer is called African. The Africanness of Egypt is not controversial although the issue is sometimes made a topic in academic exercise. This African woman writer just happens to have Arab heritage like others in the Sudan or Libya, or even Syria. This great writer explores feminist consciousness through metafiction to let the reader appreciate the close affinity between fiction and fact in her highly polemic works. In a society where women are terribly marginalised, oppressed and relegated, Saadawi has been at the vanguard of gender awareness and mobilization. Her personal oppression and political victimization are very visible in all her works. She does not pretend to be gender-neutral but reveals herself as a mouthpiece for women and for other groups on the periphery of human existence due to class, political, or religious oppression. Her protagonists are generally socio-political rebels or downtrodden.

In *Maru,* the unique regional dimension of the woman's problem is highlighted. Bessie Head exposes and condemns all form of bigotry. She equally castigates racial, class, ethnic, and cultural discrimination. The heroine, Margaret Cadmore, is an outcast, as a Masarwa (Bushman). As she is tossed around from place to place after being abandoned on the outskirts of the village, she spends the rest of her life on the social periphery of existence. Dikeledi's love and togetherness signifies a new kind of female bonding that is common in works by many female writers of Africa and the diaspora. Forced to marry the man who humiliated her, Maru reveals the woman's vulnerability. This brings out the issue of unequal yoke in marriage. Marrying into a higher class to avoid social castration and marginalization is a recurrent issue in African reality.

As in several works in this category, marriage is a major theme. Margaret's marriage to Maru instead of Maleka, the man she loves, is a common kind of dilemma that many African writers have problematized. This kind of preoccupation highlights the status of marriage and the family in the reality of the African woman. But many of these writers focus on the tension rather than the sense of fulfillment that the family represents.

Saadawi has gone further than most other African women in castigating women's marginalization, oppression, suppression, exploitation, and degradation. From the zero point of women's dilemma, she creates rebellious heroines violating social conventions and refusing to be tools in the hands of men. Saadawi's heroines, such as Zakeya, are pathetic figures that also expose the woman as a victim of social decadence, reinforced by Islamic religious beliefs. Her image corroborates that of Firdaus in *Woman at Point Zero. The Circling Song* and *Searching* further highlight religious hypocrisy and political intimidation. In all these works, the woman is portrayed as an individual with no right, no option for self-definition or self-assertion. Fouada's search transcends individual quest as it becomes a yearning for the self and for meaning by women in her society.

The Circling Song is a meeting point between autobiography and metafiction, while memory plays an important part in the reproduction of this dreamlike story. It is often difficult to discern dream from vision and reality. Saadawi admits that she wrote the story at a time when she was a victim of high-handed political injustice and so was embittered. She was dismissed for offences including her radical creative writing. The penchant tone therefore reveals the usually harsh condemnation of undue political/religious intimidation, gender brutality, and military terrorism. Her victims are generally females, her oppressors male. She did not deny the disillusion and despair and how the impact of her experience informed this book, as she admits, "I felt that this world and I were utterly incompatible, and the novel was simply an attempt to give that incompatibility concrete form" (3).

Linda Hutcheon's position, as adopted by Gayle Green, is that metafiction embraces a "commentary on its own narrative identity." Consequently, it removes to a large extent the veil between the authorial reality and the fictional world. Saadawi is so visible in the fictional process that one can not identify the end of her comment and the beginning of her fiction in *The Circling Song:*

> But everything does have a beginning, and so if I am to tell this story I must begin. Yet I do not know the starting point of my tale. I am unable to define it precisely, for the beginning is not a point that stands out clearly. In fact, there is no beginning, or perhaps it would be more accurate to say that the beginning and the end are adjoined in a single, looping strand. Where that thread starts and where it ends can be discerned only with great difficulty. (8)

Saadawi's preoccupation with reality, actuality, and truth is not disguised and fictional distancing is minimal. She is not apologetic about authorial intrusion:

> Here lies the difficulty of all beginnings, especially the beginning of a true story, of a story as truthful as truth itself, and as exact in its finest details as exactitude itself. (8)

We see Saadawi as a writer that has gone much further than most in her critique of real life process. Using the narrative mode as her axis, she launches penchant attacks on a society where gender oppression has become a matter of fact. Her heroine, Hamida, is not only a victim of male cruelty, she is rejected by her mother and family after being raped as a child. Her innocence and ignorance are explored at every move in her escape. The mythic circling song is as circuitous as the endless search for each other by Hamida and Hamido.

Searching is as polemical on gender discrepancy as it highlights the socio-political trauma of Fouada on the disappearance of her lover, Farid. Her personal search exposes the deep-rooted corruption and exploitation of women, as in several other works by Saadawi. This work, as a major preoccupation in her literary production, is indicative of this author's unending circular search for meaning against all odds in her society. The portrait of the artist as a woman activist is vivid in all her writings without exception. I disagree with Gayle Green's contention that women's fiction has always been circuitous. But the comment on Saadawi's metafictional technique of stories within the story is valid: ". . . when a writer talks about narrative within narrative, she unsettles traditional distinctions between reality and fiction and exposes the arbitrary nature of boundaries."[6]

Emecheta, Head, and Saadawi are three writers with unique backgrounds that differ from the exposure or experience of several other African women writers. The majority of other African females fit into a more conventional image in that they use fiction for the purpose of cultural awareness, as well as for gender construction to varying degrees. Each of these three writers functions from a unique environment that enhances a close link between their personal life and their fictional setting and characters. Often, the unique peculiar problem and experience make them focus much more on biography and the creation of fiction than cultural values. On the whole, the portrait of the African female artist is a versatile one. It is largely biographical at the personal and collective levels. What makes these three writers unique is their open revelation and/or declaration of the indissoluble link between the process of fiction and personal as well as social experience.

NOTES

1. Gayle Greene, " Feminism, Fiction and the Uses of Memory," *Signs,* Vol. 16, No. 2 (Winter 1991), p. 293.
2. Toni Morrison in Cheryl Wall, *Changing Our Own Words* (New Brunswick: Rutgers,1991), p.1.
3. James, p. 12.
4. Susan Gardener, "White Sugar, Coke and Feminism," a paper delivered at the International Conference on "Women in Africa and the African Diaspora: Bridges between Activism and the Academy," University of Nigeria, Nsukka, July 12-19 1992, p. 6.
5. M.E.M. Kolawole in an interview with Tseja Mmopi who was a student in the Serowe school where Bessie Head was a teacher. She knew Head personally. The interview took place at Maplewood apartments, Ithaca, N.Y., March 1992.
6. Gayle Greene, *loc. cit.*

Chapter Ten

Repossessing African Space: Self-healing and Self-Retrieval in the Diaspora

... only barbarians are not curious about where they came from, how they came to be where they are, where they appear to be going, whether they wish to go there, and if so, why, and if not, why not.[1]

The authentic quest for roots in the African diaspora has a long history, and Alex Haley's work is a consolidation of this long-standing desire for true self-knowledge. Many women writers emerged in the African diaspora largely because of the need to correct errors in history which, as a colleague confessed, made many Africans unsure about their heritage. How could a people identify with a culture if all they knew about it came from the clips from Tarzan movies about Africans jumping after monkeys on treetops? History could be unkind, if not deliberately false. Not even the revelation that Tarzan movies did not take place in Africa but were shot in the Florida Everglades could convince a curious young African American that there might be something to be proud of in African heritage. It took years of genuine search and the re-writing of Africa by many Africans in the diaspora to heal the wounds inflicted on the self-perception of many who have been fed on the invention of Africa from the Florida Everglades.[2]

Women writers have occupied the front burners in this attempt to rekindle true self-retrieval of Africans in the diaspora through literature. The literary renaissance that came with the Black Power movements brought many male writers onto the American scene. The baton has, however, passed on to women as the African-American literary scene becomes inundated with the flood of women writers. Similar consciousness informs much of the literature by women or about women elsewhere in the diaspora. The multiple ethno-cultural variables in the African diaspora have motivated many to lean more about their origin and search for cultural identity. This is explicit in the recent work of Maureen Warner-Lewis, *Guinea's Other Suns*. In recent decades, Africans in the Caribbean and the Americas have consequently renewed the search for their African matrix. Although Alex Haley's *Roots* is the magnum opus in this positive quest, it is by no means an exception. Maureen Warner-Lewis' critical work, based on extensive research in parts of Africa and the diaspora, corroborates this yearning.

CULTURAL ROOTS AND GENDER ISSUES

African themes could be traced to early writers of African descent, such as Olaudah Equiano, Phillis Wheatley, W.E.B. Du Bois, and Frederick Douglass, among others. The recent resurgence has, however, placed African interest in the forefront of much of the fiction, music, and art of the diaspora, giving it the focus it deserves, as Rex Nettleford comments:

> The gem of a Caribbean civilization giving to the African presence the centrality it commands is a special kind of reality hovering on the consciousness but yet to be fully acknowledged, despite the pervasive psychic energy with which it invests the region's ontologies, epistemologies and world-views.[3]

The process of cultural renaissance is inseparable from a sense of self-discovery and self-esteem, and these issues are recurrent in fiction. The Africanization of issues is not without attendant cultural explosion and conflicts. Both male and female writers have conceptualized the rewarding experience as well as the inevitable nostalgia, hope and regret. Because of historical elision and assimilation, many of these writers emphasize both the domestic as well as the public areas of preoccupation. Writers such as Zora Neale Hurston, Toni Morrison, Maya Angelou, Alice Walker, and Maryse Conde have recreated the paradox and tension caused by the erosion of their African values in their literary works. Inevitable multiple identity is at the heart of this ambivalence.

Male writers have generally focused on male heroes, as in the works of Richard Wright, Ralph Ellison, James Baldwin, and Amiri Baraka. Critics do not focus attention on the South American African diaspora because of the barrier of language. Yet, some profound messages of retracing the African origin have emerged from the works of writers male and female. Antonio Olinto is one of such Black writers in the diaspora who have placed women and Africa in the center of their fiction. An African Brazilian writer, Antonio Olinto has presented strong women in the epic novel *The Water House*. Women writers like Maryse Conde have also underscored the women's experience by building bridges in settings that span the diaspora as well as the African continent. Her works *Segu* and *The Children of Segu* are set mostly in Africa. *A Season in Rihata,* however, presents the dilemma of an African-Caribbean married to an African and the classic culture clash that often attends such. Buchi Emecheta represents Africans in the voluntary diaspora, and her work *The Family* is a complex fictionalization of the problem of alienation by a Caribbean family emigrating to London. Linto, Conde, and Emecheta represent three decades, three regions of the African world, and both male and female perceptions and perspectives; they are representative and classic.

Olinto's novel *The Water House* presents the woman questing for cultural integration, having her quest largely fulfilled. Maryse Conde's *A Season in Rihata* dramatises the woman in search of cultural, political and personal integration; her quest is aborted and only partially fulfilled. Emecheta's novel *The Family* portrays a young woman in search of self-integration and self-definition whose dream is completely thwarted, perverted and decimated. Many writers base the woman's invisibility on the public sphere. Cultural parameters are not always considered and, consequently, lop-sided and one-sided conclusions emerge about the lack of enablement of the African woman. These three writers, however, juxtapose the personal and the collective, the private and the public, the individual and the communal, the present and the prophetic.

Antonio Olinto's work in translation is unique in many ways. The literary production of writers from the African diaspora in South America are not easily accessible to English-speaking people for linguistic reasons. This work also presents women's strength of character that is unique in the same vein as writers like Ngugi Wa Thiong'o, Driss Chraibi, and Sembene Ousmane, among others. He depicts a much more positive picture of women than some female writers. His works also construct a bridge in time and space linking the continent with her diaspora culturally, ideologically, and politically. In *The Water House,* Antonio Olinto's representation of African femininity is unique. He dramatizes the lives and experience of three generations of African women from Brazil, their quest, courage, and zealous return to their motherland. They are women amazons in the sense of pulling down every obstacle and exhibiting exceptional strength in political, family, social, and economic matters. With this dynamic potential, they ignite, activate, and recreate social change, first in Bahir, then in Peor, Brazil and eventually Lagos and Ouidah, Benin Republic. Olinto's fiction excludes abject romanticisation but focuses on these women's pragmatic resourcefulness, determination, insight and foresight in a singular manner. Catarina dos Santos, uprooted from Abeokuta via Lagos at 18, is a visionary whose imaginativeness and tenacity enable her to shape the private and public life of herself, her family, and her societies in Brazil and Africa. She becomes the nerve center of social change and a motivating force for Brazilians returning to Africa. Fifty years of trauma as a slave and later a free Black in Brazil have not decimated her vision and African dignity.

Memory of home remains vibrant in her mind as she insists on returning to Africa. Years of partial and temporal separation have not cooled her affection for her cultural matrix as she persistently declares, "I must go back and I want to take my daughter and my grandchildren"(3). In spite of the long wait for her quest to materialize, Caterina becomes the focal point in directing the sail and destiny of the social ship. She is the moving force behind the epic journey. As Olinto admits in this fiction, the journey motif is identical to the personal quest for self-definition and cultural integration: "it is the story of a journey." But it transcends a physical journey as it becomes a journey of self-discovery, self-recovery, and self-restoration. So, to Catarina, space and time dissolve into each other to give time and existence a single continuum:

> Catarina was in the past and in the present, she was here and she was in that other ship, the difference in time dissolved, it seemed to have grown less and less until suddenly she saw that she had not even boarded the ship but was still in Abeokuta. (17)

Catarina's quest for a new self, a new identity, a new collective consciousness and a new space for relocation spans three generations and two continents. Olinto consistently reiterates Catarina's yearning for a new identity and image and self harmony that coincides with the communal desire, "she needed to remake herself, restore herself," (p 18). She sees the past, the present and the future as a stretch. The flood that dispossesses many Africans at Piau heightens her desire to return to Africa. Like the ship itself, *Esperanca,* Catarina is a symbol of hope. Inspite of uncertainty, arduous waiting, peril, epidemics and hazards, she survives the journey to Africa. She remains a source of encouragement throughout the journey just as she is undaunted during the initial problems of settling down in Lagos. Her daughter, Epifania, may not tower above others like Catarina but she too makes dynamic marks. She symbolizes the inevitability of dual inter-cultural change and exchange and gives up her initial resistance to the assimilation of African values. She therefore represents a progression in consciousness. Through a merger of private and public roles, Olinto concentrates on women's empowerment. These women remake history and recreate gender myths. Putting African women at the core of socio-political dynamics is the hallmark of Olinto's work. However, Mariana, Epifania's daughter, becomes the fulcrum around which the rest of the story revolves. Like her grandmother, Catarina, Mariana is a bundle of strength, determination, and unique resourcefulness.

Mariana, as a child, perceives the journey to Africa as symbolic, "for Mariana, the flood and the journey went on together" (p. 10). The flood, having swept away the old possessions, paves the way for a new beginning. Catarina is symbolic of survival and a new start, like her grandmother. Mariana's eventual water-selling business sustains the symbol of water as a regenerative force. Water also becomes a source of self-retrieval as much as social retrieval since the homecoming involves crossing the Atlantic. It is Mariana's perceptive mind that motivates her to caution her mother about the intervention in Amilia's choice of a Yoruba spouse by insisting that the next generation will be African. Her economic resourcefulness builds the foundation for economic hope for her and all the Brazilian returnees in Lagos and Dahomey (Ouidah). Having crossed cultural and economic frontiers, she gets involved in the political arena. She is instrumental in the transformation of the social life in Lagos through Brazilian ways, lifestyle, architecture (the Sobrado) and agriculture; importing cassava and other crops, she maintains the need to "search for new grounds and a different horizon."

Taking a cue from her grandmother, her horizon transcends cultural, national, ethnic and regional boundaries. Whereas her son's political ambition is thwarted, she remains the formidable pillar behind Sebastian while his political career lasts, and after his death she exhibits fortitude. She allows collective interest to veil her personal tragedy. She symbolizes legendary African giants such as Moremi, Yaa Asantewa of Ghana, Nehanda of Zimbabwe, Nzinga of Angola, Madame Tinubu of Lagos, and Amina of Hausaland. She remains a vital political rallying point and first lady. Olinto's fictional female protagonists are *invincible* but not *invisible,* physical, political, cultural, and spiritual giants. He vivifies his heroines without excessive romanticization or idealization. They are simply true to life.

Maryse Conde's novel *A Season in Rihata* reiterates the quest for Mother Africa as represented by the experience of a female protagonist. Marie-Helene's life is an apt typification of the experience of many people's desire and attempt to relocate by returning to their African matrix. Her yearning for self is frustrated further by ethnocentricity and the problem of assimilation. However, the core of her predicament is her divided loyalty. She is caught in the wheel of social and political change. The ideal Africa she has envisioned as a student and political-cultural activist in Paris is threatened by a new political dictatorship in Rihata. Her choice is between domestic-family happiness by accepting the offer of Zek's politician-brother, Madou Malan, and a poverty-ridden existence. Her husband, Isiaka Malan (Zek), is a pitiable individual as he is intimidated by his brother's love for his wife and his offer of a diplomatic job. Marie-Helene opts for a maintenance of her political principle and the rejection of personal comfort.

This is significant as Conde's novel encodes the subtle empowerment of the woman and her commitment to political issues. She has opted for the socio-political identification that has meant much to her. Her motive for marrying Zek is the desire for Africa. "To be quite honest the idea of going to Africa had a lot to do with it." This ideological decision is intertwined with the personal quest. After the death of her mother Alix, she seeks "a womb in which she could retreat from her suffering .... So, Mother Africa had appealed to her imagination and raised her expectations." She did not go back to Guadaloupe in the Caribbean but married Zek to return and re-turn to Africa.

The issue of unfulfilled hope caused by unequal yoking together in marriage is compounded and excruciated by the personal and political intrigues all around Marie-Helene. She falls into the category of women who are scapegoats of socio-cultural bigotry, as we see in the attitude of her in-laws. In the crucial problem of her relationship with Madou, we are told that as a woman and an outsider, she does not matter. "She was the only one who had been punished for the crime she had committed with Madou, if crime there had been. That was what women were for: scapegoats" (73). Yet, after a tortuous expectation of a son, her seventh child, a boy, is given the symbolic name 'Elikia,' meaning "hope." Both Olinto and Conde predicate the conclusion of their fiction on hope, in spite of apparent obstacles and despair.

Buchi Emecheta represents the ambivalent heritage of African women, and her experience is a symbol of the dual heritage in a practical way. Most African writers of diasporic origin are writing from a consciousness informed by a life lived mainly in the diaspora. Emecheta's background and immersion in African tradition as well as her acquired life in Britain gives her a different orientation. Many of her works present an African woman's views mediated by living in Britain. In *The Family,* Buchi Emecheta shifts her creative searchlight to the diaspora. This novel is different from her other works in this choice of setting. The convergence of the individual's quest for self-identity, self-consciousness and family/social acceptance and integration is at the heart of the matter. The quest by a Jamaican family for a new space and relocation in "Moder Kontry" begins to create a new desire in their daughter, Gwendolen. She is a victim of rape by Uncle Johnny and she suffers further humiliations as a victim of incest. Her father's act devastates her dream of an ideal life and self-realization in England. Her quest is frustrated and perverted as she is threatened with self-disintegration. Therefore the dreamland, England, presents a destructive influence on whatever dignity and self-perception she had left.

All the sustained family values brought from the African-Caribbean consciousness are destroyed in England. Gwendolen is a victim of racial, gender, and class oppression, intimidation, violation, and subjugation. She tries to grapple with the confusion by creating her own set of moral values and her own space, in vain.

Gwendolen's vulnerability in England, and her ultimate acquiescence to degenerate conditions, end in resignation. She is a misfit and cultural apostate in her new environment, as she feels rejected by the society. Her quest for acceptance and identification fail because of a tragic conspiracy at both domestic and public levels. Sonia's sense of duty and family commitment which necessitate her journey to Jamaica and long absence are the very causes of her tragedy and the destruction and decimation of the life of her daughter, Gwendolen. Whereas the journey and return to root motifs have created strength in Conde and Olinto's personae relatively, the journeys in Emecheta's novel act as catalysts to the tragic experience of the female characters. The initial shadow cast over Gwendolen's childhood innocence hangs over the rest of her life. Uncle Johnny and her father, Winston, the architects of her predicament, are unrepentant. Johnny rejoices in his social credulity; it's his word as a male and an adult against hers as a young girl. Winston's attitude after violating his daughter is incredible; he is shocked that she has lost her innocence earlier. He shows no sincere remorse. His self-righteousness heightens the girl's sense of defeat. Her paradoxical quest remains unresolved at the end.

These three novels are a departure from the pattern of tragic heroism in works by several African writers of the early phase. The inability to transcend personal commitment or strike a balance is responsible for the abundance of thwarted tragic heroines such as Efuru and Idu by Nwapa, Celina by Njau, and many of the heroines of Emecheta's other works who are bent double by the multiple yokes they carry. It is also a departure from the "mythologization of motherhood." The image of the iconoclast at war with the society often places too much emphasis on individualism. These writers have de-emphasized individualism by highlighting the consequence and presenting the strength in collectivism. African writers, as inevitable mouthpieces for a people diminished by the implications of 'a triple heritage,' in Ali Mazrui's words, are recreating positive images of the Everywoman. bell hooks in fact contends that, "Black women need to construct a model of feminist theorizing and scholarship that is inclusive, that widens our options, that enhances our understanding of Black experience and gender."[4]

The technique of composite heroism used by Olinto and Conde in some of her works is effective. This device has been used by other African writers, such as Ayi Kwei Armah, Sembene Ousmane, and Ngugi Wa Thiong'o to enhance collective consciousness. This coincides with African sense of collaboration and communalism. The tragic predicament of many protagonists of African literature emanates from the limitations of individualism. African writers in the diaspora, particularly females, have engaged in an unrelenting effort to encourage positive self-consciousness. The kaleidoscope on African womanity has encompassed the entire African world. They are highlighting the African woman's formidable strengths in creating spaces of empowerment. In the words of Maureen Warner-Lewis, `Guinea's other suns' are shining across the passage to be viewed by continental writers while diaspora writers continue a reciprocity that enhances the understanding of the common bonds and bonding. The Africanization of literary production by diaspora writers encourages cross-fertilization of ideas, consciousness, and the ethnocultural pluralism of the African woman globally.

It is not only in fiction writing that Africa and the reality of Africans in the diaspora is being objectified. Maya Angelou's autobiographical work, *All God's Children Need Travelling Shoes,* clearly reveals the yearning for Africa and the quest for a reconciliation of the conflicting multiple identity. The search for meaning and relevance in a multi-cultural environment is a continuous process for the African in the diaspora. In America, certain facts of the American democratic experience remain problematic for these people. Questions of root, national identity, self-expression and the meaning of freedom as well as the quest for a cultural matrix remain ubiquitous. This group is confronted with conflicts and ambivalence in daily realities as they contemplate the American dream. So, several African-American writers consider themselves as the articulate voice of the inarticulate, passive or active majority. It is significant that women writers of African descent are at the vanguard of this attempt to discover themselves and, to them, gender is inseparable from the collective concern. It is no accident that the 20th century has witnessed an explosion in the emergence of African-American female writers like the 1993 Nobel prize winner Toni Morrison, Alice Walker, Toni Cade Bambara, and Maya Angelou, among others. Most of them have found fiction an appropriate mode of self-realization as well as a paradigm of group and gender articulation.

Maya Angelou concentrates on the biography sub-genre as a vital tool of self-expression at the personal as well as the collective levels. By drawing attention to her personal experience, Angelou, like many African-American writers, deploys individual reality to give expression to the collective awareness, to support Lawrence Levine's view that "It is time for historians to expand their consciousness by examining the consciousness of those they have hitherto ignored or neglected." Maya Angelou's works are mostly autobiographical, as she reveals personal experience to explicate certain basic yearnings of her people in general and the African-American woman specifically. From the growing consciousness of her novel *I Know Why the Caged Bird Sings,* Angelou shifts her exploration of the search for identity and self-appreciation to mother Africa. She goes beyond the fictional detour to Africa. Angelou's novel *All God's Children Need Travelling Shoes* is a recast of actuality: from the romantic or psychological illusion of the African dreamland, from expectation to reality, from myth to a physical contact with Africa. Her experience in Ghana shifts her focus of cultural alienation and seeks full integration.

Angelou's personal experience in Ghana unveils certain truths about the cultural ambivalence of African-Americans:

> We had come home, and if home was not what we expected, never mind, our need for belonging allowed us to ignore the obvious and to create real places, befitting our imagination.[5]

Angelou finds avenues for her African quest in diverse ways as she sees herself on the periphery of things without feeling fully integrated. She is shocked that her homecoming, like that of other "revolutionary returnees," does not attract communal celebrations or national reception. Yet, she feels exalted as local Ghanaians identify her to be a Bambara woman from Liberia, because of her partial mastery of Fanti and possibly her look. Sometimes her experience is spectacular and nostalgic. During her visit to Keita the local inhabitants swear that she is a descendant of one of their relatives lost to slave raids long ago. This creates in her mixed emotions as much as it is a sense of self-restoration. Her quest becomes palpable through diverse contacts and interactions. Certain basic truths underscore the inalienable impact of Angelou's Americaness as she assesses the naivety of over-idealization. She acknowledges being one of the "naive travellers who thought that an airline ticket to Africa would erase the past and open wide the gates to a perfect future." Like her, several others are in search of an elusive Africa but American values constantly intrude on their yearning. Although the real Africa of her experience is more accessible than the fictional Africa of works like *The Color Purple,* the ambivalence of a double heritage is identical to her longing for a return to American life and the struggle for democratic ideals.

A conscious effort is being made by women of African heritage in the diaspora to construct a bridge in spite of centuries of forced alienation. History is no longer an immovable barrier; now these women are transcending history to reconstruct the ties that bind us together as Africans. The diverse stumbling blocks created by centuries of forced dispersal of the Black race are being demolished to turn them to stepping stones, even corner stones in the search for Black people's emancipation and self-restoration, globally. Women writers in the diaspora are at the frontline in this effort. It is no coincidence that the Black literary production of America has been dominated by women giants in the last three decades. Toni Morrison, Alice Walker, Andrea Rushing, Mary Helen Washington, Gwendolyn Brooks, and Toni Cade Bambara are some of the other numerous creative giants. These women and critics such as Ann Adams, Carole Boyce-Davis, Bell Hooks (Gloria Watkins), and Joanne Braxton have accepted the ambivalent complex heritage and the need to bring out the best of the two worlds by enhancing and not effacing African cultural traits.

NOTES

1. Isaiah Berlin, Quoted by Rex Nettleford in a foreword to Maureen Warner Lewis's *Guinea's Other Suns* (Dover, Mass.: The Majority Press, 1991), p. xv.
2. A colleague who is now a professor at the Africana Studies Center at Cornell University had this experience as a child. He started doubting the Tarzan image of Africa when he read in the newspapers that some monkeys escaped from the site of Tarzan movies in the Florida Everglades. This gave him the hope that the real Africa may be different. Thanks to this revelation he determined to work hard and visit Africa in the future.
3. Rex Nettleford in Warner Lewis, *op. cit.,* p. xviii.
4. Bell Hooks, *op. cit.*.
5. Maya Angelou, *All God's Children Need Travelling Shoes* (New York: Random House, 1986), p. 19.

Umoja: African Women's Alterity and the Dialogic Location

African women are at an important intersection in their awareness and in the search for self-definition, self-valuation, and self-retrieval. As the empire writes back, African women locate themselves at various epistemological positions that are relevant to this process in various ways. They are deconstructing imperialistic images of the African, rejecting liminal and negative images of women that are prevalent in African literature by men and they are reacting to mainstream western feminism. Having broken the yoke of voicelessness, these women are speaking out. They are moving away from any externally imposed, condescending ideology which negates this process of self-inscription, self-retrieval, and self-healing. The African woman's strength derives from within and her culture forms the foundation for a wholesome self-appreciation. William James identifies "a certain blindness in human beings" which leads to false self-esteem and a condescension in perceiving others. African women are seeking to change such attitudes.

There is no single way of achieving this because of the diversity in human consciousness. Many African women globally are looking for African women's self-definition and self-enhancement through several complimentary avenues. Nevertheless, there is a consensus that the woman's question can not be divorced from racial, national, class, and other problems that undermine the Black race.

African women's consciousness is not fixed or static but protean and dynamic. This also depends on national, ethnic, political or religious interventions. The voicelessness of African women is sometimes more of a myth than reality because one can not aver that all categories and classes of African women have been voiceless all the time. This myth is easily confused with actuality and it becomes an imperative for African women to unfold hidden or neglected areas of visibility and empowerment. Positive self-determination as recorded in history is progressively being reconstructed in this process of re-definition and re-writing of African women. There has to be a shift from the erroneous invention of Africa and African women even as one recognizes the need to reconstruct the world's cultural maps. African women have been active in charting a new cultural map and gender direction.

Umoja, the Swahili concept of togetherness, unity, or coalition, is appropriate and relevant to the current quest for an authentic and acceptable African womanist theory. This idea of *Umoja* enhances the accommodation of diverse attitudes to the woman's question without undermining one's African identity. It underscores harmony in diversity and underlies our theory that African women's consciousness is a mosaic. *Umoja* also corroborates the African world-view of negotiation of values and space. It also coincides with the fact that African thoughts derive largely from the trope of the world as a market place, a place of bargaining and give-and-take (Sekoni, 1994). Obioma Nnaemeka has consistently reiterated this philosophy of give and take. This is particularly significant because the African woman is a hybrid of the traditional and the modern, the indigenous and the exotic, the inherent as well as the acquired values. Willy-nilly, she is caught between many worlds. Her Africanness is not less important to her than her womanhood as she struggles to negotiate both identities by asserting her dignity and rejecting marginalization and subjugation. We can not run away from history; our history has been one of fragmentation. As many nations acquire independence, post-colonial issues continue to mediate the reality of the African continent. Post-colonial Mr. Big is revealed with his hydra-head as multi-nationals, the International Monetary Fund (IMF), and the World Bank, among other agencies that still control African socio-political and economic status. Women as a group have been more influenced by the impact of these agencies than has any other single group. Gloria Emeagwali rightly affirms that women pay the price of structural adjustment. Confirming that various problems and maldevelopment accompany structural adjustment policies all over Africa, she underscores the plight of women: "Women are directly affected by the perpetuation of these symptoms of maldevelopment and have a formidable battle to fight to move into the 21st century."[1]

Continental African women have for too long been circumscribed and subsumed by other people's perceptions and agendas. Many condescending Western Africanists have continued to invent their own versions of Africa and African women's reality. For the African woman to "hop on-board" the feminist agenda is to perpetuate this process of having others inscribe her identity and self-evaluation. For too long, Africa has been treated as a *tabula rasa* for other people's signatures. Africa remains a dream to many and a nightmare to others quite in the same tone as the one that emerged from Joseph Conrad's darkened heart (or heart of darkness?). As many western feminist scholars inscribe African women, they reflect "more about themselves and their culture than about Africans and theirs."[2] I was asked by an enthusiastic young Black Zimbabwean [then Rhodesian] student in Birmingham, U.K. in 1972 if there were women teachers, university graduates, lawyers or doctors in Nigeria. He was genuinely surprised at my positive answer, having been taught by the white Rhodesian propaganda that the highest educational achievement accessible to African women outside white-controlled Southern Africa was nursing. But it was rather sobering when in 1992, exactly 20 years later, I was again asked by an African-American female student, in New York, if there are female lawyers in Black Africa! Another African-American undergraduate enthusiastically asked me at a conference in Cincinnati, Ohio, in 1992, if there are cities and towns in Africa! These innocent students have not had the privilege of alternative perceptions of Africa beyond the Tarzan images. The invention of the African woman, like the invention of Africa, has continued progressively in some quarters.

The African woman is not impervious to these problems emerging from the invention of African women. She is actively seeking channels of self-definition in a changing society. Many see feminism as imperialistic while others are comfortable with it as they seek to locate themselves in global feminist agenda. Those who reject feminism are looking for alternative terminologies that are relevant to their specific cultural experience. The most dominant concept acceptable to those rejecting feminism as a term of reference is womanism (or African womanism). Womanism does not deny the natural biological God-given traits and characteristics, but rejects the manipulation of such traits to hold women down. It seeks to enhance women's strength in positive, wholesome ways by highlighting and not effacing femaleness. But this does not call for dogmatism. Josephine Donovan confirms the diversity in women's experience: "I believe that there are common denominators that unify women's experience... but we must be aware of the diversity in our theory."[3] African womanist aesthetics seek to make a unique contribution to existing scholarship by re-inscribing positive women's bonding, mobilization, and self-definition that cut across gender, racial, and class lines. I agree with Donovan that any theory about women "is at its best when it reflects the lived experience of women, when it bridges the gap between mind and body, reason and emotion, thinking and feeling."[4] African women are reassessing issues so as to build bridges and shift frontiers in human relationships by fostering true self-emancipation for all Africans.

A dialogic dispensation is then the most appropriate in accommodating the three dominant categories; the non-conformist, the receptive, and the transformational approaches to womanist issues by African scholars. Maggie Humm confirms the dialogic nature of African women's feminine visions: "African critics celebrate hybridity but not in any superficial way.... In addition, African feminist criticism is dialogic" (Humm,1994:207). Certain African women may not easily fit into various categories, and caution is needed in identifying groups. Human awareness is not static and a scholar who is liberal at the beginning of her career may become more radical with time and a change in consciousness. Some African women have shifted from one position to the other according to the epistemological growth. One can also identify a difference in the ideological position of some of their works according to the canons of intervention. This justifies the call for a dialogic approach to modern criticism as a wholesome one. The inter-locutory trend is more valid, as advocated by Mikhail Bakhtin in his dialogic theory.[5] Tzevetan Todorov also maintains that modern criticism is inevitably a dialogue. Audre Lorde and Josephine Donovan also recommend a dialogic approach. This is the position of many African critics, including Ropo Sekoni and Obioma Nnaemeka.

I have located this discourse within a dialogic framework in positing African womanist theories because the underlying principle is one of accommodating different but relevant approaches to African women's self-definition. Dogmatism and relativism are inadequate in giving expression to the pluralistic African setting. One increases the options by revealing African women's multiple voices. Black women are rejecting being circumscribed by definitions and ideologies created by other people or by Africans in a dogmatic way. Since gender is a vector of social transformation, the ultimate goal is not to replace one form of separatism with another, however. It is important for African women to explore common fronts for struggle in the existent dichotomized world. The majority of African women can not search for autonomy and self-fulfilment in the same manner as the Western woman because their criteria of values are sometimes poles apart. Many Africans still celebrate conventional family values and they believe that the breakdown of the family system and its replacement with other "politically correct" and acceptable set-ups is responsible for the rate of crimes, drug use, alcoholism, suicide, and many perversions that are the hallmark of modernized societies today. Feminism celebrates many of these values that Africans consider problematic and this explains the attitude of non-conformist African scholars.

African women's self-definition focuses on positive collectivity as opposed to individuality. It also endorses the overt manifestation of womanhood and motherhood with no apologia. Consequently, the average African woman's exaltation of marriage and family values and assertion of feminine outlook are important canons of African womanhood. Nonetheless, these women are crying out for justice where these values and traditions are abused or when the ideals of African culture are perverted in the patriarchal structure. To many, female bonding therefore consists of bringing out and enhancing common and positive African values, as opposed to building a wall around women in exclusion of men. Womanism then articulates certain unarticulated premises that appear to be outside dominant discursive systems in Western academia. Okey Ndibe draws out the contrast vividly in commenting that "made-in-the-West feminism appeared to have declared a war against the family. For her (African woman), a cohesive family life could never pose a threat or constitute a contradiction."[6]

African womanism also identifies problems relating to the male dominance in the society while seeking solutions to women's marginalization by looking inward and outward. It further seeks to create a conducive social space for the woman from which she contributes to the larger struggle of her gender, race and/or class. Her struggles are closely intertwined with other levels of self-assertion and she needs self-definition for a total personal and group emancipation. Consequently, after self-knowledge, she attempts to identify with the group's needs. Womanism is therefore inclusive and the positions of African women bear similarities globally. Bell Hooks identifies this:

> Black women need to construct a model of feminist theorizing and scholarship that is inclusive, that widens our options, that enhances our understanding of Black experience and gender.[7]

I agree that self-recovery, self-restoration, and self-wholeness are minimal starting points for the Black woman's liberation to be meaningful. This view is identical to Toni Cade Bambara's call for an inward-looking change in her affirmation that "revolution begins with the self and in the self." The African woman's level of consciousness is therefore central to her self-recovery. This can not be enhanced by re-writng negative images and areas of invisibility and voicelessness. The time is now ripe for unveiling areas of strength in traditional and modern African women's reality as a motivator.

One identifies a growth in awareness that makes it possible to delineate a distinct female voice or plurality of female voices. Literary production is one of the avenues for self-expression and women have published works that are not intertexts to men's literature or western feminist writing. African women writers, like many African women, are not passive to their condition but seek to ameliorate it. If the resistance is not as radical as elsewhere, it is often a matter of different reactions to stimuli. Culture, too, has a lot to do with the differences in the definition of power and empowerment. Many have therefore focused on issues of paramount interest to women. A major preoccupation is the chasm between women's roles in the home and their public or other economic occupations. This sometimes overemphasizes the conflict which is more of a problem for the middle-class women than others. Generally, African women's activities and empowerment are more dominant in the private sphere than in the public, but domestic empowerment sometimes shapes public issues. Women are becoming increasingly visible in the public sector too. Although, as Emeagwali identifies, there are usually no overt written policies to exclude women from the public sector, the truth is that they are being excluded by invisible codes of practice. But women are getting mobilized to change this in many countries. The interdependence of private and public spaces is central to any valid study of African womanism. This is recurrent in many African women's literature as they dramatize the tension or the attempt to resolve it.

African women's literary theory is inevitably intercepted by several extra-literary determinants. Writers and critics such as Nawal El Saadawi, Molara Ogundipe-Leslie, Micere Mugo, Tessie Onwueme, and Abena Busia are more radical in their perception of the woman's question largely because of their socialist and other radical cultural or ideological positions. Ama Ata Aidoo, Buchi Emecheta, and Bessie Head have at one time or the other dissociated themselves from feminism as a concept. Yet, their works reveal strong womanist qualities and their voices are loud and uncompromising in decrying women's oppression and liminality. Others such as Zulu Sofola, Ama Ata Aidoo and Mariama Ba are sometimes more subtle and at other times outgoing but always effective in speaking for their race and gender. Flora Nwapa, Tsitsi Dangarembga, and Zaynab Alkali reveal feminine consciousness effectively at varying degrees of commitment from one text to another. The need for a "simultaneity of discourse," in the words of Barbara Christian, is significant in the light of this situation. Mae Gwendolyn Henderson recommends "social difference with gender identity and gender identity within racial identity."

The process of transformation should start from within and has to be within a historical and cultural context. In "An Overview of Women and Power in Africa," Karen Sacks observes that, "Any discussion of women's exercise of power needs to be placed in historical context, for the options and possibilities of any one time and place are clearly governed by the past." The search for a historically sound Afrocentric women's poetics transcends facile definitions. The African woman's quest is for a space within the collective room. One needs to break down essentialist terms and concepts that dominate modern pedagogy. Since art shapes consciousness, oral tradition and some categories of African literature have created negative images of the African woman. But women's genres have also been used for positive self-assertion. Women writers are now attempting to recreate new myths and archetypes to enhance positive depictions. Women who transcend gender, race, cultural, ethnic and class borders are being highlighted. Socially constructed partitions need to be demolished. Bakhtin observes that each social group speaks in its own "social dialect." This calls not for antinomic theories but proper cultural contextualization. We need to be reminded that African world-view is largely dialogic and the place of negotiation of values is important in conceptualizing the world as a market that can be reached through several routes.

One needs to stress—constantly—cultural idiosyncrasy in a study of this nature. A Yoruba proverb is relevant to the conceptualization of African womanism.

> Bayi lawa nse ni ile wa, ewo ibomiran.
> "The norm in this family is a taboo elsewhere."

Among the Nuba of Southwest Sudan and Ethiopia, for example, the body is not a sex object. It is a symbol of artistic beauty that these people proudly show off. Motherhood is considered a burden for many people in the West, but in many parts of Africa, women are respected—and among the Mende people, women are almost worshipped—for being the bringers of life. Ifi Amadiume's comprehensive work highlights the unique structure of power among Igbo people that unveils unique modes of female empowerment. In many parts of Malawi, women do not adopt their husband's name and both male and female children take their mother's surname. In divorce, wives take custody of the children.

The plurality of the African woman's reality requires the creation of a space for diversity. Another contigency is the need to accommodate the yearnings of the various class divisions. For too long, the plight of the middle-class has been equated with the general condition while the lower class has been subsumed under the agenda of an elite that is basically alienated and not representative. One needs to bridge the chasm created currently by numerous polarities, west/east, male/female, white/black, mainstream/minority. Womanism recognizes the meeting point of all women's struggle but underscores Africaness. The larger concern of all African people globally centers on self-esteem and the assertion of the Black wo/man's dignity and in this, men and women need to form a coalition. Many horizons of emancipation are interdependent.

Okey Ndibe recommends a more profound and resourceful approach:

> The burden of the African feminist is, in part, to rehumanize the struggle, to suffuse old concepts with new, never-before considered meanings, nudge the struggle in the direction of paring down all kinds of jingoisms instead of exacerbating them; to ultimately move us towards the creation, neither of a man's world nor a woman's, but of a human world.[8]

No form of gender separatism can solve African problems, and Ndibe rightly castigates male chauvinism: "Eager to act the role of master, the African man often opens up a sector of war with his womenfolk that he can hardly afford, a war... that enervates his and her struggle to throw off the yoke that keeps both of them down."[9] African world-view is syncretic and accommodationist. Like elsewhere, gender issues will remain on the front burner of scholarship for a long time. But African thought and philosophy cannot be muted in such discursive frameworks. The rectifying of the hiatus of womanist studies does not rest on the search for a room of one's own in the Virginia Woolf sense. A cult of womanhood that creates suspicion and/or aversion to normal male-female interaction is considered alien to African thought by many.

AFRICAN VALUES, NEGOTIATION, AND A DIALOGIC POSITION

The myth of African woman's invisibility is being decoded. But the reality is that the ordinary African woman does not live in some subterranean world. She is dynamic on the farm and in the market place. She is only less visible in the public sector and this has changed considerably in many parts of Africa. Complementarity in role sharing is important and several writers, male and female, have fictionalized the changing status of African women's empowerment. Indeed, some male writers express a more positive female image than female writers. Dialogism focuses on this divergence and complementarity. In discussing African women's awareness, the task is two-pronged. One elucidates her existent level of consciousness in order to further raise her consciousness. The view of Molara Ogundipe-Leslie is pertinent here:

> Certain issues are clear, such as that there is no one 'African' aesthetic; that to study indigenous aesthetics we must look at discrete communities and cultures, each of which has its own aesthetic universe: the Yoruba as opposed to the Tiv or the Gikuyu or the Tutsis. Then we must attempt to elicit the aesthetic criteria of the people themselves and not impose European ideas as was done to African sculpture.[10]

The African woman's visibility varies according to class, ethnicity, and level of awareness. Even religion determines the level of awareness in some cases. African women still enjoy some measure of empowerment conferred by religion, which cannot be disregarded. This centrality in religious role has been maintained in many modern Christian churches, and in some cases women play certain roles that are still reserved for men in western churches.[11] Consequently, many churches are founded and led by women in an overt show of empowerment that uniquely highlights African women's spirituality. In cultural production, women are at the cutting edge of change also. Nevertheless, the women have a long way to go along the road to total self-emancipation and assertion. Vital areas of decisionmaking in the public arena still exclude women. But they need to create their own terms of emancipation rather than adopt externally imposed criteria of struggle. Self-definition is the beginning of true freedom. The African woman's increasing awareness will enhance genuine self-retrieval.

Womanism is accommodating and it is not a transcendental or immanent concept. Its cultural and geographical relativism is wholesome. It takes root in the same cultural Afrocentric demands that motivate our sisters in the diaspora while drawing sustenance from the continental peculiarity. Writers are playing the role of social arbiters to retrieve lost dignity and reinscribe a new positive ideality of African womanhood. This involves transcending facile conceptions and perceptions of African women. The chasm between the woman as object of admiration, adoration, worship, and ornamentation on the one hand, and condescending humility, distrust, and elimination from certain public duties that subsisted since pre-colonial times, is being bridged. In some parts of Africa, women are recovering lost ground in the public sphere.

The African scene is centrifugal while the region's literary scene is largely a reflection of reality. The woman writer's role includes the decoding of disparate but inter-related concepts, a process described by Tillie Olsen as the documentation of, "inequalities, restrictions, penalties, denials, leechings."[12] This is achieved with a keen sense of history. Womanism is not ahistorical. African women's experience is a continuum; the woman's struggle is not divorced from the larger problems. The African woman needs to be conscious of her unique role; that of speaking to her gender, for her gender, and on behalf of her gender without solipsism. What is needed is positive coalition or *Umoja,* to enhance self-knowledge. She, however, transcends the self in the larger struggle for class, group and collective gender, racial but not racist self-retrieval.

African womanism strikes the balance between the inner reality and the sociological determinants, but it emphasises the impact of the collective values and not individualism. It highlights female bonding and collective actions as a part of the larger struggle of all Africans, all Blacks, all women and indeed all dispossessed, undermined or oppressed groups. It respects the family unit and motherhood. It does not seek to achieve emancipation by hating men or non-Africans or people of other races. The African woman's spirituality is being positively harnessed. African womanism is centered on the need for positive gender self-definition within historical, geographical and cultural contexts. The historical backcloth gives meaning to the cultural.

Abena Busia's recent discourse, "In Search of Chains Without Iron: On Sisterhood, History, and the Politics of Location," is thought-provoking. Although her focus is sisterhood across diverse boundaries, it is relevant to the search for an authentic African womanist theory:

> We need to negotiate our way, not around, but through the long shadows of our histories. Those histories have been histories of separation, of fragmentation, and they have been necessarily constructed as such. And speaking as an African woman, it is a painful thing to acknowledge the 'success' of the strategies.[13]

Being female is the waistcloth, the *oja,* that binds African women together.[14] The African reality includes colorful outfits: the *kente,* the *akwete* or the *aso ofi* are generally colorful and it is unnecessary to discard the multi-colored African outlook of African wrappers by imposing some dull shades of feminism on all African women. Unless one respects the viability of a multiple presentation of viewpoints, in the words of Abena Busia, "we will be building alliances on quicksand rather than rock."[15] African womanism can not be separated from humanism. Rather, it seeks to enrich the female gender through consciousness-raising while giving a human touch to the struggle for the appreciation, emancipation, elevation and total self-fulfilment of the woman, in positive ways.

The sum total of this multivalent womanist outlook is that it enhances African women's alterity. African women can still remain themselves in a changing cultural, and socio-historical setting. African women can take whatever is positive in the encroaching modern values and simultaneously retain the essence by preserving what is good in their culture and establishing it. Indeed, in manifesting cultural exteriority and maintaining their feminine selves, they sustain their alterity in a positive way. By refusing to be subsumed and submerged in externally imposed feminist philosophy, they enhance rather than negate their African values both on a personal and collective levels. African womanist configuration derives from this culturally wholesome self-expression and not any polemics that are extraneous to the consciousness of the majority of Africans.

Because literature is an imitation of reality, it is one of the major avenues of decoding African women's yearnings and encoding her alterity. Women writers are reacting against Eurocentric portraits of Africa by Western writers. But they are also correcting the African world of male heroism presented by male writers. Literature as an imitation of African women's reality and inscription of their values, inevitably underscores gender uniqueness which is encapsulated in cultural difference. Difference or otherness has been manipulated by feminists and patriarchal structures to situate African women in marginal or liminal social positions. African womanism embodies a set of values that reconstructs a more accurate, a more valid and a more authentic wholesome African feminine consciousness and actions. African women cannot remain the same within traditions that undermine them. But they need to maintain alterity to resist myths, theories and any reality that erodes their humanity, encourages self-deprecation, and undermines their ability to be their own voices and act for themselves as agents of culture and of change.

NOTES

1. Gloria Emeagwali, *Women Pay the Price: Structural Adjustment in Africa and the Caribbean* (Trenton, N.J.: African World Press, 1995), p.10.
2. John Gruesser, *White on Black: Contemporary Literature About Africa* (Chicago: University of Illinois Press, 1992), p. 1.
3. Josephine Donovan, "Towards a Women's Poetics," in S. Benstock, ed., *Feminist Issues in Literary Scholarship,* (Bloomington: Indiana University Press, 1987), p. 99.
4. *Ibid.*
5. Mikhail Bhakthin, Caryn Emerson, and Micheal Holquist *The Dialogic Imagination,* (Austin: University of Texas Press, 1981).
6. Okey Ndibe, *African Commentary* (Amherst: Mass., 1991), p.3.
7. Bell Hooks, *Talking Back,* (Boston: Southend Press, 1989), p. 182.
8. Ndibe, *loc. cit.*
9. *Ibid.*
10. Ogundipe-Leslie in James, p. 66.
11. An example is the international Christian group, Full Gospel Businessmen's Fellowship International. In Nigeria, this fellowship is more of a family fellowship and in many chapters, women are registered in their own right and very often their roles are indispensable. This is a marked contrast to the situation in Great Britain where the fellowship is much less visible than in Nigeria and women are not actively involved in the core programmes.
    Another illustration is that of the numerous indigenous churches founded by and/ or led actively by women.
12. Tillie Olsen, in Mary Eagleton, *Feminist Literary Theory.* (Oxford: Basil Blackwell, 1986), p. 1.
13. Abena Busia, "In Search of Chains Without Iron: On Sisterhood, History, and the Politics of Location," African Studies Association Women's Caucus Annual Address, published in ASA Women's Caucus Newsletter, June 1994.
14. *Oja* is the Yoruba word for the long piece of cloth used to tie babies securely on their mothers' back. It is symbolically any strong cord that binds people, things, or ideas together; a symbol of unity.
15. Busia, " In Search of Chains Without Iron," *loc. cit.*

BIBLIOGRAPHY

Abraham Francis and Abraham Subhadra. *Women, Development and Change: The Third World Experience.* Bristol, Indiana: Wyndham Hall Press, 1988.

Achebe, Chinua. *A Celebration.* Portsmouth, Heinemann, 1991.

——. *Arrow of God.* London: Heinemann, 1980.

——. *Anthills of the Savannah.* London: Heinemann, 1987.

——. *A Man of the People.* London: Heinemann, 1966.

——. *No Longer at Ease.* London: Heinemann, 1980.

Afonja, S & Bisi Aina. *Women in Social Change in Nigeria.* Ife: O.A.U. Press, 1994.

Akinjogbin, I.A. *Dahomey and its Neighbours,* Cambridge: Cambridge University Press, 1967.

Amadiume, Ifi. *Male Daughters, Female Husbands.* London: Zed Books, 1987.

Angelou, Maya. *All God's Children Need Traveling Shoes.* N.Y.: Random House, 1991.

Asante, Molefi. *Afrocentricity.* Trenton, NJ: Africa World Press, 1989.

Asante, Molefi. *The Afrocentric Idea.* Philadelphia: Temple University Press, 1987.

Asein, Sam. and A. O. Asaolu. *Studies in the African Novels.* Ibadan: University Press, 1986.

Awe, Bolanle ed. *Nigerian Women in Historical Perspective.* Ibadan: Sancore/Bookcraft, 1992.

Awoonor, Kofi. *The Breast of the Earth.* New York: Anchor Doubleday, 1976.

Baker, Houston, Jr. *Afro-American Poetics.* Madison: University of Wisconsin Press, 1988.

Bakhtin, Mikhail. *The Dialogic Imagination.* Trans., Caryl Emerson and Michael Holquist. Austin: University of Texas, 1981.

Bhasin, K. et al. "Some Questions on Feminism and Its Relevance in SE Asia." New Delhi: Kamla Bhasin, 1986.

Barthes, Roland. *The Rustle of Language.* Berkeley: University of California Press, 1989.

Beneria, Lourdes. *Women and Development.* New York: Praeger, 1985.

Benstock, Shari, ed. *Feminist Issues in Literary Studies.* Bloomington, Indiana: Indiana University Press. 1987.

Booth, Wayne, C. *The Rhetoric of Fiction.* Chicago: University of Chicago, 1983.

Boyce-Davis, Carole & Anne Adams Graves, *Ngambika.* Trenton, N.J.: African World Press, 1986.

Braxton, Joan & Andre Nicola McLaughlin. *Wild Women in the Whirlwind.* New Brunswick, N.J.: Rutgers, 1990.

Brown, Lloyd. *Women Writers in Black Africa.* Westport, Conn.: Greenwood 1981.

Bryce, Jane. "A Feminist Study of Fiction by Nigerian Writers." Ph.D. thesis, Obafemi Awolowo University, Ile-Ife, 1989.

Campbell, Jane. *Black Mythic Fiction: The Transformation of History.* Knoxville: University of Tenessee, 1986.

Charleton, Sue Ellen. *Third World Development.* London: Westview Press, 1984.

Christian, Barbara. *Black Women Novelists.* Westport, Conn.: Greenwood Press, 1980.

Clarke, John D. *Teacher and Friend. Memoirs of an Education Officer in Colonial Nigeria.* Pittsburgh, Pa.: Allies Behavioral Center, 1993.

Coles, Catherinie & Beverly Mack. *Hausa Women in the Twentieth Century.* Madison: University of Wisconsin, 1991.

Conde, Maryse. *A Season in Rihata.* Oxford: Heinemann, 1988.

Calvin C. Horton. *The Sexual Mountain and Black Women Writers.* New York, N.Y.: Doubleday/Anchor, 1984.

Chraibi, Driss. Heirs to the Past. Trans. Leo Ortzen. London: Heinemann, 1980.

Crowley, David. *African Folklore in the New World.* Austin: University of Texas, 1977.

Cudjoe, Selwyn. *Caribbean Women Writers.* (Essays from the First International Conference.) Wellesley, Mass.: University of Massachusetts Press, 1990.

Davis, Miranda. *Women's Struggles and National Liberation.* London: Zed, 1983.

Diop, Cheikh Anta. *Black Africa.* Trenton, N.J.: Lawrence Hills, 1987.

——. In *Great African Thinkers.* Ivan van Sertima, ed. New Brunswick, N.J.: Transaction Books, 1986.

——. *The Cultural Unity of Black Africa.* Chicago: Third World Press, 1978.

DeLauretis, Teresa, ed. *Feminine Studies.* Bloomington, Ind.: Indiana

University Press, 1986.

Dube, Leela, Eleanor Leacock & Shirtley Ardener. *Visibility and Power.* Delhi: Oxford University Press, 1986.

Eagleton, Mary. *Feminist Literary Theory.* Oxford: Basil Blackwell, 1986.

Ebeogu, Afam. "Feminism in Oral Literature: The Example of Igbo Birthsongs." in *Folklore and National Development.* Lagos: Nigerian Folklore Society Publication, 1984.

Edelman, Marion. *Portrait of Inequality.* Washington, D.C.: Children's Defense Fund, 1980.

Egejuru, Phanuel. *Towards African Literary Independence.* Westport, Conn.: Greenwood Press, 1980.

Eko, Ebele, *Elechi Amadi, The Man and His Work.* Lagos: Kraft Books, 1991.

Emenyonu, Ernest ed. *Critical Theory and African Literature,* Ibadan, Heinemann, 1987.

Emenyonu, Ernest ed. *Literature and Black Aesthetics.* Calabar Studies in African Literature. Ibadan: Heinemann, 1990.

Evans, Mary. *The Woman Question.* London: SAGE, 1994.

Fausto-Sterling, Anne. *Myths of Gender.* New York: Basic Books, 1988.

Finnegan, Ruth. *Oral Literature in Africa.* Nairobi: Oxford Univ. Press, 1976.

Frye, M. *The Politics of Reality: Essays in Feminist Theory.* Trumansburg, N.Y.: Crossing Press, 1983.

Gaidzanwa, Rudo. *Images of Women.* Harare: The College Press, 1985.

Gates, Henry Louis, Jr. *Reading Black, Reading Feminine.* New York: Meridian (Penguin), 1990.

Gates, Henry Louis, Jr. *Race, Writing and Difference.* Chicago: Chicago University Press, 1986.

Gilligan, Carol. *In a Different Voice: Psychological Theory of a Woman's Development.* Cambridge, Mass.: Harvard University, 1982.

Godwin, June. *Cry Amandla! South African Women and the Question of Power.* New York: Africana Press, 1984.

Hall, Margaret. *Women Unliberated.* Washington: Hemisphere Publication, 1979.

Hall, Majorie. "The Position of Woman in Egypt & the Sudan as Reflected in feminist Writings since 1900." SOAS Ph.D, 1977, Thesis 1123.

Harding, Sandra, ed. *Feminism and Methodology.* (Milton Keynes, Open Univ.) Bloomington: Indiana University Press, 1987.

Harding, M.E. *Women's Mysteries, Ancient & Modern.* London: Riders, 1977.

Hilkka, Pietila and Jeanne Vickers. *Making Women Matter: The Role of the United Nations.* London: Zed Books, 1990.

Holquist, Michael. *The Dialogic Imagination: Four Essays by Mikhael Bakhtin.* Austin: University of Texas, 1981.

Hooks, Bell [Gloria Watkins]. *Ain't I a Woman.* Boston: South End

Press, 1981.

Hooks, Bell. *Talking Back* Boston: South End Press, 1989.

Hooks, Bell. *Yearning.* Boston: South End Press, 1990.

Hudson-Weems, Clenora. *Africana Womanism.* Troy, Mich.: Bedford Publishers, 1993.

Humm, Maggie. *Contemporary Feminist Literary Theory.* London: Harvester-Wheatsheaf, 1994.

Humm, Maggie. *Feminism: A Reader.* London: Harvester- Wheatsheaf, 1992, p.122.

Hutchinson, Linda. *Narcissistic Narrative: The Metafictional Paradox.* New York: Methuen, 1984.

James, Adeola. *In Their Own Voices.* London: Heinemann, 1990.

Keller, Frances, ed. *Views of Women's Lives in Western Tradition.* New York: Edwin Mellen, 1990.

Kirsten, Holst Petersen and Anna Rutherford. *Chinua Achebe, A Celebration.* London, Heinemann, 1990.

Koedt, Ann, et al, *Radical Feminism.* N.Y.: Quadrangle, 1973.

Kolawole, Mary E. Modupe. "An African View of Transatlantic Slavery and the Role of Oral Testimony in Creating a New Legacy" in *Transatlantic Slavery: Against Human Dignity,* ed. Anthony Tibbles. London: H.M.S.O./National Museum & Gallery, 1994.

——. "Gender and Changing Social Vision in the Nigerian Novel." in *Women in Social Change in Nigeria.* Mt. Saint Vincent University and Women's Studies Group, Obafemi Awolowo University Press, 1993.

Levine, Laurence. *Black Culture and Black Consciousness.* Oxford: Oxford University Press, 1978.

Lorde, Audre. *Sister Outsider.* The Crossing Press, 1984.

Macdonald, Sharon et al. *Images of Women in Peace and War.* Madison: University of Wisconsin, 1987.

Mai Thi Tu. *Women in Vietnam,* Hanoi: Foreign Language Publishing House, 1978.

Mama, Amina, " Black Women, the Economic Crisis and the British State," *Feminist Review* 17 (1984).

Mazrui, Ali. *Cultural Forces in World Politics.* Portsmouth, N.H.: Heinemann, 1990.

Mazrui, Ali and Toby Levine. *The Africans.* New York: Prager, 1986.

Mcwatt, Mark, ed. *West Indian Literature and its Social Context.* Cave Hill, St. Michaels: University of West Indies Press, 1985.

Mba, Nina. *Nigerian Women Mobilized.* Berkeley: University of California Press, 1982.

Mbiti, J.S. *African Religion & Philosophy.* London: Heinemann, 1969.

Miller, R. Baxter. *Black American Literature.* Lexington, Kentucky: University of Kentucky Press, 1981.

Mohanty, Sandra. *Third World Women and the Politics of Feminism.* Bloomington: Indiana University Press, 1991.

Mutiso, G.C.M. *Socio-Political Thought in African Literature.* London: Macmillan, 1974.

Newton, Judith and Deborah Rosenfelt, eds. *Feminist Criticism and Social Change.* London: Methuen, 1985.

Nilsen, Alleen et al. *Sexism and Language.* Urbana, Illinois: National Council of Teachers of English, 1977.

Ogden, C.K. and I. A. Richards. *The Meaning of Meaning.* New York: Harcourt Brace, 1989.

Ogundipe-Leslie, Molara. *Recreating Ourselves.* Trenton, N.J.: Africa World Press, 1994.

Oluwole, Lai. *Women and Social Change in Nigeria.* Lagos: Unity Publishers, 1990.

Olagunju, A. O. "Myths in Yoruba Religion Traditions: A Phenomenological Study." Ife: Unpublished M.A. thesis, 1986.

Ong, Walter. *Orality & Literacy.* London: Routledge, 1982.

Oppong, Christian, ed. *Female and Male in West Africa.* London: Allen and Unwin, 1983.

Oshungbohun, C.O. *The Place of Women in Yoruba Religious Tradition.* Ife: Unpublished B.A. thesis, 1987.

Otukunefor, Henrietta and Obiageli Nwodo. *Nigerian Female Writers.* Lagos: Malthouse, 1989.

Preminger, Geoffrey, *African Mythology.* New York: Peter Bedrick, 1982.

Parpart, Jane and Kathleen Staudt. *Women and the State in Africa.* Boulder, Colorado: Lynne Riener, 1989.

Phillips, Anne. *Divided Loyalties: Dilemmas of Sex and Class.* London: Yirago, 1987.

Pletila, Hilka. *Making Women Matter. The Role of the U.N.* London: Zed Books, 1990.

Priebe, Richard. *Myths, Realism and the West African Writer.* Trenton, N.J.: African World Press, 1988.

Romney, Ronna, et. al. *Momentum ... Women in American Politics Now.* New York: Crown Publishers, 1988.

Rosaldo, Michelle & Louise Lamphere. *Women, Culture and Society.* Stanford: Stanford University Press, 1974.

Rotimi, Ola. *Our Husband Has Gone Mad Again.* Oxford: Oxford Univ. Press, 1979.

Schipper, Mineke. *Source of All Evil.* Chicago: Ivan Dee, 1991.

Schwartz, Daniel. *The Case for a Humanistic Poetics.* Philadelphia: University of Pennsylvania, 1990.

Selden, Raman. *Practicing Theory and Reading Literature.* Lexington, Ky.: University of Kentucky Press, 1989.

Slipman, Sue. *Helping Ourselves to Power.* New York: Pergamon Press, 1986.

Smilowitz, Erika et al. *Critical Issues in West Indian Literature.* Parkersburg: Caribbean Books, 1984.

Sofola, J. A. *African Culture and the African Personality,* Ibadan: African Resources Publishing Company, 1978.

Soyinka, Wole. *Art, Dalogue and Outrage.* Ibadan: New Horn, 1988.

———. *Death and the King's Horseman.* London: Eyre Methuen, 1978.

——. *The Interpreters.* London: Heinemann, 1968.

——. *Season of Anomy.* London: Trinity Press, 1973.

Staudt, Kathleen. *Women, International Development, and Politics.* Philadelphia: Temple University Press, 1990.

Steinberg, Stephen, *The Ethnic Myth.* Boston, Beacon Press, 1989.

Sweetman, David. *Women Leaders in African History.* London: Heinemann, 1984.

Todd, Janet. *Gender and Literary Voice.* Hoddesdan: Holmes and Meier Publishers, 1980.

Todorov, Tzvetan. *Literature and its Theorists: A Personal View of Twentieth-Century Criticism.* Trans., Catherine Porter. Ithaca: Cornell University Press, 1987.

Todorov, Tzvetan. *Genres in Discourse.* Trans., Catherine Porter. New York: Cambridge University Press.

Tong, Rosemarie. *Feminist Thought.* San Francisco: Westwood Press, 1989.

Tate, Claudia. *Black Women Writers at Work.* New York: Continuum, 1985.

Thompson, Leonard and Andrew Prior. *South African Politics.* New Haven: Yale University Press, 1982.

Trinh Minh ha. *Women, Native, Other.* Bloomington: Indiana University Press, 1991.

Uchegbulam, Abalogu, et. al. *Oral Poetry in Nigeria.* Lagos: Nigeria Magazine, 1981.

Vincent, Theo. *7 Black and African Writers on Literature and Life.* Lagos: Center for Black and African Arts and Civilization, 1981.

Wadley, Susan ed. *The Powers of Tamil Women.* Syracuse: Syracuse University Press, 1980.

Wall, Cheryl, ed. *Changing Our Own Words.* New Brunswick: Rutgers, 1991.

Wallace, Martin. *Recent theories of Narrative.* Ithaca, N.Y.: Cornell University Press, 1986.

Wallace, Michelle. *Black Macho and the Myth of Superwoman.* New York: Verso, 1990.

Warner-Lewis, Maureen. *Guinea's Other Suns.* Dover, Mass.: The Majority Pres, 1991.

Waugh, Patricia. *Metafiction: The Theory and Practice of Self-Conscious Fiction.* London: Methuen, 1984.

Williams, W.M., ed. *The Sociology of Women.* London: George Allen & Unwin, 1980.

INDEX